Love and Death in Psychotherapy

Also by Robert Langs

A CLINICAL WORKBOOK FOR PSYCHOTHERAPISTS (1992)
SCIENCE, SYSTEMS AND PSYCHOANALYSIS (1992)
EMPOWERED PSYCHOTHERAPY (1993)
DOING SUPERVISION AND BEING SUPERVISED (1994)
THE DREAM WORKBOOK (1994)
CLINICAL PRACTICE AND THE ARCHITECTURE OF THE MIND (1995)
THE DAYDREAM WORKBOOK (1995)
THE EVOLUTION OF THE EMOTION-PROCESSING MIND: WITH AN
INTRODUCTION TO MENTAL DARWINISM (1996)
THE COSMIC CIRCLE: The Unification of Mind, Matter and Energy
(*with A. Badalamenti and L. Thomson*) (1996)
DEATH ANXIETY AND CLINICAL PRACTICE (1997)
GROUND RULES IN PSYCHOTHERAPY AND COUSELLING (1998)
CURRENT THEORIES OF PSYCHOANALYSIS (*editor*) (1998)
PSYCHOTHERAPY AND SCIENCE (1999)
DREAMS AND EMOTIONAL ADAPTATION (1999)
FREUD'S BIRD OF PREY (A Play in Two acts) (2000)
FUNDAMENTALS OF ADAPTIVE PSYCHOTHERAPY AND COUNSELLING
(2003)*

* Also by Palgrave Macmillan

Love and Death in Psychotherapy

Robert Langs, M.D.

palgrave
macmillan

First published 2006 by
PALGRAVE MACMILLAN
Houndmills, Basingstoke, Hampshire RG21 6XS and
175 Fifth Avenue, New York, N.Y. 10010
Companies and representatives throughout the world

PALGRAVE MACMILLAN is the global academic imprint of the Palgrave Macmillan division of St. Martin's Press, LLC and of Palgrave Macmillan Ltd. Macmillan® is a registered trademark in the United States, United Kingdom and other countries. Palgrave is a registered trademark in the European Union and other countries.

ISBN 13: 978–1–4039–3602–8
ISBN 10: 1–4039–3602–1

This book is printed on paper suitable for recycling and made from fully managed and sustained forest sources.

A catalogue record for this book is available from the British Library.
A catalog record for this book is available from the Library of Congress.

10   9   8   7   6   5   4   3   2   1
15   14   13   12   11   10   09   08   07   06

Printed in China

Contents

Introduction

Love looks not with the eyes, but with the mind,
And therefore is wing'd Cupid painted blind.
William Shakespeare: *A Midsummer-Night's Dream*

This book reflects the results of a major transformation in my thinking about the human mind and the treatment experience. Initially, I approached the much neglected but critical subject of love in psychotherapy using a fairly classical psychoanalytic and psychotherapeutic framework. The questions I asked and tried to answer with fresh perspectives were familiar and time worn. Is some form of love essential for a successful psychotherapeutic experience? Should this love be felt by the patient or by the therapist, or by both of them? What form should it take? How is love in psychotherapy related to love in everyday life? For patients, is their love for their therapists solely transferential and largely fantasy-based or are there non-transferential kinds of love as well? How are they to be distinguished?

I began to read articles and books on the subject of love in psychotherapy and found the literature to be rather vague and without a consensus on these issues. I saw that by and large, I had to find my way on my own. I therefore began to look closely at my interactions with my psychotherapy patients and at my supervisory work with these love-related puzzles in mind. And I did so at a time when my basic thinking about the many facets of emotional life and how we cope with it was in the process of changing. I'd been trained in classical psychoanalysis at a time when unconscious, intrapsychic fantasies, wishes, and memories were thought to be the prime movers of both emotional wellness and emotional ills. As time passed, ideas about interpersonal and narcissistic needs were incorporated into my thinking as well.

After a while, however, my observations of transactions within the therapeutic arena gradually led me to make some fundamental changes in my clinical and theoretical perspectives. In lieu of viewing various inner needs as the basic issues in emotional life, I began to see and

validate the idea that coping with reality, mainly with traumatic triggering events and their most anxiety-provoking meanings, actually was the
fundamental task of what I came to call *the emotion-processing mind* –
the mental module with which we, as humans, adapt to emotionally-
charged events and their ramifications. And as this new viewpoint
began to take hold and was being fleshed out, new questions about love
in psychotherapy began to emerge. Mindful of the old questions which
still needed fresh answers, my dawning insights into these new emotional issues were disquieting because they seemed to call into question
previous thinking on this important subject. Long-standing theoretical
ideas and clinical precepts seemed to be in need of revision.

To explain, the new approach that I was developing, previously
called *the communicative approach* and now called *the strong
adaptive approach*, saw the emotion-processing mind as designed
and operating on the basis of two fundamental systems. There is a
conscious system that relies on conscious perceptions and makes
conscious efforts to cope with consciously recognized emotionally-
charged events and meanings. And there is as well a *deep unconscious system* that relies on unconscious or subliminal perceptions
and makes unconscious efforts to cope with unconsciously perceived, emotionally-charged events and their most anxiety-provoking
meanings – events and implications that are too disturbing to register
in awareness. These two systems operate relatively independently
and they do so on the basis of very different levels of wisdom and
with distinctive coping strategies and capabilities. In this regard, the
deep unconscious system appears to be the far more perceptive and
effective adaptive instrument.

The question arose, then, as to whether these two systems of the
emotion-processing mind have similar or different views of love in
psychotherapy. And if differences do exist, what are they and which
position is the more reliable and affecting? In exploring these new
questions, initial indications were that significant differences do exist
in their views of love in psychotherapy and that the deep unconscious
position was far more reliable and influential than that of the conscious mind. In addition, it also began to emerge that in and of itself,
the evolved, two-system design of the emotion-processing mind has
strong effects on the vicissitudes of love in the treatment setting. The
challenge lay with defining these effects and using the insights so
gained to enhance the loving aspects of psychotherapy and the overall
therapeutic process as well.

Another relatively neglected aspect of the psychotherapy experience that came to the fore in the course of these newly directed clinical researches was the role played by the setting, ground rules, frames, and boundaries of the treatment situation in determining the vicissitudes of love for both patients and therapists. Early on, I discovered that there is an archetypal or ideal, unconsciously sought healing set of ground rules for all psychotherapy experiences. It was therefore possible to identify the features of a well-secured therapeutic framework and to contrast them with frameworks that did not meet these ideals. This classification of two basic kinds of frameworks for a psychotherapeutic experience, secured and modified, facilitated the study of the ways in which a therapist's management of the ground rules and boundaries of psychotherapy affects the vicissitudes of love for both themselves and their patients. Many unanticipated insights followed in the wake of these studies.

Perhaps the most compelling set of novel questions arose when my adaptation-oriented investigations into the human psyche and its concerns came upon the critical role played by death and death anxiety in both emotional life and in the treatment experience. It quickly became clear that the awareness of death and human mortality has led humans to experience three forms of death anxiety: *predatory* (the fear of being harmed or killed by others or by natural disasters), *predator* (the fear of being harmed or killed because of having harmed others), and *existential* (the fear of death linked with the inevitability of personal demise). It turned out that each form of death anxiety is activated by particular kinds of external triggering events and that for psychotherapy patients, most of the influential traumatic incidents occur within the treatment setting – i.e., tend to be constituted as the interventions of their therapists. For psychotherapists, I found that the behaviors of, and material from, their patients loom large as major causes of the activation of their own death anxieties. But in addition, therapists appeared to be far more sensitive than their patients to death-related traumas in their personal lives. With so much of this being experienced and mediated unconsciously, and with mounting evidence that a patient's or therapist's personal history of death-related traumas played a significant role in how these death-related issues were dealt with in therapy, there was a lot to sort out and understand. This too emerged as another unexpected challenge that arose from my newly revised view of the emotional realm.

All in all, then, it emerged that there are three generally unrecognized factors that affect the vicissitudes of love between patients and therapists in the psychotherapy experience:

The evolved architecture of the emotion-processing mind and especially its two-system design;

The nature of the setting and ground rules of a particular psychotherapy experience; and

The patient's – and therapist's – personal history of death-related traumas and the occurrence of death-related triggering events and the activation of death anxieties within the psychotherapy situation – and secondarily in the outside lives of both patients and therapists.

Operating together in various mixtures, these vital aspects of human emotional experience form a *three-dimensional matrix* out of which the vicissitudes of love in psychotherapy emerge. In addition, each of these factors appears to be more fundamental in emotional life and its psychotherapy than is love per se. Each would have to be deeply understood before I could appreciate and resolve the many issues raised by expressions of love in the treatment setting. So it was with these challenges in mind that I undertook an extended, in-depth study of love in psychotherapy and came upon results and insights never before in evidence.

1

Taking the Measure of Love

'What is this thing called love?'

This age-old question, asked so plaintively by the songwriter Cole Porter, has intrigued and baffled humans since the dawn of awareness and the story of Adam and Eve. Through the centuries, efforts to define the experience of love and to identify its manifestations have confounded the best of our philosophers, psychologists, and writers. And this uncertainty has carried over into the arenas of psychotherapy and counseling (terms I use interchangeably), where little has been written and even less has been clarified on the subject of love between patients and their therapists.[1] Like so many other abstract terms that allude to the actual transactions between the therapeutic couple – terms like transference, resistance, countertransference, and the like – the subject of love is more a source of bewilderment and consternation than illumination. This book has been written to bring light into this darkness.

The dictionary, which addresses conscious feelings, tells us that expressions of love for others range from God's beneficence on His children to the experience of strong sexual desires for another person – with countless forms in between. Love implies an intense need for another person, a strong wish for involvement or attachment, a sense of longing and caring, and a preparedness to make sacrifices on behalf of the loved one. Love may also entail commitment, passion, affection, romance, concern, exclusivity, intensely concentrated attention,

---

[1] The subject of this book is love, conscious and unconscious, between psychotherapy patients and their therapists. Although the findings generalize to everyday life, I will not explicitly explore love between patients or therapists and other people in their lives. Unless otherwise stated, then, when I allude to love per se or to love in psychotherapy, I am referring to experienced feelings and actions taken by patients and therapists towards each other.

worship, idealization and over-idealization, devotion, adoration, fondness, involvement, sexual desires, and hopes for return satisfactions and love from the person (or entity) who is the object of these feelings. Along different lines, love may be unilateral or shared, and it may be felt consciously as such or masked by conscious feelings like anger or indifference. Many of the attributes of *conscious love* also characterize the expressions of deep *unconscious love* – the form of love that is experienced outside of awareness and encoded in narrative images.

Both conscious and deep unconscious love are adaptive or maladaptive responses to triggering incidents – so-called environmental impingements – that are experienced and processed with or without awareness. In general, conscious love is evoked by consciously registered triggers and their implications, while deep unconscious love is evoked by meanings of triggers that register and are processed outside of awareness. These triggering events may come from within the therapeutic interaction – i.e., from the other member of the therapeutic dyad – or from the outside life of the patient or therapist. It is noteworthy that by and large, while in psychotherapy, patients are far more sensitive unconsciously to love-related triggering events within their treatment situation than they are to incidents outside of the therapy. In contrast, therapists, who also are sensitive to both kinds of love-evoking incidents, tend to be especially affected by triggering events in their daily lives – more so than their patients.

Anger is Easy, Love is Hard

During my many years as a psychotherapist and supervisor of other therapists, I have been struck by how easily most therapists approach the problem of patients' hostility towards them while assiduously avoiding the slightest indication of positive feelings aimed in their direction. Should a patient express outright loving feelings, they tend to be embarrassed and unable to think clearly. And if the patient's feelings have a sexual component or if they realize that they have said or done something striking that has moved the patient to act in a seemingly loving manner, they become rattled and guilt ridden and tend to avert their eyes from their clients. This is not meant to imply that the guilt is necessarily inappropriate or that therapists are without responsibility when patients express feelings of this kind. To the contrary, as we shall see, therapists have considerable accountability in this regard.

Noteworthy too is the impression that because therapists often fail to consciously notice what they have done to arouse a patient's ardor, an unconscious sense of culpability and guilt often plays a significant role in their discomfort.

For example, a male psychologist, a supervisee whom I will call Dr Stuart, came to a supervisory session eager to talk about anything but his last session with a young woman patient whom I will call Ms Trent. When I pointed out his evident avoidance of the patient's session, Dr Stuart turned beet red and said that he was very anxious about telling me what had happened in the patient's hour. It seems that midway through her session, Ms Trent described a fantasy of having oral sex with Dr Stuart and wondered if she was falling in love with him.

Dr Stuart had tried to trace the fantasy to his patient's childhood wishes towards her father, but the effort fell flat. He also brought up some sexual fantasies Ms Trent had been having about her married boss, whom she sees as very attractive, and suggested that she was displacing these fantasies onto him – again to no avail.

Could this be a positive sign that she is relating well to me in the therapy, he wondered aloud in the supervisory session. Is it an indication that she's investing her transference feelings in me? Almost as an aside, he mentioned that he couldn't see anything he had done to evoke his patient's fantasy and feelings, which had made both of them quite uncomfortable.

I asked Dr Stuart to present the session in sequence as he recalled it. (I ask supervisees to present sessions from memory, without making or using notes.) It turned out that about ten minutes into her hour, the patient had brought up her dire financial situation and said that she could no longer afford to continue in treatment. After some discussion, Dr Stuart asked if a twenty-five dollar fee reduction would enable her to remain in therapy. Ms Trent responded by saying that Dr Stuart was a love, adding that the fee reduction certainly would make it possible for her to continue. The sexual fantasy emerged soon after, as did memories of her father's extramarital affairs and his trying to buy the patient's love by giving her large sums of money with which to shop for clothing.

It seems clear that Dr Stuart's fee reduction had evoked his patient's erotic fantasy and loving feelings towards him. Much as the patient's father had tried to buy her love, the therapist was doing something similar in the therapy. What the patients saw consciously as a loving gesture was seen unconsciously as a seductive bribe. Subsequent material in this session involved recollections of her father's quasi-sexual seductiveness with the patient when she entered adolescence. This lent support to the thesis that by reducing the patient's fee, the therapist had behaved in a manner that had repeated earlier seductions by the patient's father.

Without delving further into other ramifications of this vignette, my intent in presenting it here is to emphasize that many of the most troublesome problems that therapists experience in dealing with loving feelings and fantasies within the therapeutic interaction lie with their own contributions to their patients' expressions of outright love towards them. In many instances, therapists are quite unaware consciously of what they have said or done, much of it inadvertent or seemingly innocuous, to provoke these loving desires. We can see then that the interactional aspects of love in psychotherapy loom large for both parties in the therapeutic dyad. We will be well advised to think about love in psychotherapy with this in mind.

In general, it is assumed in the psychotherapy literature that patients will love their therapists as a way of expressing some kind of transference fantasy or wish derived from past relationships (Freud, 1912b, 1913; Gabbard, 1996). As for themselves, therapists uniformly believe that they approach their patients with basic love towards them and that their interventions express that love in ways that are therapeutic (Friedman, 2005). Love seems to become a problem for therapists mainly when they inadvertently behave in manifestly unloving ways towards their patients (Gabbard, 1996; Rabin, 2003). More broadly, however, there is a growing literature on the subject of therapist-love, or as it's called in recent writings, 'countertransference-love,' a term that is currently used to allude to all types of positive feelings, inappropriate, but mostly appropriate, in therapists towards their patients (Searles, 1965; Gorkin, 1987; Davies, 1994, 1998; Gabbard, 1994, 1998; Gabbard and Lester, 1995; Rabin, 1995, 2003; Hoffman, 1998; Slavin et al., 1998; Mann, 1999; Renik, 1999; Slavin, 2002; Natterson, 2003; Friedman, 2005).

Therapists do from time to time feel consciously guilty over being openly provocative with a patient who feels or acts in a loving or hateful manner towards them. Even so, unconscious guilt caused by interventions whose incitement qualities have not been consciously recognized appears to be a far more common occurrence, and in the absence of explicit awareness, far more difficult for therapists to deal with. Helping therapists to identify such incidents in treatment and facilitating therapeutic work under these circumstances is one of the many goals of this book.

Some Basic Dimensions of Love in Psychotherapy

There are many ways of classifying love within the therapeutic interaction. Patient- or therapist-love may be fantasized or enacted; accepted as wishful and illusory or believed to be real and genuine; sexual or non-sexual; homosexual or heterosexual; demanding of satisfaction or quiet, without wishes for gratification. In more abstract terms, there are expressions of love that are genuine and caring, in contrast to love that is manipulative or defensive, or part of evident attempts to harm the other party to a given psychotherapy. There also is a patient's so-called *transference love* that is said to be derived from past relationships and misappropriated to the therapist, and so-called *non-transference love* which is said to be an appropriate response to a therapist's healing ministrations. Similarly, as noted, therapists are said to experience forms of countertransference love which may be healthy and truly loving or pathological and a way of falsely loving their patients.

Many difficulties in exploring and understanding love in the therapy situation seem to arise because love is so multidimensional. Problems also stem from the fact that the manifestations of love can take such a wide variety of forms and serve so many different conscious and unconscious functions and needs – love in psychotherapy is by no means a unitary matter. There are, for example, various types of *patient-love*, the term I use for patients' loving feelings and love-based enactments towards their therapists, and similarly, many forms of *therapist-love* that therapists experience or enact towards their patients.

Given the complexities of the situation, I have selected for initial discussion what appear to be three of the most fundamental ways to describe, define, and understand love in psychotherapy: True versus false; conscious versus unconscious; and subjectively experienced versus enacted – forms of love.

True versus False Love

Patient-love and therapist-love come in two basic forms, as either true or false expressions of love.

True love may be thought of as a reflection of genuine caring and affection that is conveyed in a manner that is in keeping with the respective role requirements of being a patient or a therapist. It also is a love that is expressed with full respect for the other party and for the conditions and boundaries of therapy that best serve the healing process. It is conveyed without efforts to modify the ideal or archetypal

ground rules and limits of the psychotherapy situation. Most importantly, true love is a feeling, communication, or behavior that is validated unconsciously by the patient's material and by the therapist's
private efforts at self-processing. Thus, it is a love that is supported by
the patient's and therapist's encoded narrative themes which emanate
from the deep unconscious wisdom subsystem of the emotion-processing mind. All in all, true love is, then, comprised of appropriate,
unconsciously validated, sincere feelings that advance or are responsive
to healing interventions within the therapeutic process – it is love in the
service of the insightful cure of the patient.

False love, on the other hand, may be thought of as a feeling or enactment of seeming care and affection that is harmful to the other party to
therapy and quite often, harmful to the perpetrator as well. This kind of
love is motivated unconsciously by wishes to seduce or do damage to
either or both parties to the therapeutic process. Such love also may be
recruited to show appreciation for the other party's offer of inappropriate defenses and thereby to support the use of denial and other costly
defense mechanisms that are invoked primarily to deal maladaptively
with unmanageable forms of anxiety and conflict. Thus false love is
secretly harmful to self and other and is mobilized in the service of
pathological satisfactions and defensiveness.

The inappropriate qualities of an expression of love in psychotherapy often goes unappreciated consciously by one or both parties to the
treatment experience. However, the deep unconscious wisdom subsystem of the emotion-processing mind encodes narrative themes that
clearly indicate the falsity and maladaptive qualities of this kind of
love. This means that in the case of a false expression of love, a manifest, conscious expression of patient- or therapist-love is refuted and
invalidated by the encoded narratives that emanate from this subsystem. All in all, then, false love in psychotherapy is inappropriately satisfying, maladaptive, invalidated unconsciously, an obstacle to a
soundly healing therapeutic process, and operates as a resistance or
counter-resistance to therapeutic progress.

The split between the conscious and unconscious views of love is
reflected in the brief excerpt from Ms Trent's psychotherapy offered
earlier in the chapter. While the patient consciously reacted to Dr Stuart's
fee reduction by seeing him as a loving therapist, the encoded story that
followed was about her father's attempt to buy the patient's love with
monetary gifts. This is not a true expression of love and it speaks for the
falsity of the therapist's well-meaning, but inappropriately seductive fee
reduction.

Conscious versus Unconscious Love

Another basic classification of love lies with the distinction between consciously and unconsciously expressed love. Conscious love entails manifest loving feelings and behaviors, while unconscious love entails non-manifest expressions of love that are reflected in encoded narrative material like dreams and stories. This differentiation has many important implications.

Because they emerge in displaced and disguised narrative imagery, unconsciously expressed loving feelings tend to be overlooked by many psychotherapists. To correct this oversight, therapists are well advised to monitor their patients' narrative themes for what they say about the course of love in psychotherapy. It has been found clinically that while conscious, manifest or direct expressions of love may be true or false, quite often they are false. In contrast, unconscious expressions of love are almost always true and deserved. The rare exception to this rule may occur when a therapist has been extremely hurtful to a patient, usually through a very damaging remark or harmful frame violation. Paradoxically, the encoded themes that initially follow this kind of intervention may be exceedingly loving in nature. Such images are unconsciously activated in the service of *deep unconscious denial*. As a rule, however, under these circumstances, devastatingly negative encoded themes soon follow and serve to set matters straight.

Subjectively Experienced versus Enacted Love

As expressed in psychotherapy, love may be confined to feelings, fantasies, and wishes or alternatively, conveyed through actions and efforts at enactment. Loving feelings, fantasies and wishes may be consciously or unconsciously experienced and they may be constrained or overly intense. The relatively controlled expressions of conscious love generally are sublimated and true, while the overly intense and exceedingly arduous expressions of love tend to be unsublimated and false. Similarly, loving actions or enactments tend to be true if they are limited in nature and carried out within the confines of the therapeutic contract – e.g., a passing offer by a patient to give his or her therapist financial advice. But these efforts at enactment are likely to be false if they are insistent, involve a breach in the ideal boundaries between patient and therapist, or are otherwise violations of the optimal ground rules of the therapy. In general, then, love that is fleeting and confined to feelings tends to be truthful, while love that is enacted and extended most often is false.

Recognizing and Evaluating Love in Psychotherapy

Given the complexities of love in psychotherapy, therapists also are faced with a variety of problems in tracking its vicissitudes and assessing its attributes in the course of a treatment experience. In light of the defensive alignment of the conscious mind and, as we shall see, its tendency to be affected and biased by unconscious guilt and unconscious needs for punishment, conscious evaluations of the actual nature of a loving expression tend to be quite unreliable. It follows then that basic decisions about the nature and classification of a loving expression in psychotherapy, whether emanating from the patient or therapist, should be based on unconscious perceptions and deep unconscious assessments of these loving gestures. Patients respond unconsciously to every loving expression made by themselves and their therapists. These unconscious evaluations are encoded in their dreams and stories and can be decoded in light of their love-related triggers – i.e., as valid perceptions of the true nature of the loving gesture to which the patient is responding. These encoded, unconscious appraisals are based on universal, archetypal values common to all humans, patients and therapists alike, and therefore tend to be highly reliable.

Similar principles apply to therapists' self-explorations *or self-processing activities*, as they are called (Langs, 1993, 2004c), when issues of love arise in their work with patients. Conducted privately, outside of the sessions with their patients, these self-processing efforts are designed to shed light on therapists' own unconscious evaluations of expressions of love by either themselves or their patients. Here too, conscious thinking is to be mistrusted, while trigger decoding unconscious perceptions is likely to be an eminently helpful guide to understanding and technically handling the love-related interludes at hand. When it comes to love in psychotherapy, as therapists, we are well advised to access and make use of as much deep unconscious wisdom as possible.

Dealing with Love in the Treatment Situation

It seems evident that the vicissitudes of love in psychotherapy deserve to be one of the many features of a treatment experience that we, as therapists, monitor with some consistency. We also need to more clearly define the various manifestations of this love so we may better understand their unconscious meanings and functions. Their more precise clinical definition will enhance our efforts to analyze, interpret and resolve pathological expressions of love, be they from our patients or ourselves. This kind of work can contribute greatly to insightful cure in that patients' displays of false love always reflect on their basic emotional problems. On the other hand, therapists' realizations that the love that they are feeling and/or expressing towards a patient is false rather than true can facilitate the insightful resolution of what is sure to be a significant obstacle to the patient's sound emotional healing.

In this connection, it is to be emphasized that, as material permits, expressions of patient-love should be explored and dealt with in the course of their psychotherapy sessions. On the other hand, manifestations of therapist-love need to be quickly examined subjectively during a session with a patient, but should be more elaborately explored and dealt with privately by therapists on their own without burdening their patients. That said, every episode of love, be it from a patient or therapist, presents a psychotherapist with challenges that call for deep understanding and the application of sound principles of technique. Errors and failures in dealing with love can cause much harm to patients and considerable unconscious guilt in errant therapists. On the other hand, discovering the triggers or stimuli that have evoked a patient's loving feelings and behaviors, whether true or false, and determining the deep unconscious meanings and functions of this love, is remarkably healing for both parties to therapy.

By and large, dealing with false expressions of patient-love poses many problems for psychotherapists. There is the natural wish of therapists to be loved, so identifying a loving expression as false threatens a therapist's self-image and feelings of worth. Also problematic are the many pressures from patients to satisfy their needs to be loved falsely in some extra-therapeutic or pathologically satisfying manner. These demands tend to be triggered by their therapists' ground rule violations and other erroneous interventions and they therefore evoke considerable unconscious guilt and may cause cognitive dysfunctions in the errant therapist.

Therapists' difficulties in dealing with patient-love tend to be compounded when therapists themselves feel love towards a loving or nonloving patient. Quite naturally, therapists want to believe that the love that they feel is genuine and if it is constrained and limited to feelings of affection and caring, this may well be the case. Nevertheless, therapists often express their love through some kind of seemingly caring, loving action, but this is a sign that their love is likely to be quite false. Therapist-love also may extend into sexual fantasies and this too should serve as a warning that it probably is false and treacherous. Any inclination in a therapist to mention these wishes to a patient, or to enact or satisfy them in a session, should be taken as a strong indication that false love is at work. In general, therapists abhor the experience of conscious guilt and degradations in their conscious self-image and as a result, they have considerable difficulty recognizing the falsity of their own false love. For this reason, as therapists, we are well advised to keep our loving feelings and wishes to ourselves. We also should avoid any enactment of that love and instead, actively and privately engage in self-processing activities geared towards the resolution of such feelings and the renunciation of these impulses when they arise.

In this context, we may be reminded that feelings of love, true and false, can arise in any relationship and interaction between a patient and therapist, be it under the rubric of counseling; cognitive, behavioral, or existential psychotherapy; psychodynamic or psychoanalytic treatment paradigms; or any of the over three hundred other forms taken by efforts to heal emotional maladaptations. Indications are that the greater a therapist's distance from a psychodynamic position, the more likely the therapy will be carried out in framework that is some distance from the archetypal ideal and thus, the greater the chances that patients' and therapists' loving feelings and enactments will convey false rather than true love. This proves to be the case even when a particular expression of love is sanctioned by the therapist's colleagues and is part of the standard therapeutic approach used by the therapist. To safeguard against the use of these errant love-related interventions, therapists are well advised to take into account the evocative triggers for all loving expressions, especially as they pertain to their own interventions, and to decode their patients' narrative themes in light of those triggers. This approach can help to insure that true love prevails for both parties to therapy, and that false love, if it arises, is insightfully resolved.

Four Traditional Components of Love

In a somewhat scattered manner, traditional psychotherapists have considered four dimensions of love in psychotherapy: The genetic, intrapsychic, interactional, and contextural components.

Love in psychotherapy has *genetic* aspects in that early life experiences with love and its polar opposite, hatred, influence its vicissitudes in the treatment setting.

Love has *intrapsychic* aspects because the character structure; inner mental state, needs, defenses, and conflicts; and the personal history of both patients and their therapists affect its vicissitudes and form.

Love has *interactional* components because an expression of love primarily is in part a product of the bipersonal therapeutic field (Langs, 1976) and a reflection of patients' and therapists' conscious and deep unconscious attempts to adapt to the words and deeds of the other party to therapy – and secondarily to outside life events.

And love is *contextural* in three inter-related ways:

First, expressions of love are affected by the nature and goals of the therapeutic relationship and the satisfactions that patients and therapists can expect from their work together.

Second, love is influenced by the role requirements for being a patient or therapist and the tasks assigned to each of them.

And third, expressions of love are affected by the physical, interpersonal, and psychological conditions within and under which a therapy unfolds – the setting, boundaries, and explicit and implicit ground rules that are established for a given therapeutic interaction.

These three components have extensive effects on the form that love takes; its fidelity or falseness; the causes of, and intentions behind, a loving expression; the needs that the love is intended to satisfy; the kinds of loving feelings and actions that are – and are not – permissible for a patient or therapist; and the range of consequences that a loving expression has for the course and outcome of a psychotherapy.

The Genetic Component

For both patients and therapists, there appear to be two kinds of early childhood experiences that affect the vicissitudes of love in a given psychotherapy. The first unfolds along a continuum of being loved or unloved by parental and other family figures and secondarily by other important childhood and later figures like teachers and religious leaders. The overall quality of these cumulative experiences for both patients and their therapists have lasting effects including many that are love-related in a treatment experience.

The second important type of love-affecting genetic experience involves another continuum, with loving rescue operations and acute care of the patient or therapist as a child when they were in dire need or in danger on one end, and on the other, the opposite experience of a harmful, acute traumatic event that entails experiences of being unloved and hurt by critical caretakers. Examples of positively-toned, loving incidents include care and concern at times of personal loss or threat and natural disasters, while examples of unloving incidents are the death or serious illness of, or abandonment by, a parental figure; the lack of care when the child was ill, injured or otherwise in acute distress; direct harm to the child by a parental figure; natural disasters that cause the child to feel unprotected and similar kinds of adverse incidents. In general, these early-life traumas are experienced unconsciously as death-related and they evoke significant forms of death anxiety that in turn, cause strong feelings of being unloved. In turn, these incidents greatly affect the course of love in psychotherapy, biasing these expressions towards false rather than true love. Thus, patients who have suffered significant unloving traumas, cumulative as well as acute, tend to love their therapists falsely and to seek forms of false love in return.

To cite a brief example, Mr Blake, whose therapy I supervised, was born in Asia and was two years old when his parents left him to live with his grandmother so they could arrange to relocate in America. In his therapy with Ms Thomas, a social worker, he repeatedly tried to express his love for his therapist by giving her inappropriate gifts and offering her financial advice regarding which he had considerable expertise. He also made incessant demands that the therapist show her concern and affection for him by changing the time of, and extending, his sessions, providing him with reading materials, allowing him to borrow or take magazines from her waiting room, and the like.

With utmost consistency, the encoded themes in Mr Blake's dreams and stories indicated that he was offering to, and demanding from his therapist, false forms of love and that their satisfaction would be harmful to both her and himself. A typical example is reflected in a dream that he had soon after he offered Ms Thomas a stock tip. In the dream, a jailed criminal is bribing the guards so he can escape prison. Associations were to Mafiosa payoffs.

These encoded themes speak clearly for the dishonesty and falsity behind the patient's seeming loving gesture. The patient evidently felt trapped in the secure framework of the therapy offered by Ms Thomas and other material from the patient indicated that the genetic connection evidently went back to the sense of imprisonment that the patient had felt when he was left behind in his native country while his parents were in America. At the time, he felt that he was being punished for his bad behavior and he wanted badly to be with them.

In general, true patient-love is grounded in a foundation built from early experiences of being truly loved and loving truly in response. In the therapy situation, this kind of patient-love is primarily an immediate response to unconsciously validated interventions made by psychotherapists – i.e., interventions that are followed by patients' positively-toned displaced, encoded narrative themes. On the other hand, false patient-love is grounded in a foundation built from early experiences of false love, received and given, and is, as noted, a common response to death-related traumas. In psychotherapy, this kind of patient-love tends to be an immediate response to erroneous, deep unconsciously invalidated interventions made by the therapist. In principle, the non-validation of an intervention indicates that the therapist's efforts have been experienced deep unconsciously by the patient as unloving and harmful.

In like manner, for therapists, offers of true love are founded on formative loving experiences. In their work as therapists, this kind of love is expressed through a basic caring attitude, securing the ground rules of treatment, and making deep unconsciously validated interventions. By way of contrast, false therapist-love is grounded in early falsely loving and death-related experiences and in therapy, it is expressed through a wide variety of interventions that do not obtain deep unconscious confirmation.

The Intrapsychic Component

There are many inner mental, characterological, and historical factors in both patients and therapists that affect the manifestations of love in psychotherapy and how they are responded to by both participants to treatment. In regard to patients, when a loving feeling or impulse is expressed towards a therapist, the therapist must define its nature and consider its sources. There is, as noted, a group of background factors that lead to intrapsychic attitudes and inclinations within patients that stem from their life histories and resultant inner psychic conflicts. These factors include such matters as the nature of their early and later-day loving experiences, the quality of parental care, the nature of early-life interactions, and their death-related and sexual traumas. Consideration also should be given to patients' preferred current modes of coping with emotionally-charged triggering events, including the extent to which they make use of defensive forms of denial and have, in the past, used loving feelings and sexual acts in the service of this denial and of gaining pathological satisfactions.

Related to these considerations, therapists are well advised to ascertain a patients' history of relationships with loving individuals like parents; their current capacity for true love in their daily lives; and the noteworthy love-related experiences, favorable and unfavorable, that they have experienced in the past and more recently. These perspectives should be applied to all expressions of patient-love, but are especially relevant to loving feelings and acts that have false qualities to them.

Negatively tinged intrapsychic structures and preferences are factors that render both patients and therapists vulnerable to turning to expressions of false love at times of trauma and stress. On the other hand, healthier and more adaptive inner mental structures favor expressions of true love by both patients and therapists.

The Interactional Component

Patients' experiences of love towards their therapists, which may be true or false and expressed consciously or unconsciously, should be accounted for interactionally by identifying the triggering event – and the meanings of that event – that has activated the patient's loving feelings and impulses. In this regard, patients' unconscious perceptions of their therapists' interventions are of prime importance, while acts of nature and the behaviors of figures outside of therapy are, as a rule, of secondary relevance. As noted, true patient-love is usually a response to an unconsciously validated, healing intervention by therapists, while false patient-love is a reaction to erroneous, invalidated, traumatic interventions, most often in the form of a therapist's uncalled-for violation of one or more of the deep unconsciously sought ideal ground rules of therapy.

The intrapsychic and interactional components of love tend to work together in the sense that patient-love, which is motivated and partially directed by inner needs, is activated and given direction by emotionally-evocative external, environmental events – a term that alludes to acts of nature and the words, deeds, and feelings of other humans. For patients in psychotherapy, these events almost always involve their therapists' interventions.

As for therapists, their loving feelings towards their patients are affected by the physical attributes and demeanor of their patients and their patient's life histories, as well as the manifest and encoded meanings of their patients' ongoing communications and behaviors. Importantly, when faced with personal death-related traumas, therapists are unconsciously driven to experience and interactionally enact falsely loving feelings towards selected patients – usually those who are unconscious sources of death-related anxieties for the therapist. On the other hand, when the personal life of a therapist is going well and he or she is in good health, there's an inclination to experience muted feelings of admiration and true love for selected patients as evoked by empathic responses to their emotional suffering and their struggle to find relief from their emotionally-founded symptoms.

Therapists who are not well loved in their everyday lives are vulnerable to feelings of false love towards their patients in a search for compensatory love and in their hunger for someone to care for them and for them to care about as well. Although they are more reactive to their therapists' interventions, patients also may show this kind of effect. The occasional interactional experience outside of therapy that arouses false love in the treatment situation almost always involves a severe death-related trauma, such as the death of a loved one or a personal illness which enormously increases the patient's or therapist's death anxieties. In these instances, feelings of false love are unconsciously activated as maladaptive attempts to deny feelings of helplessness, inadequacy, vulnerability, and hurt, and as an unconscious way of trying to use the celebration of love, however false and ill-conceived, to deny death and the terror that it evokes, much of it deep unconsciously.

To cite a brief example, Dr Thomas, a male psychiatrist-psychotherapist, suffered the death of his wife, who died unexpectedly of a pulmonary embolus after chemotherapy for lung cancer. In response, he abruptly canceled his sessions and was out of his office for two weeks. On his return, he unexpectedly found himself attracted to, and having sexual fantasies about, two of his unmarried women patients. His dreams were mainly about his incestuous, adolescent sex play with his sister who was two years older than him. In addition to these dreams, Dr Thomas experienced a large number of lapses in managing the ground rules of his sessions with these two patients. For example, he inadvertently left his office early and missed a session with one of them and he mistakenly extended the session of the other woman by fifteen minutes.

On the conscious level, Dr Thomas recognized that his attraction to these women patients was motivated by his wish to undo the loss of, and replace, his wife. He also tried to rationalize that these women were unattached and attractive, and that his loving feelings would enhance his therapeutic work with them – i.e., that there was a measure of true love in his feelings towards, and sexual fantasies about, these women. But his unconscious mind saw this love in a very different light. The encoded themes in his dreams spoke to the inappropriateness of his feelings and fantasies, stressing their incestuous qualities and characterizing them as falsely loving.

As for his frame lapses, his conscious sense was that in forgetting his patient's session, he was reenacting the loss of his wife and turning his role as the passive victim into one in which he is the active, abandoning figure. His extension of the other patient's session was viewed as an expression of his wish to undo the loss of his wife by keeping his patient as his prisoner. But here too, his unconscious mind, as reflected in several dreams he had after these incidents, saw these acts in a different light and as both unloving and hurtful. By and large, the dreams were about ruthlessly harming women and in one dream, he murdered an old girlfriend. His private associations to these dreams revealed that unconsciously, he held himself accountable for the death of his wife and that his frame violations were motivated by unconscious wishes to be punished by his victimized patients – e.g., by their leaving therapy – because of the murder he unconsciously believed he had committed.

In general, therapists have tended to underestimate the extent to which the vicissitudes of their personal lives, and especially traumatic events, affect their work with, and loving or unloving attitudes towards, their patients, including their management of the ground rules of therapy. This is another aspect of love in psychotherapy that needs further scrutiny.

The Contextural Component

The contextural aspects of psychotherapy frame the therapeutic experience both psychologically and physically, and they define the background conditions for the treatment experience and for the emergence of love, true or false. These components tend to have a settled core that is, as well, open to variations from one session to the next. They exert a continuous influence on the therapeutic couple, most of it unconsciously mediated.

Goals and Satisfactions

The primary goal of psychotherapy is to alleviate patients' emotional suffering, their maladaptations. and dysfunctions. In addition, there are a number of secondary, complementary goals that pertain to the therapists' satisfactions, such as helping patients to heal their emotional wounds; developing fresh understanding of human emotional life as it pertains to their patients and themselves; and having an adequate income through the fees paid to them by their patients. In principle, loving feelings in, and behaviors of, patients or therapists that are consonant with these goals are true and appropriate. Those that are not, fall into the false love category.

Uncertainties arise in trying to precisely define the kinds of feelings, verbal communications, and behaviors that are, in fact, in keeping with the appropriate goals and satisfactions of the treatment experience. For example, do they include opportunities for a therapist to write a professional paper about the new insights that he or she has garnered in working with a particular patient? Is it appropriate for the patient to be told about the paper so he or she can approve the material and possibly share in that satisfaction? These and many other similar questions cannot be answered through conscious system observations and thinking which are quite varied from one therapist to the next. Patients' deep unconscious experiences and adaptive processing of these satisfaction-related issues do, however, offer a consistent set of answers because they reflect universals far more than individual propensities. Therapists therefore should make ample use of trigger decoding when a satisfaction problem arises in a given psychotherapy situation and they are well advised to learn to accept the encoded pronouncements of the deep unconscious wisdom and moral subsystems in these matters. Satisfactions that stay within the boundaries of the role requirements and ground rules of psychotherapy tend to be acceptable and viewed as truly loving deep unconsciously, while those that extend beyond these boundaries are viewed as unloving and exploitative.

In regard to the question of writing a well-disguised paper or book about a particular treatment experience, for example, deep unconscious guidelines indicate that there is an unresolvable conflict between the needs of the field of psychotherapy for informed presentations of clinically-grounded new ideas in the one hand, and on the other, the therapeutic needs of patients and the appropriate satisfactions of psychotherapists. Writing about a patient, however well disguised, is seen deep unconsciously by both patient and therapist as unloving and exploitative no matter how valuable the particular contribution. This clinical finding should be given full consideration in these situations. One solution is for the therapist-writer to make up representative vignettes based on his or her collective clinical experiences so that the main points are clinically illustrated while the ground rules regarding privacy and confidentiality are sustained.

You can deceive the conscious mind, but not its deep unconscious counterpart. This is especially pertinent when it comes to love in psychotherapy because true love is seen deep unconsciously as adaptively wise and moral, while false love is viewed as maladaptive and immoral. Unconsciously mediated consequences unfold accordingly.

Role Requirements

Another set of contextural consideration regarding love in psychotherapy pertains to the prescribed role requirements for both patients and
therapists. The form that love takes, the ways in which it may be
appropriately expressed, and the limits set on these expressions are
contingent on the identity of each party to therapy and what is
required of them. This specificity is seen, for example, in the differences in the optimal and permissible expressions of love that occur
between a mother and child as compared to that between the mother
and her husband. In some cases, as with a mother and child, the nature
of acceptable expressions of love change with time as their responsibilities and expectations of each other – i.e., the role requirements of
the relationship – are altered. On the other hand, there are relationships for which the form and boundaries of expressed love are fairly
stable and persist throughout the entire span of the contacts between
the parties – and in many cases, after direct contact has ended as well.
The therapeutic relationship is of this latter type – one of several ways
in which it differs from the mother-child dyad to which it so often is
mistakenly compared.

There are significant differences in the role requirements that prevail
for the two parties to the therapeutic relationship and these differences
are pertinent to the form taken by true and false love expressed by each
of them. Although the patient's therapeutic needs are primary, the therapist nonetheless has the dominant role in the treatment situation. He
or she has the greater responsibility for framing the psychotherapy
experience and for defining the nature of the satisfactions that are consciously deemed appropriate for both parties to treatment. This role
requirement creates what is often alluded to as the 'tilted therapeutic
relationship' in which the therapist wields a measure of qualified power
over the patient. With this prerogative, however, comes the greater
responsibility for what happens in the course of the therapy.

The main role requirements for the psychotherapist include having
the necessary expertise as a therapist; setting up the consultation
session; providing the patient with a secured office for his or her sessions; establishing the patient's need for therapy; creating and maintaining the ground rules and boundaries of the therapy; informing the
patient directly or indirectly as to his or her responsibilities and role in
the treatment experience; intervening in a manner that is empathic and
healing for the patient; and placing the patient's therapeutic needs
above all else.

As for the matter of love, the therapist has the basic responsibility to define the parameters within which it can or should be expressed. This task generally is carried out without explicit instructions, but is reflected in the therapist's demeanor and ways of handling the ground rules and boundaries of the treatment. It also is expressed in the therapist's selection of material for interpretation and in the meanings that the therapist proposes in connection with the patient's loving expressions. Quite critical is the manner in which the therapist responds to a patient's loving feelings and gestures when they arise. Essentially, this entails the absence of a reciprocal response, the maintenance of the therapeutic boundaries and ground rules, and sustaining the effort to understand the sources and nature of the loving feeling or action, along with making the necessary, relevant trigger-decoded interpretations.

For their part, patients are required to have a need for and to seek help with their emotion-related problems; to work with their therapists in the manner prescribed; to cooperate with and respond to the reasonable interventions of their therapists; to attend sessions regularly and pay the therapist's fee in timely fashion; to be honest and forthright and not conceal information and feelings from their therapists; to respect the valid ground rules and boundaries of their therapy as established by the therapist, and to explore any impulse to do otherwise; and to be prepared to end treatment when their emotional problems have been resolved. Expressions of patient-love should fall within the sphere of these role requirements and not entail a departure from these requisites.

Ground Rules and Boundaries

All of the distinctive contexts in which a given psychotherapy unfolds have features that involve the ground rules and boundaries of the treatment experience, as they are explicitly implicitly defined by the psychotherapist. There are, of course, rare exceptions to this rule in which a patient sets one or more of the conditions of treatment. Nevertheless, the therapist, who has the prerogative of accepting or not accepting the patient's proposal, still has the greater responsibility in this regard.

The setting and rules of psychotherapy are called the *frame or framework of treatment* (Langs, 1998b, 2004c). The deep unconscious mind harbors an ideal, archetypal set of conditions for a psychotherapy experience and a therapy that is conducted under these conditions is called a *secured frame psychotherapy.* A therapy for which one or more of these universally sought ground rules is altered or omitted is known as a *deviant- or modified-frame psychotherapy.*

Operating with considerable influence, there are two basic ways in which the ground rules and framework of a psychotherapy affects the emergence and nature of loving feelings and impulses, true and false, in the parties to a given psychotherapy situation. The first entails the effects of the type of setting and ground rules set up by the therapist. In principle, establishing a secured-frame psychotherapy situation is an expression of true therapist-love and implicitly enhances patients' expressions of true love in return. On the other hand, creating a deviant-frame psychotherapy is an expression of false therapist-love and inherently, it promotes patients' expressions of love that are false as well. Similarly, patients who accept and work within a secured frame for their therapy tend to be truly loving, while patients who refuse to do so or press for a modified frame tend to love falsely, if at all.

As for the second major effect of the ground rules and boundaries, once established, they operate as a steady influence on the emergence of loving feelings and the form that they take, true or false. As noted, secured frames tend to create the conditions under which both patients and therapists are motivated to express true love, while modified frames motivate expressions of false love. Of note in this regard is the finding that patients' efforts to enact or gratify loving feelings directed towards their therapists, which almost always are false expressions of love, are rare in secured frames and quite common in frames that are deviant.

Finally, frame-related issues outside of treatment may play a role in expressions of patient-love, but as a rule, the effects are relatively minor. Such issues do, however, have a greater influence on expressions of therapist-love. Much of this appears to arise because deep unconsciously, patients are more invested in their therapies than their therapists, much of it because patients have but one therapist, while therapists tend to have many patients.

Is True Patient-love a Necessity?

Having framed and contexturalized the experience of love in psychotherapy, we may now ask if true patient-love is an essential requirement for an effective psychotherapeutic experience. The answer to this question is rather complicated.

By and large, patients enter psychotherapy without love for their therapists, true or false. The emergence of patient-love is contingent on the interventions of the therapist – interpretive, non-interpretive, frame-related, and otherwise – which begin with the referral and the patient's first therapeutic contact. Through it all, the hallmark of true patient-love is that it is a response to unconsciously validated interventions and is itself unconsciously validated. It may emerge consciously in one of several guises, such as a deserving respect and trust of the therapist or an appropriate admiration of his or her wisdom, empathy and therapeutic skills. Transient conscious feelings of closeness, affection, positive regard, and actual love may also express true patient-love. A patient's occasional passing sexual fantasy or other kind of wish directed towards the therapist that does not spill over into efforts at satisfaction may be a form of true patient-love as well.

However, in order to insure the truthfulness and healing qualities of a patient's loving expression, the intervention that has triggered the feeling of love must be investigated and shown to be one that the patient has, in fact, validated deep unconsciously. In addition, the patient's deep unconscious perceptions of the nature of his or her love must be determined because of the reliability of the deep unconscious system's evaluations of loving expressions themselves.

Should a therapist appear to be ill or impaired in some way, muted feelings of love or concern also may well be within bounds. This does not, however, hold when a therapist deliberately reveals that he or she, or a family member or any other personal acquaintance, is or has been suffering with an illness or injury. This kind of deliberate violation of the therapist's relative anonymity is a consciously wrought appeal for help and love, and as such is, according to deep unconscious assessments, a non-loving intervention. Any patient-love that such an intervention evokes very likely will be false and defensive.

In addition to its above-noted conscious forms, true patient-love often is experienced deep unconsciously and conveyed in patients' encoded narratives. This love is disguised in dreams and stories in which healthy and satisfying forms of love for and between others encode a patient's true love for a truly loving therapist. With a truly loving psychotherapist, unconsciously expressed true patient-love is far more common than comparable conscious feelings. This is the case because expressions of true therapist-love inevitably bring the patient face-to-face with their death-related issues and their unconscious ramifications. Some of this arises because true therapist-love often is expressed through frame-securing interventions which, while ideally holding and caring, evoke severe forms of existential death anxiety. Thus, the lovingly secured frame disturbs patients even as it offers them the exceptional opportunity to be truly loved and to experience, explore, and resolve their dreaded death-related anxieties. Similarly, valid, deeply insightful, trigger-decoded interpretations are lovingly healing, yet they also touch on or lead to patients' death-related traumas and the activation of the death anxieties and deep unconscious guilt that they have aroused. Patients working with truly loving psychotherapists therefore can be expected to alternate between expressing their true love for their therapists and pulling back and becoming resistant and fearful of them.

True love never runs smoothly in an unconsciously validated psychotherapy experience.

Summing up, true conscious patient-love is not a requisite for a successful insightful psychotherapy, whereas true deep unconscious patient-love is vital to the healing process mainly because it is a sign that the therapist is being truly loving and deeply helpful to the patient. Deep unconscious loving expressions are displaced onto other individuals who appear in patients' dreams and stories, and their associations to these so-called *origination narratives* – i.e., images that serve as sources for further narrative associations. These truly loving storied themes are, as a rule, triggered by an unconsciously validated intervention and almost always are reflections of appropriate, well-deserved positive feelings towards the deeply effective, truly loving therapist.

True patient-love of this kind greatly facilitates the well-secured, insight-oriented therapeutic process.

Is True Therapist-love a Necessity?

The love-related requisites for therapists are different from those for their patients. Indications are that muted or neutralized feelings of affection, love, and loving concern for their patients is a sine qua non for effective psychotherapy – i.e., that patients do not need to earn their therapist's true love, that it should be given freely to all. A cold, unemotional, unloving approach to patients is likely to be unconsciously perceived by them as hostile and harmful and it can interfere with emotional healing. Transient personal feelings of more intense therapist-love towards a patient may be acceptable if they are short-lived. These feelings do, however, call for private self-processing by the therapist – the strong adaptive, narrative-based form of self-exploration (Langs, 1993) – or for an interlude of psychotherapy with an effective psychotherapist. Much the same applies to persistent conscious feelings of therapist-love and to all consciously loving sexual fantasies about and wishes towards a patient. Intractable, elaborate sexual desires and fantasies of love towards a patient is an indication of a serious emotional disturbance within the therapist and calls for insightful resolution.

There are, then, a limited number of avenues for expressing the kind of true therapist-love needed for a patient's successful psychotherapy experience. On the other hand, expressions of false therapist-love are legion and probably unavoidable to some degree. They take many forms and their detection and resolution is a major challenge for all psychotherapists.

Summing up, *true therapist-love of patients should be unconditional*, even though it may wax and wane in response to a given patient's behaviors and reactions to the therapist's interventions and the treatment process. In contrast, true patient-love is contingent on true therapist-love, which in turn is contingent on intervening in ways that earn patients' deep unconscious validating responses and appreciation.

Some Final Perspectives

There are a number of basic perspectives regarding love in psychotherapy that sum up these introductory ideas and that will put us on the path to clarifying and making constructive use of loving feelings in the treatment situation.

Appropriate feelings of love in psychotherapy – and they may be conscious or unconscious – are multi-determined and basically, are part of a patient's or therapist's efforts at adaptation to emotionally-charged triggering events, most of them caused by the other party to a particular psychotherapy. Such love is highly dependent on the conditions and framework of the therapy, the nature of the therapist's interventions (for the patient) and the patient's material (for the therapist), and a variety of other factors within the patient and therapist, their interaction, and personal lives.

For patients, true love, affection, and caring for their therapists is an adaptive response to true therapist-love – i.e., it must be earned by the therapist. It tends to arise as a momentary conscious feeling that can be described as neutralized, desexualized, and sublimated. It also features respect for the therapist's interpersonal boundaries and for the ground rules of treatment, especially in regard to privacy, confidentiality, and the relative anonymity of the therapist. The truly loving patient is comfortable with, and accepting of, the restraints and limits that apply to loving gestures and shows no need to seek actual satisfaction of sexual and other kinds of extra-therapeutic fantasies and wishes. This kind of patient-love also has elements of empathy, sympathy, and tolerance for the arduous aspects of the therapist's position and role. Patient-love also may be experienced deep unconsciously and conveyed in encoded narratives. Most patient-love on this level of experience is true and has been rightfully earned by the therapist.

Therapeutic work is needed to determine a patient's deep unconscious assessment of his or her consciously expressed loving feelings and urges. True patient-love is based on positive unconscious perceptions of the therapist in light of his or her unconsciously validated therapeutic interventions, which is its defining feature. By way of contrast, false forms of conscious patient-love are marked by being triggered by therapists' interventions that are not unconsciously validated. In such instances, the displaced, encoded themes from patients speak of their therapists' interventions as inappropriate, unloving, seductive, or harmful.

For therapists, true conscious love for their patients should be a quiet aspect of their approach to all of their patients. It also should be privately experienced as a background feeling that does not demand enacted satisfaction. Essentially, it is non-sexual and sublimated, and empathic of, and sympathetic with, the patient's emotional pain and the difficulties in being a psychotherapy patient. When subjected to therapists' own self-processing, these loving feelings are supported deep unconsciously by positive, healing encoded themes. This kind of therapist-love also is expressed by establishing a sound set of ground rules and boundaries for a patient's psychotherapy and in making effective, unconsciously validated frame-securing and interpretive interventions. Failures along these lines are experienced deep unconsciously by both patients and therapists as either falsely loving or distinctly non-loving. All in all, a loveless therapeutic relationship is fundamentally cold and cruel, and unlikely to provide the backdrop for effective emotional healing.

Among the many ways of categorizing love in the therapeutic relationship, the most critical distinctions are between its true and false forms, and between loving feelings, wishes, fantasies, and thoughts on the one hand and on the other, trying to satisfy or enact such feelings in some actual manner, sexually or non-sexually. Constrained expressions of love tend to be true, while enacted expressions of love almost always are false. Whatever form it takes, these four classes of love differ in respect to their unconscious sources and their consequences for both patients and therapists.

Expressions of true and false love in psychotherapy are motivated and affected by a large number of inter-related factors. They include the emotionally relevant histories of both the patient and his or her therapist, with an emphasis on sexual and death-related traumas; the healthy mental capacities of the participants to therapy, as well as their impairments; the vicissitudes of the unfolding therapeutic process;

incidents in the outside lives of the patient and therapist, especially the therapist; and the handling of the ground rules and boundaries that are defined and managed by the therapist and accepted or rejected by the patient as the framework for their therapeutic work together.

Feelings of love in psychotherapy have both manifest/conscious sources and non-manifest/unconscious sources. Similarly, the consequences of loving feelings and enactments are mediated directly and consciously, as well as indirectly and unconsciously. The conscious and deep unconscious sources and effects of loving expressions are very different: Those that are deeply unconscious tend to be the more powerful of the two and to be of greater consequence for the therapeutic experience and the lives and mental health of both the patient and the therapist.

While all conscious expressions of patient-love call for an exploration of the therapist's contributions to this love, this search is especially vital when patients' loving feelings persist or a patient attempts to satisfy that love directly with his or her therapist. While the patient's contributions to these situations is considerable, the therapist plays a significant role as well. Recognizing their role in patient-love, especially when it is false in nature, poses special difficulties for therapists because so much of their contribution is non-manifest and mediated unconsciously. These difficulties are compounded because conscious system evaluations of loving expressions are quite variable and uncertain, and often treacherously misleading even when they are carried out by therapists. This points again to the need for therapists to develop the ability to ascertain their patients' far more reliable deep unconscious assessments of contentious loving expressions and to use these evaluations as guides to both understanding and intervening.

In general, true expressions of love by either party to therapy need not be acknowledged or interpreted. On the other hand, when an expression of therapist-love is identified as false by the therapist, he or she needs to unilaterally, or at the behest of the patient's encoded directives, rectify the situation and interpret the patient's deep unconscious perceptions of the falsity of the love. As for false love from patients, properly interpreted and rectified, these expressions, which tend to be evoked by therapists' errant interventions, can be the basis for affording patients deep unconscious insights into their love-related problems. Much depends on therapists' being able to distinguish manifestations of true versus false love from their patients and themselves.

With these perspectives in mind, let's look now at the strong adaptive approach that I shall be using to expand these ideas and probe more deeply the many issues raised by experiences of love in psychotherapy.

2
The Strong and Weak Adaptive Approaches

The insights into love in psychotherapy presented in this book are based on what I call the strong adaptive or communicative approach to emotional life, the emotion-processing mind, and the therapeutic process. It is a school of psychoanalytically oriented thought that stands in contrast to virtually every other school of psychodynamic thinking, including the various versions of psychoanalysis. I term these theories and the clinical principles and techniques that they spawn *weak adaptive (conscious system) approaches*. Neither term is used pejoratively; each is essentially descriptive.

Weak adaptive approaches acknowledge adaptation to environmental impingements such as natural disasters and the words, deeds, feelings and emotions of other humans, but they see coping with external events as one of a large group of ego functions that are of secondary importance. Their main focus is on an individual's inner mental life and his or her various emotion-related needs, emotions, fantasies, memories, and wishes, as well as inner-directed needs for relatedness, interaction, sexual satisfactions, narcissistic supplies, tension regulation, and the like.

In contrast, the *strong adaptive (deep unconscious system) approach* views adaptation to traumatic environmental events as the primary function of the emotion-processing mind and affords a secondary role in emotional life to inner needs, wishes, and the like. In addition, while weak adaptive approaches tend to be grounded in the structural theory of ego, id, and superego (Freud, 1923), the strong adaptive approach is rooted in a revised topographic model of the mind (Freud, 1900) that is configured with two operating systems – conscious and deep unconscious (Langs, 1992a, 1995, 2004c).

Weak Adaptive Approaches

Weak adaptive approaches come in many different versions: Classical psychoanalysis (Gabbard, 1996; Langs, 1998a); object relations theory; the inter-subjective, interpersonal, constructivistic, and self-psychological approaches; cognitive psychotherapy, and the like (Kohut, 1971, 1977; Hoffman, 1983, 1991, 1992, 1998; Atwood and Stolorow, 1984; Stolorow *et al.*, 1987; Mitchell, 1988, 1993, 2000; Orange, 1998; Aron, 1990; Bacal and Newman, 1990; Gabbard, 1996; Orange *et al.*, 1997; Gordon *et al.* 1998; Loewis, 1998; Miller and Dorpat, 1998; Singer, 1998). Each version has adopted a biased way of thinking and a restricted field of vision. But despite their diversities, they share much in common in regard to the focus and limits of their observations, their methods of listening to and formulating the material from patients, their basic understanding of how the human mind operates, and the nature of the transactions within the therapeutic interaction. When it comes to love in psychotherapy, they all share a basic ideology that seeks to understand its vicissitudes in therapy largely in terms of patients' inner strivings, past histories, and current psychopathology. Thus, they tend to define issues pertaining to love in psychotherapy largely in terms of instinctual drive wishes; relationship needs for nurturance, affirmation, and enhanced self-esteem; requisites for tension regulation; and the need for companionship. Interactionally, their position is that therapists play a role in patients' loving needs and ventures, but their contribution is largely coincidental – therapists are evocateurs who sometimes stimulate their patients' internally determined love-related inclinations (Langs, 2005c).

In terms of listening and formulating, weak adaptive therapists tend to focus on the manifest contents of patients' material and of their own interventions, and on the evident implications of these communications. Unconscious meaning is either by-passed or defined as those implications of a patient's manifest material of which the patient evidently is unaware. This focus on *extractable, implied meanings* takes weak adaptive therapists to a realm of emotion-related experience that is very different from that accessed through the decoding of *narrative themes* and imagery in light of their evocative *triggers* – a process that is used extensively by strong adaptive therapists. As a result, the two approaches deal with very different realms of experience and thus arrive at very different views of the emotion-processing mind and of love in psychotherapy (Raney, 1984; Smith, 1991).

When issues of love arise in a therapy session, the weak adaptive exploration tends to be straightforward and linear. The patient is asked how he or she feels and the details of these manifest responses are teased out. When therapists make openly provocative interventions, they will ask their patients about their impressions of the incident and queries are made as to what the patient is reminded of. These efforts usually culminate in the direct recognition of a connection between the love-related experience in therapy and comparable incidents with someone in the patient's earlier life. Interpretations generally center around patients' transference-based distortions of their therapists' lapses and with few exceptions, patients' responses are given little credence. Narrative material is not sought after because they are not seen as a special mode of communication. When stories do come up in these explorations, these so-called *coincidental narratives* (Langs, 1988, 2004c), which are about other topics and other people, tend to be ignored or treated as signs of resistance and as irrelevant to the love-related topic at hand. In contrast, strong adaptive therapists would see these stories as embodying invaluable encoded deep unconscious perceptions and assessments of the love-related expression in question.

The Strong Adaptive Approach

The strong adaptive approach originally was called the communicative approach because it pays careful attention to the form and nature of the communications used by patients – and secondarily, by their therapists. In regard to patients' communicative vehicles, a basic distinction is made between those that are narrative in nature (e.g., dreams and stories) and those that take a non-narrative form (e.g., intellectualizations, speculations, interpretations, commentaries). This difference draws its importance from the clinical finding that non-narrative communications essentially are single message vehicles. They convey only one, manifestly stated meaning, which does, of course, carry with it a variety of extractable implications. On the other hand, narratives are two-message communicative vehicles which convey two distinctive sets of meaning, each fraught with its own implications. The first set is manifest and directly stated, while the second set is *encoded* in the same images and themes. These encoded meanings cannot be extracted from the manifest narrative, but must be treated as disguised and displaced images that can be decoded solely in light of the triggering event or communication that has evoked the storied expression. Thus, while the surface meanings of narratives can be understood directly as such, their disguised meanings can be determined solely through the process of *trigger decoding* because they are not evident in the surface tale (Langs, 1999).

These communicative distinctions are observationally-based and play a significant role in the psychodynamic formulations and understanding of the strong adaptive approach. They have enabled the approach to derive a distinctive set of fundamental concepts regarding the nature of the emotion-related mind and its operations – and of love in psychotherapy. A key thesis of the approach, one that has been derived through its adaptation-oriented listening and decoding processes, is that the primary function of the emotion-processing mind – the postulated mental module that has evolved to deal with emotionally-charged issues – is to adapt to traumatic environmental impingements such as adverse acts of nature and the hurtful words and deeds of other living beings. While favorable incidents, such as acts of true love, tend to have positive effects and evoke salutary responses in their recipients, unfavorable, traumatic triggering events, such as expressions of false love, tend to have negative effects and evoke a variety of dysfunctional responses in those towards whom they are directed. The emotion-processing mind has evolved to cope as effectively as possible with these damaging incidents.

A Revised Model of the Mind

Much as the human immune system is basically designed to deal with microscopic predators and physical death-related threats, and only secondarily with internal threats within an individual, the emotion-processing mind is basically designed to deal with macroscopic or gross death-related external dangers, both physical and psychological, and only secondarily with internal emotional issues that threaten the survival of the individual. There is then a significant shift from the weak adaptive view that inner mental transactions drive both emotional health and emotional dysfunctions to the strong adaptive view that external events play this role. This change in viewpoint has major consequences for our understanding of the human mind, emotional life in general, and love in psychotherapy in particular.

The emotion-processing mind copes with these emotionally-charged, traumatic triggering events on the basis of two relatively independent operating systems, a conscious and deep unconscious system. Each of these systems has its own means of perception, particular sensitivities and insensitivities to various types of incoming stimuli, defenses, intelligence, adaptive processing capabilities, adaptive preferences, moral and ethical values, and mode of communication.

The Conscious System

The conscious system functions on the basis of direct, consciously registered perceptions of triggering events and their implications, and it responds with conscious appraisals of these events and manifest, undisguised responsive communications. The resources of this system are familiar to us because they are available to direct awareness; they usually are grouped under the rubrics of ego, superego, and id functions. There are, however, three generally unrecognized features of this system that can be discerned solely by contrasting manifest, conscious responses to triggering events with those that are encoded and deep unconscious. Each of these attributes has profound effects on the conscious system's operations, values, and adaptations, including the system's views on, and preferences regarding, love in psychotherapy.

The first generally unrecognized feature is the basically defensive alignment of the conscious system, which has evolved with strong protective defenses designed to block the conscious registration and recognition of many potentially disruptive triggering events and their more discombobulating meanings. Thus, the conscious system (i.e., the conscious mind) automatically and without conscious awareness makes extensive use of obliteration and denial in response to many anxiety-provoking events and meanings. This overuse of defenses severely curtails the system's knowledge-base and creates blind-spots and biases that affect its adaptive choices, preferred ways of expressing love, and its views on love as well.

The second largely overlooked feature is the conscious system's imperviousness to deep unconscious wisdom and knowledge, which has little if any effect on conscious choices and adaptations (see below). On the other hand, the conscious system is greatly affected by deep unconscious guilt which arises from having harmed others. This guilt, which operates entirely outside of awareness (but is encoded in narrative images) activates unconscious needs for self-punitive choices and actions. This means that conscious thinking is strongly biased by self-punitive needs that affect its ways of expressing love and its evaluations of love-related communications.

The third generally unrecognized feature of the conscious system is the extent to which its views of the emotional world, adaptive preferences, and ways of thinking vary from one person to another. The operations of the conscious system tend to be highly individualized and greatly affected by a given person's conscious and unconscious needs, current traumas and satisfactions, and life history, especially as it pertains to death-related traumas. Unlike the deep unconscious system, there are few archetypes and universals in the operations of the conscious mind. As a result, its views on such general matters as factors in emotional illnesses and issues in therapeutic techniques, and on specific issues pertaining to love in psychotherapy, almost always lack a clear consensus. There are, then, virtually no universally agreed-on weak adaptive, consciously-based positions regarding the subject under study in this book.

The Deep Unconscious System

For ease of discussion, I shall focus on psychotherapy patients in my initial presentation of the key features of the deep unconscious system. This system operates on the basis of unconscious or subliminal perceptions of triggering events and their implications, which the system adaptively processes using a strikingly wise deep unconscious wisdom subsystem. The nature of the perceptions and processing activities of the deep unconscious system are conveyed in encoded narrative messages. These messages can be decoded using the emotionally-charged meanings of the events that have activated the deep unconscious mind, a process called trigger decoding. While the conscious system of patients works over tolerable incidents and meanings of incidents that occur both within and outside of therapy, the deep unconscious system works over incidents and meanings of incidents that are intolerable to conscious awareness and, with few exceptions, that take place within the therapeutic interaction. Patients' deep unconscious systems are centered on their therapists' interventions, especially those that involve the ground rules and framework of the treatment situation. This focus makes considerable sense because it has been found that the framework of a psychotherapy experience has extensive effects on the participants to, and the vicissitudes of, a given psychotherapy.

The deep unconscious system has three subsystems and each plays a significant role in evaluating love in psychotherapy and expressing its deep unconscious form:

A *wisdom subsystem*, which is extremely intelligent and adaptively wise, and whose recommendations are encoded in displaced, narrative communications. Because this wisdom is built around experiences that are intolerable to awareness, its perception and adaptive processing efforts attain conscious representation solely in disguised form and this is why it has little effect on conscious decisions and actions. Nevertheless, the subsystem carefully and with great clarity evaluates and responds adaptively to all love-related gestures made by patients and their therapists, doing so in light of the triggers that have evoked a given loving gesture.

A *subsystem of morality and ethics*, which speaks for and unconsciously endorses a universal, ideal, archetypal set of human values. In psychotherapy, the morality of both patients and therapists is reflected in their position on, and behaviors pertaining to, the ground rules of treatment. Adherence to the ideal frame is deep unconsciously viewed as highly moral, while modifying an archetypal ground rule is viewed as immoral. This subsystem, which has, as noted above, a strong unconscious influence on conscious thinking and behavior, evokes an experience of deep unconscious guilt when its precepts are violated. In turn, this guilt unconsciously orchestrates self-punitive and self-harmful conscious decisions and actions whose true sources usually go unrecognized consciously. This subsystem evaluates the moral implications of all love-related gestures by both patients and their therapists. By and large, it sees securing or accepting the ideal ground rules of therapy as truly loving and moral, and modifying the ideal frame as falsely loving and immoral.

A *danger-sensitive subsystem*, which is activated by death-related traumas and the death-related meanings of seemingly non-traumatic events, behaviors, and comments. This subsystem, discovered through the strong adaptive focus on external reality, plays a significant role in human emotion-related adaptations and the vicissitudes of love in psychotherapy. This subsystem does so because emotionally-charged traumas arouse death anxieties that have powerful unconscious effects on emotion-related thoughts, feelings, and behaviors. The death anxieties activated by this system in response to traumatic triggering events are the main cause of conscious-system-denial and the deepest source of most resistances in psychotherapy. These anxieties also are the basis for much that is unloving or falsely loving in the treatment situation on the part of both patients and therapists. They also are the underlying basis for many of the consciously-wrought misconceptions about love in psychotherapy that can be found in the weak adaptive literature. When the death anxieties evoked by this system are insightfully resolved by means of therapists' truly loving interpretive and frame-securing interventions, expressions of true patient-love are a common response.

Each of the subsystems of the deep unconscious mind has a set of fixed, archetypal or universal viewpoints, preferences, and adaptive responses. This renders deep unconscious positions on love in psychotherapy not only extremely wise adaptively, but also remarkably consistent across individuals. For example, the deep unconscious wisdom subsystem of every patient knows and seeks the archetypal or ideally healing set of secured and truly loving ground rules for a psychotherapy experience. Every deep unconscious system of morality and ethics views departures from these ideals as immoral and unloving, a view that is softened but not eliminated when a departure is unavoidable – e.g., the presence of a third-party payer in an insurance-funded psychotherapy. And every patient's danger-sensitive subsystem sees a therapist's invocation of an unneeded frame modification as an unloving or falsely loving predatory act that arouses deep unconscious predatory death anxieties. Conscious views on all of these matters tend to vary greatly from one patient to another.

We can see, then, that while therapists are unable to agree consciously on love-related issues such as whether it is truly loving for a therapist to touch a patient at times of urgent need or to be selectively self-revealing to patients, their deep unconscious positions on these issue tend to be unanimous. As we shall see, its position on these two questions is that both physical contact and deliberate self-revelations are falsely loving or unloving acts that are harmful to patients.

Forms of Death Anxiety

Death and death anxiety are, then, the most fundamental issues in emotional life and its dysfunctions, as well as its interludes of health and creativity. They also are major determinants of expressions of love, true and false, in psychotherapy.

There are three basic forms of *death anxiety* and each may be experienced consciously and/or deep unconsciously (Langs, 1997, 2004a,b,c, 2005a):

Predatory death anxiety – which arises when there is a threat to one's life from natural causes or other living beings, especially other humans. The main response to these threats is the mobilization of resources, mental and physical. In psychotherapy, frame violations, which are unconsciously experienced as immoral and unloving acts, are unconsciously perceived by both their perpetrators and recipients as predatory acts.

Predator death anxiety – the fear of being killed or harmed as retribution for harming or destroying natural resources or other living beings. This form of death anxiety is linked with conscious and deep unconscious guilt and prompts self-punitive decisions and actions. In psychotherapy, enacting a frame violation generally entails behaving immorally and in an unloving or falsely loving manner and such actions activate this type of death anxiety.

Existential death anxiety – the universal dread of ultimate personal demise. This form of death anxiety is dealt with through denial in its myriad forms in thought and deed. In psychotherapy, existential death anxieties are experienced within the ideal, secured, healing, and truly loving frame as an entrapment anxiety. Efforts to deny or escape existential death anxieties are major unconscious motives for frame violations and for expressions of false forms of love in psychotherapy. On the other hand, the resolution of existential death anxieties is an essential prerequisite for expressions of true love by both patients and therapists.

Two Viewpoints on Love in Psychotherapy

Because they operate relatively independently and are built on very different foundations, the views and adaptive positions of the two systems of the emotion-processing mind are radically different in regard to virtually every important issue in emotional life. In general, the deep unconscious mind appears to be more perceptive, meaning-sensitive, effective adaptively, morally centered, non-defensive, and reliable than its conscious counterpart. We are, then, far wiser and ethical, and far more truly loving, when we have no conscious idea of what we are thinking and are unaware of the meanings of what we are doing than we are when we know exactly where we stand on an emotional issue – love included. This means that encoded, deep unconscious positions on love in psychotherapy are far more reliable than unencoded, manifest, conscious positions. While conscious thinking may be on the mark regarding a love-related issue, more often than not it is well off the mark. On the other hand, deep unconscious thinking on such issues usually is sound and only rarely off-base.

The problems inherent in trusting conscious thinking about love in psychotherapy are compounded because, on the manifest-content level of experience, there is no clinical means of reliably validating and confirming the healing qualities of an intervention and the theoretical constructs on which it is based. The absence of a reliable arbiter is another reason why conscious opinions on love-related issues tend to vary from one therapist to another. This variability is reinforced by their use of direct inquiries when a love-related problem arises in therapy, an approach that extends personally biased impressions without drawing on trigger-decoded, archetypal deep unconscious wisdom.

The strong adaptive perspectives on love have been developed by trigger decoding patients' narrative communications when a love-related issue arises and thereby accessing consistently wise, universal deep unconscious system observations, perspectives, and evaluations. While still open to personal bias or error, the adaptive approach's use of a method in which interpretations are repeatedly subjected to efforts at encoded, unconscious validation or refutation tends to minimize their frequency. *Validation* of an intervention is signaled by the subsequent emergence of narratives with positive themes such as those of helpful, wise, sensitive, or understanding individuals and by the appearance of stories that extend and elaborate the unconscious implications of a therapist's interpretation or frame-securing effort. In contrast, *non-validation* is signaled by the emergence of negatively-toned displaced narrative themes such as those of people who are unhelpful, deaf or blind, harmful, insensitive, and the like.

It can be seen, then, that there are many critical differences between the prevailing weak-conscious system and strong adaptive-deep unconscious system views on love in psychotherapy. And in general, because it draws on deep unconscious wisdom, the strong adaptive view tends to be more consistent across patients and therapists and more reliable than weak adaptive viewpoints (Langs, 2004c, 2005a,b,c).

A Clinical Vignette

In order to highlight the similarities and differences between the weak and strong adaptive positions, let's look at the opening moments of a psychotherapy session in which love became a major issue.

Mr James, a man in his mid-30s, is in psychotherapy with Dr Ford, a male psychologist, because of episodes of depression. About a year into the therapy, he begins a session with a dream in which a man with a dark complexion is handing him a bag full of money. It seems like a terrific gift, but he realizes that the man is trying to entice him into becoming a partner in some kind of crime, perhaps a murder. He takes the money and throws it into a trash can.

Associating to his dream, Mr James says that the man looks like someone whose picture he had seen in the newspaper on the day of the dream. When the comptroller of his company inadvertently left the door to the company's safe open at the end of a day of collections, the man emptied the safe of money and disappeared. While it was no excuse for what the man did, it was really stupid of the comptroller to forget to lock the safe.

This brings to mind an incident regarding Mr James' father, who also has a dark complexion. His father was an aloof man who traveled a lot for business and often spent weeks at a time away from their home. A few years ago, his father fell ill with a cancer of the large bowel that was removed surgically. When the patient visited him at home after the operation, the father openly expressed his guilt and remorse for having been such an uncaring parent and for not having been there for his son. He told the patient that he was going to make amends and show the love he has for him by giving him a gift of 20,000 dollars. To his amazement, his father immediately handed him a check in that amount. However, when the father told the patient that he had earned the money through a series of illegal stock trades, he gave the money back to him. Mr James had been very depressed at the time, and he also is feeling depressed at the moment. Somehow, these feelings seem to have something to do with a kickback he gave to one of his customers to persuade him to not move his business to a competitor and to continue to buy his electrical equipment from the patient's firm. Maybe he feels guilty about being involved in this kind of dirty business.

Before analyzing this vignette, let's note that in principle, because they virtually always adopt a narrative form, dreams are important carriers of both manifest and encoded meanings. In addition, they serve as markers for additional storied material, narrative associations that are brought to mind by the dream elements and that usually are drawn from the life of the dreamer. These storied *guided associations* almost always are more powerful and significant than the images in the dream itself. Together, a dream and a patient's guided associations to the dream form an invaluable *dream-associational network or pool of themes* that encodes the dreamer's deep unconscious perceptions and adaptive processing activities in response to emotionally-charged triggering events.

Weak Adaptive Formulations

That said, how might a weak adaptive therapist formulate and understand this patient's material to this point in the session? While many different psychodynamic conjectures are possible, the following seems more or less representative. The patient has been involved recently in giving his client an illegal financial kickback. At first, he denies feeling guilty, but then acknowledges it. The manifest dream suggests that unconsciously, the patient sees himself as a criminal and is fearful of being found out and prosecuted. He may be thinking of fleeing the therapy before his crime is discovered, in part because in his unconscious fantasies, taking a customer away from a rival company is viewed as an act of oedipal murder.

The associations to the dream seem to reveal Mr James' unconscious identification with his father as a criminal. His superego and conscience seem to be trying to goad him into finding a way to undo and reform his own dishonest ways, as seen by the allusion to his having given back tainted money in both his dream and in reality, with his father. In this connection, we might also speculate that, as seems to have been the case with his father, Mr James uses money to express the love that he is unable to give to others in more personal ways. The imagery also suggests that in the therapy – i.e., in his relationship with Dr Ford – Mr James is experiencing a father-transference in which he is projecting his own and his father's dishonesty onto the therapist.

Finally, were a weak adaptive therapist to think about issues of true and false love, the thought might be that offering love through the giving of illicitly gained money is a type of false love. It follows then that there also may be an unconscious father-transference here in which the patient, based on his experiences with his father, mistakenly sees the therapist as withholding his love and as offering it through interpretations that are corrupted in a way that is similar to the father's offer of money gained dishonestly. In light of this formulation of an inner mental projective mechanism, there would be little reason for a weak adaptive therapist to look for a current love-related issue in the psychotherapy.

While a lot more could be proposed regarding this excerpt – as noted, conscious thinking in psychotherapy varies from one therapist to another – these patient-centered formulations are sufficient to allow us to compare them with those that can be made on the basis of the strong adaptive approach.

A Strong Adaptive Formulation

While acknowledging the presence of intrapsychic issues and conflicts within the mind of the patient, the strong adaptive therapist would see them as secondary and as overshadowed by the patient's need to cope with some kind of triggering event that most likely has arisen within the therapy. Thus, the strong adaptive assessment would begin with the suggestion that a vital piece of information is missing from the presentation – namely, the evocative interventional trigger to which the patient is reacting consciously and especially, deep unconsciously. Instead of trying to formulate the patient's fantasies and wishes, the strong adaptive therapist would be searching for a trigger that would allow the patient's narrative material to be formulated as valid deep unconscious perceptions of the meanings this trigger and as reflections of the earlier life events (genetics) to which these perceptions are linked.

Because false love is a major theme in this patient's narrative material, the strong adaptive therapist would be looking for a triggering intervention that he or she had made that could be viewed as such an expression. This search would reveal that at the end of the previous session, Dr Ford had given the patient his bill for the previous month's sessions. That month, Mr James had had to cancel a session because of a business trip that he was obligated to make. The ground rule regarding absences from sessions that Dr Ford had established at the outset of the therapy called for the patient to be responsible for all missed sessions – the time that had been allotted to him. On a previous occasion of this kind, the patient had complained that it was unfair to hold him responsible for sessions that he had to miss because of his job. The exploration of this issue was, however, confined to the conscious level of communication and experience. The patient's encoded narratives were not decoded or addressed even though they spoke for the need to keep this aspect of the ground rules in place and secured. As a result, Dr Ford had decided this time to forego the fee for this recently missed hour. When he saw the bill, Mr James was enormously grateful for the waiver of the fee and as he left the session, he thanked the therapist profusely for his kindness and consideration. The material presented above is from the opening moments of the following session.

We may now trigger decode Mr James' dream in light of Dr Ford's triggering intervention – his seemingly loving decision to forgive his fee for the recently missed session. The method calls for undoing the disguises in the dream and associated narratives by using this adaptation-evoking trigger as the decoding key. This effort shows that, in contrast to Mr James' conscious feelings that the therapist had acted in a truly caring and loving fashion, forgiving the fee was experienced deep unconsciously as an illicit act, a falsely loving gift of illegally gained (frame-violating) money. The therapist's seemingly caring and thoughtful intervention was seen deep unconsciously as a thoughtless failure to properly secure the frame – cf. the comptroller's not locking the door to the safe. It also was validly perceived as an invitation to the patient to steal money that belongs to the therapist – i.e., the unpaid fee to which he was entitled. As encoded in the dream and in the associated offer from the patient's father of dishonestly gained money, deep unconsciously, the patient rightfully felt that the therapist was making him into a criminal through his falsely loving gesture. In addition, as reflected in the story of the business payoff, the intervention was seen unconsciously as an attempt by the therapist to bribe the patient into staying in the therapy. The allusion to the thief's disappearance may well convey the patient's thoughts of leaving treatment because of this falsely loving attempt at bribery.

While the conscious mind usually has one or two experiences of, and opinions about, an emotionally-charged incident, the deep unconscious mind has multiple experiences and develops a strikingly large number of viewpoints of the same incident, each of them quite valid. We can see too that conscious experience tends to be restricted by the extensive use of denial and that conscious concerns tend to be off-center. Thus, conscious thinking is inclined to be relatively thin, over-intellectualized, naïve, defensive, and drained of meaning and emotional impact. In contrast, deep unconscious thinking is inclined to be wide ranging, detailed, powerful, disturbing, and of great import, with effects that are unconsciously mediated.

Clinical experience indicates that as a rule, modifications of ground rules that manifestly satisfy patients' wishes and superficial needs are experienced consciously as loving. However, the patient's deep unconscious experience is quite the opposite. With great consistency, this system insists that such gestures are falsely loving, largely because the therapist has failed to meet the patient's basic needs for an ideal, archetypal, truly loving secured frame. This is a valid viewpoint that has strong effects on patients because deep unconsciously, they feel over-indulged and corrupted by such interventions and begin to mistrust their frame-violating, immoral therapists. For their part, while feeling satisfied consciously over their misguided generosity, therapists who gratify patients with deeply unloving frame modifications experience a strong measure of deep unconscious guilt which then unconsciously drives them towards self-punitive decisions and actions.

The dream theme of the patient being asked to cooperate in an act of murder is notable because it shows how a falsely loving intervention that is entirely non-violent on the surface can be experienced deep unconsciously as having murderous qualities. In this situation, the accompanying themes suggest that the therapist's frame-modifying intervention has ramifications that actually could destroy both the patient and his therapy. In addition, with due respect for the patient's own conflicts and issues, the theme of murder also may reflect the patient's justified murderous anger against the therapist for his over-indulgent and deeply harmful, falsely loving intervention. All of these deep unconscious experiences will have profound adverse effects on the patient in both his therapy and private life.

All in all, then, a seeming expression of therapist-love that would be supported and sanctioned by many weak adaptive psychotherapists turns out to be experienced deep unconsciously by the patient as a falsely loving intervention that does violence to both himself and his psychotherapy. These insights come to us solely through the use of trigger decoding. It is well to realize, however, that such decoding is possible only when a patient is allowed or encouraged to communicate displaced and disguised narrative themes. Conscious system therapists tend to explore love-related triggers directly by asking patients for their conscious thoughts and intellectualized associations to the trigger. But deep unconscious system therapists do the exact opposite: Implicitly, they ask patients to tell a story about anything but the triggering inter-vention. Dr Ford did this by being silent and allowing the patient, who began the session with a dream, to associate other stories to his dream. If Mr James had not done so, Dr Ford could have asked him to associ-ate to the dream with incidents from his personal life. One approach restricts the patient to his conscious thoughts, the other opens the door to deep unconscious thinking. It is this door that I shall soon open for our investigations of love in psychotherapy. But before I do so, let's turn to the existing literature, beginning with the subject of patient-love, to see where matters stand regarding love in psychotherapy as seen from a weak adaptive perspective.

3

Patient-love: The Literature

The writings on love in psychotherapy tend to deal far more with patient-love than therapist-love. Freud established this trend by writing extensively on patient-love, which he explored in the context of his ideas about transference (Freud, 1912a,b, 1913, 1915a). In contrast, he had far less to say about therapist-love, which he touched on only sparingly in terms of countertransference, a term he used to allude to emotional problems in the analyst that created obstacles to cure (Freud, 1910). In the many years that followed Freud's initial writings, the subject of love in psychotherapy was explored mainly by psychoanalysts who therefore account for almost all of the writings that I shall discuss here. Nevertheless, the theoretical ideas offered by these writers clearly are meant to apply in some way to patient-therapist interactions in general. From a strong adaptive perspective, such generalizations are well justified in that therapeutic interactions in both psychoanalysis and psychotherapy tend to unfold with comparable love-related forces and motives in play, especially on the deep unconscious level of experience.

Freud on Patient-love

Psychodynamic efforts to understand the sources and meanings of love in psychotherapy begin with two of Freud's seminal papers on the technique of psychoanalysis (Freud, 1912a, 1915a) in which he linked the subject of patient-love to his concept of transference. Defining transference as intrapsychic templates that are imposed on the contemporary relationship with the analyst, Freud suggested that it has two basic forms – positive or loving and negative or hostile. Positive transference is either conscious or unconscious. The former takes shape as affection and is a sublimated form of erotic love that tends to advance the analytic work. The latter is sexual in nature, repressed, expressed through evident displacements, and operates in the service of resistance. The analyst's task is to enable the patient to consciously experience his or her unconscious transference wishes by removing the obstacles that block them from direct awareness. In Freud's thinking, these repressed wishes break through whole cloth into awareness once the resistances opposing their expression are removed.

Freud explicitly stated that these historically-genetically determined templates of patients' needs for love and for 'love objects' are the unconscious source of patients' neuroses. Their presence makes it inevitable that patients will fall in love with their analysts. While this love is recruited by patients as a distraction or effort to resist and sabotage the analysis when infantile complexes are being recovered from repression, the analytic exploration of the nature and genetic sources of this love can be used to advance the analytic process as well.

All in all, then, Freud placed love at the center of the psychoanalytic experience. He saw the analysis of a patient's transference-love for his or her analyst as the central vehicle through which a patient's neurosis is cured. This love was understood to be intrapsychically determined and inevitable once a patient entered analysis. It was transference-based in that it does not arise from the person and actions of the analyst, but from the patient's fixed templates for his or her conditions for falling in love. There was little or no interactional component to Freud's view of patient-love – transference-love essentially arose from within the patient and was interjected into the analytic relationship. It was projected onto the analyst who was advised by Freud to neither accept nor reject the patient's love, but to subject it to analysis. This meant tracing the love back to its unconscious infantile roots. It was the analyst's task to show the patient that her love for her analyst, which feels real to her (Freud wrote of women patients), actually is unreal or illusory because it belongs to the patient's earlier life.

Freud's ideas about transference-love have been generally accepted and elaborated on by many later-day psychoanalysts (Gabbard, 1996). By and large there has been one major addendum to Freud's thinking that has arisen largely in reaction to his stress on the role of forbidden instinctual-drive wishes in transference-love. This entailed a shift from Freud's so-called one-person, drive-oriented view of the analytic interaction to a two-person, person-oriented view in which the analyst is understood to play a role in shaping the patient's transferences (Kohut, 1971, 1977; Atwood and Stolorow, 1984; Stolorow *et al.*, 1987; Aron, 1990; Bacal and Newman, 1990; Orange *et al.*, 1997; Gordon *et al.*, 1998; Miller and Dorpat, 1998; Mitchell, 1988, 2000). These interactional or interpersonal elements are, however, viewed in general terms and attributed to the presence of the analyst and the nature of the analytic setting. A role also is afforded to the analyst's interventions, but the stress is on their manifest meanings and extractable implications. The essential idea is that, driven by their inner needs and fixed ways of relating and seeking satisfactions, patients recruit their analysts' interventions as justifications for their inappropriate, transference-based feelings of love – or hate – for their therapists (Gabbard, 1996).

Missing from these formulations is the idea that patient-love is an adaptive or maladaptive response to the specific conditions of therapy and to the particular interventions of therapists; interventions that are perceived and experienced both consciously and deep unconsciously. A full picture of patients' love in psychotherapy seems to require a deeper understanding of therapists' interventions and their patients' deep unconscious perceptions of their implications. This picture can be developed solely by the process of trigger decoding described in the previous chapter. Without such considerations, we are left with a conscious-system literature with proposed insights that are based almost entirely on the evident, conscious meanings of the therapist's interventions and patients' manifest responses to their extractable implications. There are many pitfalls in exploring patient-love working solely with this level of communication and meaning.

Further Historical Perspectives

A study of the historical basis on which the concept of transference-love was first invoked illuminates some of the unappreciated problems with this theoretical construct. Some years ago, Chertok (1968) investigated this matter in detail. He describes how, in the 1890s, Freud was privileged to hear about the psychotherapeutic work that his mentor, the internist Joseph Breuer, had carried out with a patient called Anna O. (Breuer and Freud, 1893–1895). These efforts included hypnotic regressions with visualizations of the traumatic incidents that had evoked his patient's various hysterical symptoms. These regressions enabled his patient to abreact the bottled-up emotions connected with the conflicts aroused by these precipitating events; evident symptom relief then followed. Freud adopted this hypnotic method and used it with his 'neurotic' women patients, visiting them in their homes, usually in their bedrooms, and adding full body massages to the regime.

According to Chertok, the inciting incident for the invocation of the transference idea took place during a home visit by Freud to a young woman patient. Freud had completed his therapeutic ministrations when she woke up from her trance and threw her arms around him and expressed her undying love for him. Deciding that he had not done anything to arouse his patient's ardor – i.e., invoking denial – Freud reasoned that the love that the patient felt towards him was undeserved and must belong to her father rather than his 'charmless self'. He reasoned that the patient had unconsciously transferred her love for her seductive father onto himself, her innocent physician.

Experiences of this kind, in which the contributions of the therapist to the patient's feelings towards him or her are blatant but not recognized and thus denied, are part of the clinical basis for the concept of transference to this day. This type of situation flies in the face of the idea that patients' love for their analysts is unprovoked and that although the love feels quite real to them, it is, in fact, quite unreal (Freud, 1912a, 1915a; Gabbard, 1996; Friedman, 2005). The claim is that while the love is believed to be genuine by the patient, it actually is illusory because it does not really apply to the analyst but to an earlier person in the life of the patient. In classical forms of psychoanalysis patients are expected to understand and accept this confounding and unreal aspect of their loving feelings towards their analysts – the so-called 'as if' qualities of their love. Failure to do so is thought to be a sign of serious psychopathology in the patient and evidence that he or she not only is resistant, but may be unanalyzable.

Both Little (1951) and Szasz (1963) have pointed out that the concept of transference implies the innocence of the analyst. Their main point is that labeling a patient's loving attitude or behavior vis-à-vis their analyst as transference-based carries with it a denial that the analyst has made an intervention that has evoked the patient's loving feelings. Clearly, as detailed by Chertok, this was not the case at the moment when transference was invented. It seems far more in keeping with the clinical evidence that this patient's loving feelings towards Freud arose because of the immediate interventions by her physician which had aroused her sexual needs, perceptions, and wishes. This arousal appears to have been both a response to the current stimulus and a consequence of the patient's earlier experiences with her father and the intrapsychic template that they had left within her psyche. But the past was not motivating her to distort her present view of her therapist, as is conjectured in the concept of transference. Instead, the present seductiveness of Freud, her therapist, was reminiscent of and repeated the past seductiveness of her father. Repetition and accurate perception, be it conscious or unconscious, rather than distortion and misperception appear to have been at play.

While later-day analysts have not attempted to revise Freud's basic thinking about the intrapsychic basis of transference, they have, as noted, made some efforts to correct his oversight in respect to his general contributions to his patient's loving feelings. But even as they bring the therapist into the picture, they still view a patient's love for his or her therapist as a form of transference, which implies that it is neurotic, inappropriately directed at the therapist, primarily rooted in past relationships, fantasy-based, disingenuous, and linked to the patient's fixed inner template for love and his or her internally driven emotional problems. At most, a therapist's interventions are thought of as shaping the form and timing of a manifestation of transference-love, an idea that insists on the neutrality of the analyst except for blatant countertransference-based errors. Transference also continues to be thought of as an inevitable happening in the course of an analysis or dynamic form of psychotherapy because it is a fixed aspect of the patient's psyche, interpersonal needs, and interactional ways of relating to others that is always prepared to find cause for its expression.

We may note again that there are no formulations built around patients' valid unconscious perceptions of the specific meanings of a therapist's interventions. There is as well an emphasis on verbal comments and the therapist's gross behaviors to the neglect of his or her more subtle ways of intervening and managing the rules, frames, and boundaries of the psychotherapy. Also unappreciated are the basic effects that the status of the frame has on patients' expressions of love for their therapists. The relevance of the conditions of a psychotherapy is suggested by the realization that the first expression of patient-love, which Freud labeled as transference, arose when he was not in his office, but in his patient's home and possibly her bedroom, and after he had intervened by making physical contact with, and hypnotizing, her. Today's strong adaptive psychotherapist would expect an outpouring of false love from a patient treated in this manner.

Breuer's Experience with His Patient

Freud's mentor, Josef Breuer, had an experience with his patient, Anna O., that was comparable to what happened to Freud. He too saw his patient in her home, although it's unclear if he also offered her full body massages. In any case, Anna O. suffered from a variety of severe, so-called hysterical symptoms and many of them were resolved through hypnotic regressions to their exciting incidents. It was the patient herself who had proposed the shift from Breuer's use of direct hypnotic suggestions of symptom removal to allowing her to tell her story and move back in time mentally to the precipitating events for her symptoms – a process she called 'chimney sweeping', which proved to be the beginning of the talking cure (Breuer and Freud, 1893–1895).

After many months of therapy, Breuer decided that Anna O. was sufficiently well to terminate her treatment and he held a final hypnotic session with her. But that night he was called back to see his patient because she was writhing on the floor of her home in the throes of a pseudocyesis (false pregnancy), crying out 'Here comes Breuer's baby'. Breuer used hypnosis one last time to remove this symptom and never again tried hypnotherapy with any of his patients.

We do not know what went through Breuer's mind or what actually happened between him and his patient. Clinical experience using the strong adaptive approach with present-day patients has validated the thesis, mentioned in the previous chapter, that patients' dreams and stories first and foremost embody and encode valid, accurate unconscious perceptions of the underlying meanings and implications of their therapists' interventions – many of them seemingly innocuous on the surface. Anna O. certainly found an unusual way to reveal her unconscious perceptions of Breuer's therapeutic ministrations: The development of an hysterical symptom that told a tale of having been seduced and impregnated by her therapist so that the termination of her therapy entailed the delivery of their child. While these are only informed speculations, we are well advised to take a lesson from this symptomatic narrative because as yet, there is no way of knowing how many symptoms experienced by patients to this very day tell a comparable story.

We can only wonder if Breuer's likely seductiveness was physical in nature or verbally expressed either in an indirect way or explicitly stated through open expressions of love for his patient. It also is possible that his patient's unconscious experience of his seductiveness may have been inherent to his therapeutic methods – i.e., to his use of hypnosis and his seeing his patient in her home. We do, however, have good reason to infer that Breuer was not able to mobilize the kind of denial and claim of innocence that Freud used in invoking the concept of transference. Even though his patient's pregnancy was imagined, Breuer treated it as a reflection of the real events that had transpired between him and his patient. He was unable to conjure up the idea that the true meaning of the pregnancy fantasy was that the patient imagined that she'd been impregnated by her deceased father. On some level, consciously or unconsciously, Breuer evidently knew that he'd been seductive with his patient and in the absence of denial, he saw only one way to resolve the situation: Remove the patient's falsely loving false pregnancy through hypnosis and leave a field that probably was causing him far too much conscious and deep unconscious guilt to continue on.

Whatever the truth of the matter, there are several lessons for us in this tale:

First, the conditions of treatment and the methods used by psychotherapists appear to play a major role in the evocation of loving feelings in their patients. The details and specificity of these contributions have been relatively neglected to this day.

Second, it is quite easy for therapists to deny and overlook the ways in which they have been seductive with their patients and thereby have stimulated feelings of false love towards themselves – i.e., there are generally unrecognized, unconsciously transmitted seductive features to many presently accepted therapeutic interventions. Paradoxically, Freud's use of denial by inventing the concept of transference enabled him to continue his work as a psychoanalyst, even through it gave psychoanalysis an evidently false foundation that has yet to be recognized and revised. The use of conscious-system denial appears to have played a major role in the creation of psychoanalysis and has been a continuing feature of its historical evolution.

Third, Anna O's pseudocyesis shows that patient-love is not always confined to fantasies, but may be enacted in the relationship with the therapist or with figures outside of therapy, to the detriment of all concerned. This kind of harmful enactment of false-love has a grain of deep unconscious truth to it because it is, as a rule, a reaction to falsely loving, frame-modifying interventions by a psychotherapist. By and large, these enactments of false patient-love do not occur in response to frame-securing interventions and other expressions of true therapist-love.

Patients' Demands for Satisfaction

Freud recognized that some patients demand that the analyst satisfy their cravings for love towards them and that they insist on having their way with it. The love experienced by these patients became known as the *erotized transference*. In an elegant piece of writing in his paper on transference-love, Freud stated:

> There is, it is true, one class of women with whom this attempt to preserve the erotic transference for the purposes of analytic work without satisfying it will not succeed. These are women of elemental passionateness who tolerate no surrogates. They are children of nature who refuse to accept the psychical in place of the material, who, in the poet's words, are accessible only to 'the logic of soup, with dumplings for arguments'. (Freud, 1915a, pp. 166–167)

With these patients, Freud went on, the analyst can either return the patient's love or evoke her scorn by refusing to do so. The result is that the analyst must withdraw unsuccessfully and wonder how a capacity for neurosis is joined with such an intractable need for love.

This unilateral, patient-centered view of patient-love is especially common when it materializes in its more unyielding forms (Blum, 1973; Lester, 1985; Trop, 1988). Indeed, even with the recent shift to ill-defined interactional considerations, holding patients almost totally accountable for the love-related resistances and regressions that they experience in the course of their therapies is inherent to all of the present-day weak adaptive theories and practices of psychotherapy and psychoanalysis. This defensive posture on the part of therapists seems to have impaired their ability to openly investigate the problem of love in psychotherapy and has interfered with their arriving at sound insights and effective principles of technique that do not harm their patients on the deep unconscious level of experience. There seems to be a strong need for therapists to more fully appreciate the role played by their own interventional triggers in evoking patient-love, true or false.

Later-day Writings

In 1923, Freud abandoned the topographic model of the mind and replaced it with the structural hypothesis (Arlow and Brenner, 1964;

Langs, 1992a, 2004c). In the topographic model, Freud (1900) envisioned an essentially two-system mind – the systems Ucs. and Pcs.-Cs. These hypothesized mental entities were defined by the status of their contents, which were either unconscious or conscious and/or easily accessible to consciousness Also distinctive was the proposed nature of the contents of the two systems – unconscious-primitive or conscious-sophisticated. Another distinguishing feature was the kind of thinking carried out by each system – the irrational, drive-dominated, discharge-seeking primary processes for the system Ucs. and the rational, controlled, secondary processes for the system Pcs.-Cs.

In changing to the structural model of the mind, Freud (1923) envisioned an essentially three-system mental entity of ego, id, and superego. Each system was defined according to its functions – the ego as the executive and defensive agency of the mind, the superego as the seat of the conscience and ideals, and the id as the source of sexual and aggressive drives. Each system was thought to have conscious and unconscious contents and functions.

Among the many far-reaching consequences of this fundamental shift, several are important to the subject matter of this book (Langs, 1992a). For one, the term *unconscious*, which no longer was a defining feature of the systems of the mind, became a waste-basket term that was – and is to this day – used in many different ways. Most often the term now refers in an ill-defined manner to such entities as thoughts of which patients are unaware at any given moment; thoughts that emerge in the course of a discussion with the therapist about conflicted subjects like loving feelings; unrecognized connections between such loving feelings and feelings towards earlier persons in the life of the patient; and the implications of patients' material of which they are unaware but which are, nevertheless, recognized by their therapists. These are highly arbitrary categories that are all but impossible to define clinically.

This loss of a precise definition of the unconscious realm and of unconscious communication has spilled over to the concept of transference. Freud had stressed its unconscious component and its basis in unconscious fantasies and memories that distort and misrepresent the patient's view of and feelings towards the analyst. But today, based on manifest, conscious communications and responses, the term transference is used in a variety of ways: To characterize the entire relationship that a patient has to his or her therapist; to allude to patients' neurotic ways of relating to the therapist; to refer to patients' attempts to draw therapists into enactments of past relationships; to describe patients' characteristic ways of relating to others and gaining a wide range of satisfactions from them; to refer to the ways in which patients misperceive what their therapists are doing; and to the unreal and undeserved, misplaced feelings patients have towards their therapists. In some sense, most of these usages imply that patients' relationships to their therapists are fundamentally illusory and unreal – and that patients must recognize them as such. Their failures to appreciate and accept the essential unreality of their love for their therapists are seen as reflections of severe psychopathology.

This is the kind of patient-love that has been termed the erotized transference because these patients insist that their love is sincere. These patients are believed to be suffering from impairments in reality testing – actually, in 'unreality testing' – because they wish to have their love satisfied in some manner by their therapists (Blum, 1973; Lester, 1985; Trop, 1988; Bolognini, 1994). Their relatively intractable transferences are accounted for almost entirely on the basis of attributes shared by these patients, such as borderline personality features; fragile egos; early childhood seductions, often of an incestuous nature; and a history of severe abuse by parental figures (Gabbard and Lester, 1995).

Some Final Thoughts

The all-encompassing use of the transference idea implies that it has both conscious and unconscious features. By and large, it is believed to be expressed manifestly in patients' conscious thoughts and feelings about their therapists. As for the unconscious component, this is seen as involving thoughts and feelings about the analyst that come through unexpectedly in the course of direct and manifest explorations of an expression of patient-love. But in addition, it may be reflected in implications of patients' comments about their therapists of which they are unaware. There also are early-life, genetic experiences that sponsor the patient's transference feelings, wishes, and attributions about the therapist.

The related concept of so-called transference-dreams alludes to dreams about the therapist or about minimally disguised substitutes for the therapist. In general, their contents are extracted and transposed whole cloth into the therapeutic relationship and viewed as unconscious commentaries now made conscious – that is, dream contents are taken at face value as messages from the unconscious mind. Attention is paid only to the most obvious ramifications of therapists' interventions in evoking such dreams. In addition, dreams that are well disguised and the stories about other people and other matters that patients tell in the course of their sessions are seen as resistances and are not trigger decoded for deep unconscious perceptions of the therapist. All in all, the writings on transference make little or no use of displaced, heavily encoded deep unconscious perceptions, feelings, and thoughts about the therapist. Much insight is lost in this manner.

All in all, there appear to be important limitations to the value of the existing literature on patient-love in psychotherapy. There is an absence of extensive, in-depth investigations of the hallmarks of true versus false patient-love. The basic view on patient-love is that it is primarily transference-based; patient-caused; inappropriate in respect to the interventions of the therapist; brought up in the service of resistance; and therefore a kind of false love in the sense that it is misdirected. Side by side with this thesis is a conception of a desexualized form of transference-love that facilitates the therapy, yet as such, it too is said to have a false foundation.

It also needs to be reiterated that even though the components of this love are thought of as unconscious, the ideas offered are based mainly on manifest communications from, and the conscious feelings of, patients. Thus, these writings fail to give in-depth attention to the therapist's role in evoking loving expressions in his or her patients or to the facets of the therapeutic setting and interaction that also play a part in loving interludes. The overall result is a limited and somewhat erratic literature that is in great need of revision and expansion based on explorations of patients' deep unconscious experiences of their therapists' interventions as the therapeutic interaction unfolds, be it with or without love, true or false, as the case may be.

4

Two Approaches to Patient-love

Having reviewed the theoretical literature on patient-love in psycho-analysis and psychotherapy, I turn now to writings that include presentations and discussions of the techniques called for in dealing with loving – and unloving – interludes in the treatment experience. In the main, I shall explore several representative, weak adaptive, love-related clinical vignettes in order to identify the features that they share in common and to distinguish them from the approach to love in psychotherapy used by strong adaptive psychotherapists.

As reflected in recent on-line discussions among American psycho-analysts and in a recent paper by Friedman (2005), true-therapist love is assumed to be a feature of therapists' attitudes towards their patients and is thought to be reflected in their specific interventions. Thus, short of a blatant, consciously recognized unloving countertransference-based intervention, therapists are assumed to be appropriately caring and loving at all times. The recognition of non-loving interventions is left to the conscious mind of the therapist and their definition depends on his or her theoretical orientation and technical preferences. By and large, the only broadly acknowledged expression of false therapist-love is that of sexual contact with a patient; every other intervention in word or deed is assumed to be loving until proven otherwise.

As for how to handle interludes of falsely loving countertransference-based expressions, this too is left to the individual therapist. In general, therapists are advised to engage in some form of self-analysis when they identify an error in intervening. As for acknowledging the problem to the recipient-patient, writers are divided. Hampered by conscious-system uncertainties, some therapists advocate acknowledging their errors and untoward feelings towards their patients, while others believe that these revelations are harmful to the patient because they entail unwarranted, anti-therapeutic frame violations of therapists' relative anonymity and neutrality. There is, then, no settled weak adaptive answer to this dilemma.

In regard to explorations of patient-love, they tend to be undertaken when a patient openly and consciously expresses some form of loving feelings towards, or raises an issue regarding love with, his or her therapist (see for example, Gabbard, 1996; Rabin, 2003). At such times, the technical rule is for the therapist to ask the patient to explore or reveal his or her thoughts and fantasies about what was and is happening in this regard. Should a dream appear with evident connections to these issues, its contents are brought directly into the discussion. These are ways of bringing out patients' unmentioned manifest responses to the love-related issue and whatever emerges is treated and interpreted by these therapists as expressions of the patient's inner-directed transference. Should the patient connect the present love-related feeling or problem to an earlier relationship or incident with an early-life figure, this is seen as the genetic source of the misguided expression of transference-love and the earlier figure is understood to be the person towards whom the patient's feelings towards the analyst are really meant.

For example, Gabbard (1996) writes of a woman patient who tells him that she doesn't believe that he cares for – i.e., loves – her. He responds by asking her to say more about it. The patient then describes how she doesn't like people very much and the analyst says that she might feel the same way here in her analysis. The exchange then goes on in this manifest, patient-centered vein until there is some direct kind of seeming closure to the matter.

Along different lines, Rabin (2003) briefly describes a session with a woman patient, Julia, with whom he shared mutually loving feelings. The session begins with the patient expressing her anger over the therapist's having made an error in scheduling a session that was to be held at a time other than the patient's regular hour. With tears in her eyes, she then says that nevertheless, she realizes that her expressiveness and female self are being accepted by the therapist who affirms who she is with him, which helps her so much.

These brief clinical examples are representative of weak adaptive therapeutic work. They show the extent to which the explorations are direct and manifest, and the results taken at face value. With Rabin's patient, there is a distinctly unloving, frame-violating therapeutic lapse which is not important enough in the therapist's thinking for him to describe or consider what had happened and how it had affected his patient. Manifestly, the therapist's error leads to expressions of the patient's implied feelings of love for, and being loved by, her therapist. This imagery is understood as such and seen as a valid expression of her love for the therapist, without any thought of the evident defensive and denial-based qualities of the communication.

Most critically, in the course of these direct explorations, little or no attention is paid to the coincidental narratives that are vehicles for patients' unconscious perceptions of the more anxiety-provoking meanings of their therapists' interventions. As a result, there is a loss of critical aspects of the therapeutic interaction and of patients' deep unconscious assessments of the loving or unloving qualities of their therapists' efforts. Lacking perspectives on the actual implications of their own interventions, weak adaptive therapists can formulate patient-love in terms of self-objects, internal objects, transferences, patterns of relating, and the like. Without the pressures of reality registering in their minds, they do not hear or address issues of life and death or the role of death anxiety in patient-love. This is a critical omission whose importance I shall soon develop further.

Two Views of a Reported Vignette

For weak adaptive psychotherapists, in one form or another, love-related issues are at the heart of patients' neuroses and their therapeutic experience. Natterson (2003), for example, offers a brief for the centrality of love in psychotherapy, doing so on the basis of a modern-day, interactionally-oriented, intersubjective approach in which the mutual sharing of experiences and insights between patient and therapist is seen as a key facet of a psychotherapy experience. In so doing, he offers a clinical vignette that gives us another opportunity to compare weak and strong adaptive formulations (see also Rabin, 2003).

The patient is a married woman whose 16-year-old son attempted suicide. Natterson helped her to find a therapist for the young man. As for his therapeutic work with the mother, we are told that a loving intersubjectivity developed, one that enveloped the patient's entire family but was centered in the therapeutic relationship. Natterson presents two dreams from the patient, of which I will cite and discuss the second. The dream was reported after nearly three years of therapy during which the patient and therapist had developed a loving mutuality and the patient had worked on the inner meanings of her current life issues and those of her developmental years. As a result, she had become more confident as a mother, wife, daughter, sister, and artist. The dream was:

> 'I am lying in my bed. You enter the room, sit bedside me, lean over me. We kiss passionately, your wife is outside the room, looking on ambiguously, unenthusiastically. Then I come to your office for an appointment. Your wife is in the outer office and tells me in an unfriendly way that you are busy and can no longer see me.' (Natterson, 2003, p. 519).

Natterson indicates that the dream occurred as the patient was becoming less submissive and at a time when she and he sensed the immanency of her strivings for love. The dream was triggered by a visit from the patient's sister during which the patient recognized the happiness that the sister had had with their father in contrast to the patient's own marginal relationship with him. The rivalry with the sister was linked by the patient to her rivalry with Natterson's wife in the dream. This seeming insight enabled the patient to recognize that her impasse with her father was derived from her oedipal guilt in connection with her mother and her guilt over her unconscious longings for her father which both parents had provoked. The patient then realized that these dynamics were being relived in the transference with the therapist and she also saw that her submissiveness to him was an indirect repetition of her erotic experiences with her father. At this point, Natterson made a spontaneous and empathic, but decisive intervention:

> 'You have a right to have a loving relationship with your father.' (p. 519).

Natterson indicates that the intervention came from the patient's dream which he saw as demonstrating how the intersubjective circumstance between himself and the patient had evolved. In the dream the patient was asserting her ability to give and receive love to and from him. The dream also showed that she recognized his appreciation for her womanliness. As a result, the dream led to an increase in autonomy and individuality for both the patient and therapist, which was achieved through the reciprocity of their loving relationship. The dream also set the stage for the patient's finding love with and for her father.

Natterson's understanding of the implications of this dream is both strongly affirmative and highly speculative. Nevertheless, the view of this excerpt from the strong adaptive vantage-point differs radically

from that of the writer. To highlight these differences, in lieu of analyzing this dream in a broad intersubjective context, the strong adaptive
therapist would explore this dream as a response to recent, specific
triggering interventions from the therapist within the therapy situation.
The visit from the patient's sister, which is an outside-of-therapy
triggering event for the dream, would be thought of as a minor or
inconsequential stimulus for the patient's deep unconscious level of
experiences. As for therapy-related triggers, strong adaptive clinical
studies have shown that manifest dreams of therapists tend to be
evoked by one or more blatant frame violations on their part. Thus, a
search for frame-violating triggers would be an essential part of the
strong adaptive effort to understand the unconscious meanings of this
dream (Langs, 1998b).

The idea that the patient's dream has been triggered by her therapist's
interventions finds support in the dream's manifest contents which
directly involve the therapist. And the strong adaptive thesis that unloving frame modifications are likely to have played a role here finds
support in the rather pervasive frame violations that also appear in the
manifest dream. For one, the therapist is in the patient's home and in her
bedroom where he sits beside her on the bed and kisses her passionately.
These are modifications in the ground rules that pertain to the locale of
contacts between patient and therapist, which should be confined to the
therapist's professional office, and to the requisite of an absence of personal physical contact between the parties to the treatment experience. In
addition, the therapist's wife is nearby observing them and later, she
appears in the therapist's office, speaks to the patient, and tells her that
the therapist is terminating her therapy. Her presence modifies the
ground rule related to the total privacy of the therapy, which precludes
the presence of an intrusive, third party. Her presence also may imply a
lack of relative anonymity for the therapist and her comment to the
patient involves a forced termination which also speaks against the ideal
ground rule of therapy that indicates that termination should be a cooper-
ative decision made by the patient and therapist together – and certainly
not by a third party to the treatment (Langs, 1998b).

Strong adaptive therapists would give serious consideration to these
frame violations and search for the frame-modifying triggering interventions that had evoked them. They would not take these images as
alluding, first and foremost, to the patient's struggles with her ability to
love and be loved by her therapist and father, nor would they see the
therapeutic situation as one in which the patient's loving oedipal struggles were being relived in the transference – i.e., being repeated with,

or projected onto, the therapist in some unprovoked manner by the patient.

An adaptive therapist would, then, be striving to trigger decode and interpret these frame-violating images, which would be seen as distinctly harmful to and unloving of the patient – they include the therapist's being seductive with the patient and his wife dismissing her from the therapy. In searching for real triggers, the adaptive therapist would wonder if the therapist had introduced his wife to the patient, if the patient had run into the wife inadvertently, or if the therapist had brought his wife into the therapy in some other way. They would ask the therapist if he had carried out a home visit or seen a member of the patient's family and if he had touched or even kissed the patient. Dream images are drawn from real-life events within and outside of a therapy, but they always pertain deep unconsciously to events within the treatment situation (Langs, 1999).

While some of these triggers are very likely in light of the patient's dream, none of them are alluded to in Natterson's presentation. Again we see that, from the weak adaptive vantage-point, particular triggering interventions, especially those that are frame-related, are not considered to be relevant to the vicissitudes of love in psychotherapy. Yet the dream suggests that whatever the therapist had done in the way of modifying the framework and ground rules of this therapy, the patient had deep unconsciously experienced it as seductive and as threatening the continuation of her treatment. For the adaptive psychotherapist, the entire constellation of the patient's unconsciously experienced meanings that accrued to these frame breaks would be seen as sorely in need of not only interpretation, but also rectification – the therapist would of necessity be called on to correct these frame violations to the greatest extent possible.

As for love, Natterson sees this dream as an expression of true patient- and true therapist-love. In contrast, the strong adaptive therapist would see the dream as having been triggered in some real way by one or more expression of frame-violating, false therapist-love to which the patient had responded with false love of her own. It seems clear then the weak and strong adaptive clinically derived formulations about the vicissitudes of love in psychotherapy can differ markedly from each other. This divergence arises largely because of the vast differences in conscious and deep unconscious experience and adaptive processing efforts.

Finally, we may note that the material offered by Natterson is used to validate the position that psychotherapy is about and driven by love, actual and potential. But this is a patient who sought therapy because her son attempted suicide. Even though the article is about love, a strong adaptive therapist inevitably would present material from this patient in which predator death anxiety – the patient's conscious or deep unconscious guilt and fear of punishment through death for having harmed her son – played a notable role. As we shall see, observations from the strong adaptive vantage-point have consistently shown that under these circumstances, dealing with conscious and unconscious death anxieties and guilt would play a significant role in the vicissitudes of this patient's loving feelings, true and false, towards her therapist.

Hypothetically, then, Natterson's approach to this patient's therapy has removed death and death anxieties from the therapeutic experience scene – i.e., there is a likelihood that a shared denial of death is at work in this treatment experience. Had Natterson allowed this patient to associate to her dream with displaced narratives – i.e., stories from her life that came to mind on the basis of the various dream elements – clinical experience indicates that it is almost certain that death-related events and issues would begin to emerge as prominent themes in the patient's material – and life. These themes also would greatly illuminate the patient's deep unconscious experiences of the therapist's seemingly loving interventions and her own seeming feelings of love towards her therapist. On both accounts, her deep unconscious view that this love is false rather than true would most likely find clear expression.

Rabin (2003) reports a strikingly similar, seemingly loving manifest dream, from his patient, Julia, that is replete with contact with her therapist outside of sessions; physical contact with an assistant of the therapist's; and third party contact as well. The dream was dreamt at a point in the patient's therapy when she was planning to reduce the frequency of her sessions. The patient immediately associated to the dream by indicating that she loves her therapist and describing how alive she feels sexually. This occurred at a time when the therapist was falling in love with the patient and entertaining elaborate loving fantasies about her, some of them openly sexual in nature. Rabin's discussion of this therapeutic interaction centers on the importance of mutual love – i.e., true love expressed by both patient and therapist – in psychotherapy and on the natural and real qualities of the love that both he and his patient were experiencing.

Here too the abundance of frame violations indicate to the strong adaptive therapist that false love abounds here in both patient and thera-

pist. But love is, in principle, genuine true love to weak adaptive therapists and on the manifest, conscious level of experience there is no way
to garner evidence to the contrary. Yet in principle, therapists cannot be
so pristine and patients so healthy and caring without conflict to preclude false expressions of love. Indeed, the strong adaptive approach
shows that there is much truth to this realistic assumption.

Another Weak Adaptive Vignette

Having compared weak and strong adaptive viewpoints on the same
clinical material, I turn now to a comparison of weak and strong adaptive to two clinical vignettes in which the triggering intervention for
the patient's material was similar: In both cases, there was contact
between the patient and a third party and therapist-love was at issue.

In discussing transference, Gabbard (1996, pp. 123–128) reports a
vignette in which he delayed beginning a session with a Ms C because
he was talking on the telephone to a colleague from Europe. While his
usual practice is to leave ten minutes between patients, on this occasion
he ended Ms C's session ten minutes late and immediately called for
his next patient, Ms D.

At the beginning of her session, Ms D is silent for ten minutes and
then says, 'I know it's ridiculous, but I can't help feeling that you
staged that. You're hardly ever late. I think you wanted me to see your
other patient leave your office so I would be jealous' (Gabbard, 1996,
p. 124).

Ms D describes the other patient as shocked to see her, as if she'd
been caught doing something forbidden. The incident reminds Ms D of
situations she had with E, her ex-lover, in which he was involved with
other women and sneaky things were going on.

Gabbard writes:

> 'I replied: "So you felt that I would engineer such a situation to make you
> jealous".' (Gabbard, 1996, p. 124).

Further manifest discussion of the incident ensues and eventually Ms D
connects her jealousy of the other patient as a charmer of the analyst to
her jealously of her sister who was a charmer with their father.

The following session continues in this vein, with the patient again
talking about how she felt about the incident with the other patient and
the analyst picking up on these conscious feelings. Ms D then objects

to a word used by the analyst and they move on to discuss this issue. In subsequent sessions, the analyst stresses the connection between this incident and the patient's failed rivalry with her sister for her father's affection and attention. He also acknowledges that his lateness had contributed to the patient's feelings, but he did not confirm the patient's conscious image of him as cruel or as having staged what had happened. On engaging in private self-analysis, much of it also undertaken directly and manifestly, Gabbard recognizes that the patient had picked up the unconscious hostility reflected in what he had done because he should have ended the telephone call in a timely fashion.

The triggering intervention in this excerpt is the analyst's frame violation that took form as the exposure of his patient, Ms D, to another patient, a third party, which is a modification of the total privacy of both patients' analyses. In dealing with this trigger, it is striking that the entire series of exchanges between this patient and analyst regarding her wish to be loved by her analyst and her perception of his unloving gesture takes place on a conscious, manifest, directly stated level of communication and exploration. There is no indication or consideration of an unconscious experience of the trigger by the patient in this exchange between patient and analyst.

The analyst's discovery of his hostility seems best described as the recognition of a transparent implication of speaking on the telephone to a colleague so as to delay the beginning of two patients' sessions. Gabbard proposes that his patient was reacting to a perception of a real act of hostility on his part, but the perception is entirely conscious. The purported unconscious component of the patient's reactions – her supposed transference-love and transference-based disappointment – is manifestly identified by connecting the incident with the patient's recent experiences with her boyfriend and especially her past rivalry with her sister for her father's affection.

Most importantly, there are no dreams or other kinds of narratives in this patient's material – the entire session unfolds as an intellectualized discussion. And even if the patient had told a seemingly coincidental story, indications are that it would have been either ignored or brought into the discussion in linear, manifest fashion. Yet, as I have been emphasizing, these are the very narratives that reflect the powerful, anxiety-provoking, deep unconscious perceptions and meanings that are evoked by these kinds of unloving, frame-modifying incidents.

Strong adaptive studies show that, in principle, whenever there is a significant frame violation, patients who are not engaged by their therapists in direct discussions of the incident and are allowed to free-associate virtually always report dreams or tell stories that encode their deep unconscious experiences of the most disturbing meanings of the event and their compelling view of the therapist in light of the violation. The themes so contained also encode – i.e., reveal yet conceal or disguise – powerful, affective, and emotional links between these current incidents and significant past traumatic incidents in the patient's life. These events are quite specific and deeply disturbing and they are far more grim and death-related than the broad experience of sibling rivalry for a father's affection.

All in all, then, direct intellectualized discussions of love-related triggering events are relatively unempowered and of only minor consequence emotionally, no matter how awful the discussion. Narratives are the mode of expression for the most threatening and compelling aspects of human emotional life and its love-related vicissitudes – and their psychotherapy.

A Comparable Strong Adaptive Vignette

For comparison, I offer a vignette that was presented to me in the course of supervising a strong adaptive psychotherapist, Dr E. His patient, Ms F, begins an hour by mentioning that after the previous session, she found on leaving the office bathroom, that a woman was sitting in the therapist's waiting room. Ms F had had the fantasy that the woman was the therapist's girlfriend. She herself felt exposed and embarrassed on being seen by her; she had the feeling that she had been let in on a secret of the therapist's. That night, she had a dream about a woman who looked like the woman in the waiting room. In the dream, the woman looked dangerous even though the woman in the waiting room looked lovely.

Dr E remains silent and the patient continues to ruminate about the woman in the waiting room, who she might be and such, and eventually gets around to saying that the woman reminded her of one of her college roommates, the one who stole her boyfriend from her in their junior year. With the therapist still silent, the patient goes on to describe the college incident in some detail and then speaks of her rage against her roommate at the time. The patient moved out of the dormitory in which they were living immediately after she caught the two of them in bed together in the boyfriend's apartment. That was all she needed those days – a friend taking a man away from her much as her sister had done with their father.

Eschewing an evident interpretation for the moment, Dr E senses the need for more narrative material so he points out that Ms F has not described her dream or associated to it. The patient laughs and says it was a short dream in which she and this dangerous-looking woman were opening a door to someone's apartment. It felt like they were going to rob it.

The patient pauses and says that now that she thinks of it, the woman in the dream also reminds her of a woman who was in a television movie that she had seen that week. She was the mistress and cohort of a Russian spy, beautiful but an evil, ruthless killer. The film opened with her luring another woman, an enemy counter-spy, into her apartment and then holding her prisoner and killing her. There also was a scene in the movie that took place in a hospital in which a man under police protection was in his room in bed and this woman spy managed to get in there and kill him too. The police should have been more alert than that. She commits suicide at the end of the film, but she'd taken a lot of people with her. The hospital suddenly reminds the patient of the time she was in a hospital trying to save her first pregnancy, but had a miscarriage.

The therapist intervenes at this point in the session. He points out that patient evidently unconsciously perceived the woman in the waiting room after her last session – the intruder – as an evil ally and girlfriend of his who had come to spy on and murder the patient. He goes on to say that the patient also is telling him through her associations that like the police with the man in the hospital, he had failed her in his responsibility to protect her from dangerous intruders. He then indicates that he accepts her remonstration that he should have been more alert to the dangers involved and more protective than he had been – he will make every effort to do so in the future.

The patient goes back to the television movie and describes the brilliant detective work of the head counter-agent who solved the two murders and tracked down the woman killer spy and was on the verge of capturing her at the time she killed herself. There then follows more narrative material connected to the patient's miscarriage. The therapist then interprets that the patient's unconscious perception of the intruding woman as a killer appears to be based on her view of herself as a killer in having lost her first pregnancy. The suicide image must reflect her unconscious guilt over that loss and her belief that she deserves to die for what she had done. At the same time, it seems to reflect the self-punishment she advocates for him – the therapist – for his having exposed her to an unconsciously experienced threat of murder.

The patient comments that oddly enough, she had had a suicidal thought as she entered the therapist's consultation room for her session today and she had wondered where it came from. She recalls too that she'd been suicidal for weeks after her miscarriage.

Comparing the Two Vignettes

As was true of the first vignette, the triggering event here is the intrusion of another woman into a female patient's psychotherapy space. As was the case with Gabbard's patient, this patient also at first ruminated consciously about the intrusion and connected the intruder with a rivalry with a girlfriend over a boyfriend in which she – the patient – was the loser.

Differences between the two sessions begin to materialize, however, when Dr E did not join with the patient in an intellectualized discussion of the transparent and unempowered link between the woman intruder in the waiting room and the college roommate who stole the patient's boyfriend from her. He remained silent, awaiting more powerful narrative associations. The patient continued to ruminate and to offer a kind of implied self-interpretation that her rivalry for the therapist's love was linked to her rivalry with her sister for her father's love. Thus the patient herself was able to generate an interpretation similar to that made by Gabbard (1996) with his patient under similar circumstances. Nevertheless, the therapist treated this self-interpretation as either incomplete or a resistance to expressing sterner stuff, so to speak. He also rightfully suspected that the stronger issues were connected to the patient's dream and that her avoidance of telling and associating to the dream was a significant resistance. He therefore intervened by pointing out that the patient had not told her dream nor had she associated to it. This was an implicit confrontation with the patient's resistance and an invitation to the patient to overcome it and generate more narrative imagery – material that was likely to reveal the patient's more powerful, deep unconscious experience of this particular frame break.

This is indeed what proved to be the case. The dream and the patient's narrative associations to the dream are death-related, with murder and suicide as the most prominent themes. And most notably, instead of linking the trigger to an obvious, clichéd parallel experience from her college years and childhood – a link that says almost nothing about the unconscious meanings of the present frame violation – the genetic connection revealed through the encoded themes is to a miscarriage that the patient had experienced after her marriage. The patient had deeply unconsciously experienced this event as a punishable act of murder on her part. Indeed, her deep unconscious guilt and fears of punishment through death, as seen in the allusion to committing suicide when found out – was a major factor in the patient's emotional difficulties which involved repeated, inexplicable job failures.

The therapist's first trigger-decoded interpretation of this material was met with the deep unconsciously validating story about the smart counter-agent. His interpretation found cognitive validation in the patient's recollection that she had thought about suicide as she entered the therapist's waiting room that day and in the patient's recall of having felt suicidal after her miscarriage. It would appear that deep unconsciously, the patient knew where her dream would take her in the session. We may note in this connection that the deep unconscious basis for the patient's communicative resistances appears to have been her fear of communicating narratives that would mobilize her deep unconscious guilt and its ramifications. The therapist's unloving, murderous frame modification that allowed a third party into the patient's therapeutic space had evoked terrible memories of a moment in the patient's own life when she too felt unloving in a murderous manner. This too is a far cry from sibling rivalry and a far more grim and affecting issue for the patient as well.

There are, then, dramatic differences in technique, thinking, and level of insight shown by these two therapists. In the weak adaptive sessions, there are no displaced narratives, no power themes, and an unempowered conscious discussion prevails. In the strong adaptive situation, the therapist does not engage the patient in an intellectualized discussion, waits and then asks for narrative material in connection with the patient's dream which generates extremely grim and telling associations to the triggering event. We can see firsthand the dramatic differences in the emotional worlds that are explored by weak and strong adaptive psychotherapists. It also seems clear that the tendency of weak adaptive therapists to focus on manifest contents and to use intellectualized interventions is unwittingly designed to close off from the therapies that they conduct – i.e., from both their patients and themselves – the death-related traumas and horrors of emotional existence that would otherwise emerge in patients' narrative material when love-related issues arise. In this way, weak adaptive techniques also serve to preclude the revelation of the connections between patients' death-related traumas and the death anxieties that they evoke and their issues with love in psychotherapy.

This discussion also sheds light on factors in patients' conscious loving feelings towards their psychotherapists. With few exceptions, patients tend to consciously love weak adaptive therapists because they help them to avoid and deny the death-related nightmares with which they unknowingly suffer. They also, as we have seen, enable patients to avoid the death-related traumas that so strongly affect love in psychotherapy. But as we've come to expect, these loving attitudes are accurately perceived deep unconsciously as false and ill-gotten, even as they are cherished consciously.

In contrast, patients seldom express conscious love towards strong adaptive psychotherapists, largely because the therapeutic work painfully but necessarily centers around patients' death-related traumas and anxieties. Instead of focusing on patients' love and loving per se, which are secondary issues, adaptive therapists move from love to death because the latter so strongly affects the former. Nevertheless, when a strong adaptive therapist makes an unconsciously validated intervention, their patients' deep unconscious, encoded imagery consistently speaks for the experience of the intervention as truly loving and healing. And patients tend to respond to these expressions of true therapist-love with true love of their own; most often they do so deep unconsciously rather than consciously. This kind of patient-love is not transference-based love because it is not displaced from past figures onto the therapist. Instead, it is a genuine form of appreciative love felt in response to a truly loving intervention by the therapist. There is, of course, a link to the past, but it serves mainly to shape the patient's own expressions of love, the manner in which it is conveyed to the therapist, and their sensitivities to the love-related meanings of their therapists' interventions.

Summing Up

There are many inter-related problems with weak adaptive thinking about love in psychotherapy. The following, however, seem most critical:

Short of blatant errors in technique and open seductiveness, therapists are assumed to behave well and intervene correctly. Thus, they are assumed to be good, truly loving 'objects' for their patients. Similarly, without examining the details of the setting and ground rules, the therapeutic situation is assumed to be safe for the patient and lovingly constructed. This is the case even when a therapist has not invoked the deep unconsciously sought ideal frame or modifies one of the ideal ground rules of treatment. An appreciation for deep unconscious experience shows that this position is untenable. This is based on the consistent finding that all therapist-evoked frame modifications, including those that patients see as loving consciously, are experienced deep unconsciously as unloving and as such, have harmful effects.

As for therapists' contributions to their patients' love-related experiences, weak adaptive psychotherapists now recognize that patient-love is the creation of both patient and therapist. But the therapist's contribution is seen as secondary or coincidental, and understood in general, manifest-content terms. The prevailing idea is that what the therapist says and does merely gives form and timing to a patient's expression of love and that this love is transference-based. The patient is held almost entirely accountable for the nature of this love because it unfolds from his or her template of past loves as it is directed towards the therapist. The love therefore is assumed to belong to a past relationship and not to the present and the relationship with the therapist. Even though it is somehow evoked by the therapist, it lives only in the past. These ideas seem to defy logic and are not confirmed by strong adaptive clinical observations.

With this in mind, it is time now to look more closely at the role that love plays in the treatment process and in the search for deep meaning and insightful, effective cure. In so doing, we will be called on to consider the question as to whether love or death is the central issue and dynamic in the psychotherapy process and experience. But in looking at love versus death and the death anxieties death-related traumas evoke, we shall soon see that the more critical question is not is it one or the other, but instead, how death and death anxieties affect love – within and outside of psychotherapy.

5

Therapist-love: The Literature

Largely because therapist-love has been taken for granted as part of every therapist's approach to his or her psychotherapy patients, the literature on this subject is relatively sparse. In the more abundant writings on countertransference, issues of love seldom are linked to therapists' errors in intervening nor are they often connected to problems in responding to their patients' therapeutic needs when such difficulties arise. Nevertheless, there is a literature on therapist-love that deals mainly with four questions:

Is there a universal form of love that analysts and therapists experience towards their patients and how is it to be defined and characterized?

Are sexual liaisons between therapists and their patients expressions of therapist-love?

Are non-sexual physical contacts between therapists and their patients expressions of therapist-love?

And are selected personal self-disclosures by therapists to their patients acts of caring and love?

Explorations of these last three issues tend to center around the question of whether such gestures by therapists are appropriate and helpful to their patients. There is however the implied question as to whether they express true or false forms of therapist-love.

As noted, short of blatantly unloving, seductive, or hostile feelings and interventions, which in many but not all instances are viewed as countertransference-based, therapists generally are assumed to be naturally loving towards, and appropriately caring of, their patients (Gorkin, 1987; Celenza, 1991; Greenberg, 1991; Gabbard, 1996; Mann, 1999; Natterson, 2003; Rabin, 2003; Friedman, 2005). As a result, little effort has been made to identify and distinguish true from false forms of therapist-love. And because therapist-love is taken as an ever-present backdrop to psychotherapy experiences, there have been few if any attempts to clinically explore the moment-to-moment vicissitudes of therapist-love in the psychotherapy interaction or to identify the factor that influence its expressions.

With this in mind, I shall discuss the literature on therapist-love in an historical context. I do so for two reasons: First, because the ideas on these issues put forth by, and the actual behaviors of, the pioneering psychoanalysts, including Freud, have had profound effects on the love-related thinking and interventions of later-day psychotherapists. And second, because these early psychoanalysts are nature's children, so to speak. That is, their behaviors with their patients and their ideas about love in psychotherapy and psychoanalysis reflect their relatively naive, natural inclinations. Thus, the consistent trends that they reveal can be taken to reflect the evolved, archetypal propensities of their conscious minds – and by implication, of conscious minds to this very day, be they of patients or therapists.

Historical Attitudes towards Therapist-love

As we go over these long-past writings, it is well to keep in mind that once again, we will be dealing with a conscious system literature written by psychoanalysts who actually had a very limited understanding of deep unconscious communication, experience, and processes. This was especially the case when early-day analysts turned to look at themselves because they were concerned that they had intervened or behaved badly – itself, a relatively rare occurrence despite the blatancy of many of their more questionable interventions. On the whole, these writers had little to say about the qualities of appropriate or true therapist-love and even less about unloving or falsely loving efforts that unmistakably were based on pathological countertransferences. Indeed, many of the interventions that these weakly adaptive psychoanalysts accepted as appropriate and healing for their patients, including their own expressions of what they believed to be expressions of loving care, are viewed today by strong adaptive psychotherapists – and by the deep unconscious minds of all therapists and patients – as inappropriate, pathologically countertransference-based, unloving, and harmful to all concerned.

The early decades of psychoanalysis were dominated by Freud, who, quite remarkably, showed an implicit sense of the need for true therapist-love and was able to recognize the related need for secured ground rules and boundaries that would insure this love for his patients (Freud, 1912b, 1913). In his view, however, securing an ideal analytic frame was needed largely to insure the purity of patients' transference fantasies and projections. By implication, then, the optimal frame was seen as a way to set limits on analysts' falsely loving interventions. Even so, Freud never explicitly addressed the role and functions of the ground rules in psychoanalysis, nor did he define a fully ideal frame for analytic patients. In actual practice, he often failed to adhere to the frame-related precepts that he did define, such as patients' need for privacy and analysts' needs for relative anonymity. Furthermore, in terms of the archetypal frame, Freud was frame-deviantly loving in a variety of non-sexual ways that would today be recognized as falsely loving by some weak adaptive psychotherapists and most certainly by all strong adaptive therapists as well.

To cite some examples of the kind of false frame-deviant therapist-love Freud offered to his patients, he arranged for funds to be donated to the Wolf-man (Freud, 1918), fed the Rat-man during analytic sessions (Freud, 1909), and invited patients to lunch or dinner as reported by Helene Deutsch (Gay, 1988; Gabbard and Lester, 1995). Most of his students and colleagues behaved in similarly frame-violating, falsely loving ways.

It would appear, then, that offering false forms of love is the default position – the natural, evolved inclination – for the conscious system of the emotion-processing mind. This reminds us again that in order to offer their patients truly loving interventions, therapists need to find the means of overcoming these in-built tendencies and to do so insightfully if they are to sustain such efforts.

Among early psychoanalytic pioneers, Freud appears to have been an arch conservative when it came to therapist-love and Ferenczi was the radical experimenter (Ferenczi, 1950, 1955; Blum, 2004). Even so, Freud sanctioned countless actions and interventions by his followers that can only be viewed today as not only frame-violating expressions of false love, but also as definitively harmful to all concerned. As we shall see, there were strong tendencies in analysts towards being deliberately and manifestly loving and notable inclinations to openly convey their feelings of love, sexual and non-sexual, towards their patients. As a result, there were many sexual liaisons and non-sexual extra-therapeutic affiliations between these early psychoanalysts and their patients, some of whom were married colleagues.

Freud (1912a, 1915a) came to psychoanalysis with the idea that sexuality and in some sense, love, are the basic issues underlying emotional life and its failures. He stressed the role of libido or inner sexual drives, wishes, and memories in so-called neuroses. Furthermore, after initially neglecting the role of aggressive drives in neuroses, he came to see them as a factor in emotional illness, but claimed that it was subservient to the role played by core sexual needs. In this context, we can understand why, as he wrote to Jung (McGuire, 1988; pp. 12–13), Freud believed that psychoanalysis heals through love. And it also is why, based on his belief that incestuous, oedipal sexual conflicts universally are the main unconscious source of emotional dysfunctions, he was also convinced that erotic feelings in patients towards their analysts are inevitable. For this reason, he tried to help analysts deal with the danger of responding to the erotic upsurges of feelings from their patients with erotic reactions of their own. His main tool in doing this was to point out to analysts that their patients' sexual feelings towards them were transferences and thus quite misdirected.

In Freud's thinking, only the more sublimated or neutralized form of patient-love – positive transference or non-transference love – has a realistic basis. He thereby implied that patients had good reasons to love their analysts non-sexually, but poor reasons to desire them sexually. By implication, analysts were thought to be in a comparable position – neutralized, non-sexual love was permissible, while unneutralized, sexual forms of analyst-love were not. All in all, analysts were advised to remain calm and collected when their patients expressed or sought sexual responses from them. They were told that they should not try to satisfy either their patients' or their own non-therapeutic desires in the analytic situation, especially when they were sexually cast and even when they were not sexually tinged. This was one aspect of the rule of abstinence that Freud included in his outline of the ground rules of psychoanalysis (Freud, 1912b, 1913).

Freud's considerations of analyst-love and his efforts to protect analysts from enacting inappropriate loving responses to their patients entreaties were grounded in his belief in the unreality of patients' loving fantasies about, and wishes towards, the analyst (Friedman, 2005). There is, however, a strong sense of denial built into the concept of transference in that the central idea is that in the psychoanalytic situation, love for the analyst is not love for the analyst. As Gabbard (1996, p. 35) put it years later:

> A more contemporary view would be that [analytic patients'] love is both real in the sense that it involves a unique current relationship and unreal, or

displaced, in the sense that it has elements of past object relationships that have been internalized and then reactivated in the analytic dyad.

There also is a sense of denial regarding the evocative sources of patients' loving gestures that is reflected in Freud's neglect of his own often flagrant contributions to his patients' loving feelings and wishes towards him. This disregard for triggering interventions has not been sufficiently corrected by later-day interpersonal and interactional writers (Gorkin, 1987). Along different lines, Davies (1994, 1998), Rabin (2003) and others have recently taken exception to the claim for the unreality of patients' so-called transference feelings. They suggest that loving feelings in both patients and therapists often are quite real – and appropriate – although the criteria on which their real aspects are established are manifestly defined and seem to be quite arbitrary.

Freud's evident problems in dealing with love in psychoanalysis also are reflected in his attitudes towards sexual forms of love between his analytic followers and their patients (Blum, 2004). In substance, Freud sanctioned the gratification of this love for some of his followers, while questioning its sincerity and appropriateness with others (Gabbard and Lester, 1995). The basis on which he differentiated these two sets of cases is quite unclear.

There are many reported instances of Freud's approval of sexual love, so-called, between the parties to a psychoanalytic therapy. Most well-known is his reaction to Jung's affair with his woman patient, Spielrein (Carotenuto, 1982; Kerr, 1993; Gabbard and Lester, 1995). On the one hand, Freud cautioned Jung about the dangers inherent to his having a sexual liaison with this patient. But on the other, he evidently responded to complaints by Spielrein's mother regarding Jung's sexual contact with her daughter by pointing out that Jung did not charge a fee, so what did the mother expect would happen. Freud also failed to be critical of Ferenczi's love for a married woman patient, whom Ferenczi eventually took as his bride, and evidently did not question his love for the woman's daughter as well. The daughter eventually rejected Ferenczi's advances, after which he sent her to Freud for further analysis (Gay, 1988; Grosskurth, 1991; Gabbard and Lester, 1995; Blum, 2004).

Summing up, Freud warned analysts to be wary of their patients' erotic love for themselves. He advised them to recognize it as transference-based, undeserved, and unreal, and he warned them to not respond to it erotically and to keep their distance and analyze its intrapsychic sources. That said, he nevertheless allowed his followers a wide latitude of satisfactions in this regard. For his part, Ferenczi (Blum, 2004; Ferenczi, 1950, 1955) advocated and practiced a form of openly and deliberately loving psychoanalysis, in which sexual, and more often non-sexual, physical contact played a significant role. He had patients sit on his lap and share kisses and embraces, basing these ministrations on his belief that the source of their neuroses lay with parental failures at loving and that the analyst's offer of such love, supposedly true to the core, would be reparative and healing. Freud was highly critical of these practices and believed that they gratified the patient's neurotic needs and interfered with their analytic resolution – by implication, that they were forms of false analyst-love.

As far as is known, although he did confess a close call to Jung, Freud did not express love openly and directly to his patients and he did not become involved with them sexually (Donn, 1988; Gay, 1988). But in addition to the falsely loving expressions already noted, he did, however, behave in many ways that could be taken to imply feelings of love, most of them deeply false, for his analysands and he also showed implied wishes to be loved – again, quite falsely – in return. For example, he was openly loving with his patient, the Wolf-man (Freud, 1918), whom he saw without a fee, advised regarding marriage after meeting with the patient's potential bride, and for whom he raised money at times of need. He also shared personal information, much of it distressing to himself, with many of his patients and invited patients to lunch and dinner in his home. He thereby set a tone that implicitly sanctioned and advocated falsely-loving, frame-deviant interventions by therapists and set the tone for later discussions of these issues. He has, then, had notable effects on explorations of subjects like therapists' personal revelations to their patients, non-sexual physical contact with them, and the use of other seemingly loving gestures – subjects presently under considerable scrutiny and debate.

As for Jung, he evidently believed that he had fallen in love with Spielrein, and he appears to have subsequently engaged in supposedly loving sexual acts with several other patients (Donn, 1988; Gabbard and Lester, 1995; McLynn, 1996; Hannah, 1997). When he suffered from an extended, evidently psychotic episode, he turned for his analytic cure to Toni Wolfe, one of his former patients who had become a psychoanalyst (Carotenuto, 1982; Kerr, 1993). His so-called supposedly loving therapy entailed Wolfe's living with Jung and his family in what is reported to have been a ménage-à-trois – an evident expression of false love for all concerned. Jung had been strongly influenced by

Otto Gross (Green 1999), an analyst-patient with whom he engaged in marathon, in-hospital psychoanalytic sessions in which mutual analysis was the rule. Gross believed that repression was the cause of neuroses and that removing its inhibitory effects was the cure – a thesis that led to his own promiscuity and to sexual contacts with his patients. It was after working with Gross, who left his so-called analysis abruptly and unexpectedly, that Jung became sexually involved with his patients. In their mutual efforts at 'cure', Gross' permissiveness, as promoted unconsciously by Jung's permissive frame-modifying practices, appears to have strongly moved Jung towards extensive expressions of false analyst-love. This appears to be paradigmatic for how analysts and therapists naturally tend to express their love, however falsely, towards their professional patients. Let the therapist-patient beware.

Summing up, we may think of the natural attitudes towards love in psychoanalysis and psychotherapy that are found in these conscientious, pioneering psychoanalysts as a reflection of the evolved, universal needs of the conscious system of the emotion-processing mind. It would require far more extensive study of the individual lives of these analysts than is possible here to identify the particular death-related traumas and other deep unconscious factors that made these falsely loving and unloving behaviors so common an intervention. Fortunately, because therapists are as human as their patients, our study of deep unconscious factors in patients' needs for and expressions of false love can be used to shed light on why their therapists behave in similar fashion.

Many of these early-day psychoanalysts were without notable restraints and eager to rationalize and justify falsely loving forms of seduction between themselves and their patients, seeing them not only as permissible but supposedly curative. In the middle of the 20th century, there were psychiatrists who openly advocated having sexual liaisons with selected patients as a similarly rationalized effort to cure their inhibitions. This is the kind of unfounded and inappropriate pathological thinking that conscious minds are capable of when it comes to therapist-love in psychotherapy and the kinds of irrational rationalizations that they can conjure up to justify the exploitative satisfaction of their own falsely loving needs. These extreme examples should serve therapists as warnings about the inner pressures and pathological needs that must be insightfully resolved and renounced in order to do effective, truly loving psychotherapy.

By design, then, it appears that the adult human mind is geared towards expressions of false love and it's fair to say that while most therapists today do not engage in sexual acts with their patients, non-sexual forms of seduction are still rampant – and generally sanctioned by many weak adaptive writers. As we have seen, patients' displaced, encoded narratives – the voice of their deep unconscious minds – raise relentless objections to this position.

As this brief historical survey indicates, there are few signs in these early-day analysts of consistent, natural conscious system capacities for delay, renunciation, sacrifice, or frustration tolerance. Nor do they show any indication of having faced or dealt with the underlying death anxieties that affected their expressions of love in their work with patients. They also show a relative disregard for the ground rules and boundaries of psychoanalysis. Indeed, their expressions of false therapist-love entail multiple violations of the ideal ground rules of therapy and involve frequent incursions into patients' much-needed physical and interpersonal boundaries. False therapist-love seems to prevail and weak adaptive, conscious system forms of therapy and self-analysis have not provided therapists with well-established means of changing this situation.

Later-day Studies

In recent years, investigations of therapist-love have been largely concerned with studies of therapists who have had sexual liaisons with their patients. In addition, there have been sporadic discussions of therapists' loving feelings towards their patients, much of it dealing with the questions of its universal nature and the technical issue of whether they should or should not be revealed to the patient.

The most thoroughgoing studies of therapists who have had so-called 'loving' sexual contact with their patients have been reported by Gabbard and Lester (1995) and Celenza (Celenza, 1991, 1998; Celenza and Hilsenroth, 1997; Celenza and Gabbard, 2003). In their efforts to identify the factors that cause therapists and analysts to become sexually involved with their patients, these writers have focused on the precursors to such behaviors and the personality types and characterological problems that render them vulnerable to such enactments. These contacts are seen as blatantly boundary-violating and the purported love that is involved is viewed as inappropriate and pathological – i.e., essentially false.

Therapists who act in this manner tend to show one or more of the following features: Borderline and narcissistic personalities; exploitative, psychopathic tendencies; severe depressive trends, often with acute depressive syndromes; masochistic tendencies with needs for punishment; a history of severe deprivations in childhood with a notable absence of love and proper care; and a history of childhood seductions or severe traumas. They may also be suffering from the trauma of advanced aging or from specific illnesses, or may have endured a recent, severe personal loss that they attempt to repair through sexual involvement with a patient.

This work is informative but seems to be uncentered. It lacks the identification of one or two critical factors – e.g., key unconscious dynamics, core genetic traumas, and the like – that can account for most of these sexual encounters. And although these writers indicate that sexual contact between patients and therapists is, in all cases, inappropriate and a reflection of pathological countertransferences in the therapist, they do not extend these studies into the broader issue of differentiating true from false expressions of love in psychotherapy.

In keeping with the trends found in weak adaptive writings in this area, however, without citing extensive clinical material, these writers allow room for limited non-sexual, extra-therapeutic loving encounters between patients and therapists. In this regard, they invoke the common conscious system claim that the boundaries between patients and therapists cannot be rigidly maintained lest the analyst or therapist be overly depriving or lacking in human warmth for the patient. These are widely accepted conscious system rationalizations that once more find no support from the deep unconscious system which universally views boundary violations by therapists as unfeeling and hurtful and sees sustaining boundaries as expressions of true therapist-love and warmth. We see again that when it comes to love in psychotherapy, surface appearances can be quite deceiving.

There is as well a number of papers on therapists' subjective loving feelings towards their patients in forms, some of them sexual, that are not blatantly acted out. One group of papers deals with sexual and non-sexual, loving fantasies and feelings and writers tend to believe that such feelings are not unexpected and in general, not a reflection of pathological countertransferences, even when the therapist experiences these fantasies repetitively towards a particular patient (Searles, 1965; Davies, 1994, 1998; Gabbard, 1994, 1996, 1998; Hoffman, 1998; Slavin *et al.*, 1998; Mann, 1999; Slavin, 2002; Rabin, 2003). While sexual fantasies are the source of anxiety in some therapists, the occasional discussion of issue describes assurances from peers and colleagues to therapists who experience these fantasies that they are not pathological and need not necessarily disrupt treatment. Some writers and therapists believe that these fantasies can be the source of highly therapeutic work with patients (Rabin, 2003). The main unresolved problem in this regard concerns the question of whether feelings, fantasies, and wishes of this kind should be revealed to patients and the effects of such revelations, positive or negative, when they are made (see below).

In a recent paper, Friedman (2005) summarized and explored the issue of analyst- and therefore therapist-love, as it relates to the belief that analysts regularly develop a special kind of love towards all of their patients. Opinions were unanimous that such is the case and most of the writers whose papers he reviewed see this love as a helpful or an essential ingredient of the analytic process. Efforts were made by these writers to establish the idea that analysts' love for their patients is a distinctive form of love unlike everyday love outside of treatment.

Friedman's paper is largely devoted to the various ways that analysts have characterized this special form of love. It is viewed as a contact feeling; a mother-of-separation love; a libidinal love much like the patient's loving libidinous feelings towards the analyst; a contemplative love that reflects an appreciative understanding of the patient; a love that arises from the devoted study of others; a sublimated love; a love that is disengaged or unreceptive to the actual thrust of the patient's appeal, which is felt but not accepted because of the analyst's understanding of its transference-based qualities; and a playful kind of love with interpersonal qualities of mothering. The abstract qualities of these approaches to love in psychoanalysis and the absence of solid criteria that define this love clinically appears to limit the value of this elaborate but inconclusive survey.

Issues of Technique

Based on manifest impressions and without consideration of displaced narrative communications, there is a lopsided debate on the issue of therapists' revealing loving feelings and fantasies, sexual and otherwise, to their psychotherapy patients. Gorkin (1987) and Gabbard (1994, 1996, 1998) are convinced that self-revelations of this kind are anti-therapeutic, although Gabbard does allow for the occasional exception. All of the other writers on this subject advocate selected self-revelations and cite manifestly explored clinical examples that demonstrate their seemingly positive effects on patients (Searles, 1965; Fox, 1984; Davies, 1994, 1998; Greenberg, 1995; Rabin, 1995, 2003;

Cooper, 1998a,b; Hoffman, 1998; Slavin *et al.*, 1998; Mann, 1999; Renik, 1999; Slavin, 2002; Natterson, 2003).

This literature is an extension of the broad writings on self-revelations by therapists that entail a wide range of subjective feelings, fantasies, wishes, attraction to, and impressions of the patient. Adopting a position most extensively articulated by Renik (1993, 1995, 1999) and Hoffman (1983, 1991, 1992, 1998), with few exceptions, most therapists accept or advocate the use of supposedly judicious revelations to their patients of their feelings towards and about them. The claim is made that patients generally welcome them – albeit manifestly and consciously – with joy, pleasure, and relief (Natterson, 2003; Rabin, 2003).

All in all, a substantial number of present-day psychoanalysts and psychotherapists engage in the practice of making personal self-revelations to their patients. One rationalization for this position lies with the fact that analysts and therapists inevitably reveal a great deal about themselves and implicitly convey information about how they feel towards and about their patients. But this argument reflects a failure to appreciate the critical differences between inadvertent as compared to deliberate self-revelations as they impact on patients and their therapies. Because the conscious minds of most patients welcome these self-revelations and recruit them to justify or enact various forms of defense and resistance, the differences between these two types of self-revelations only rarely are evident in patients' conscious responses to these interventions. As we would expect, however, the unloving and harmful effects of these interventions are articulated repeatedly in patients' encoded narratives.

The current vogue is, then, to believe that intentional modifications in therapists' anonymity are a vital part of the psychotherapy process and that it is necessary for therapists to do so in order to make the therapeutic experience humane, warm, caring, and real. This position is based partly on an outcry against the supposed inhumanity, coldness, and artificiality of withholding information when patients ask personal questions of their therapists. The predominant belief is that therapists' subjective feelings towards and personal views of their patients' current situation, past life, and material from their sessions are part of the therapeutic process and need to be shared with them within limits that are quite ill-defined.

Similar arguments have been made by intersubjective and constructionist writers who see psychotherapy as a process in which the reality of patients' inner and external lives, and of the treatment experience itself, are co-constructed by the patient and therapist (Hoffman, 1991, 1992, 1998; Rabin, 1995, 2003; Loewis, 1998; Orange, 1998; Orange *et al.*, 1997; Natterson, 2003). These activities involve the definition of realities that inherently entail personal, subjective revelations by therapists that are not derived from, but are reactive to, the meanings embodied in their patients' material. These efforts, which by implication are believed to express the appropriate love of therapists for their patients, are said to be essential to enable patients to feel important and cared about by their therapists. They are thought of as a way of supporting and fostering patients' sense of reality and the analytic process, and placing it on a solid grounding. The minority of therapists who object to such revelations argue that they contaminate the therapy, over-gratify patients, and interfere with rather than enhance the therapeutic process. Each side supports their position by pointing to patients' manifest responses to these kinds of interventions, pro and con, and there is no means available to them through which these opposing viewpoints can be reconciled or one or the other position shown to be more valid than the other. The limitations of weak adaptive, conscious system clinical methods appear to make this one of the many unresolved and unresolvable love-related dilemmas we find in its literature.

These writings echo the weak adaptive literature on non-sexual contact between patients and therapists in which such contacts are advocated by all but a handful of today's psychotherapists (Casement, 1982, 2000; Goodman and Teicher, 1988; Woodmansey, 1988; Lindon, 1994; McLaughlin, 1995, 2000; Gabbard, 1996; Breckenridge, 2000; Fosshage, 2000; Holder, 2000; Pizer, 2000; Ruderman, 2000; Schlesinger and Applebaum, 2000; Toronto, 2001; Slavin, 2002). Once more, on the basis of conscious system explorations, the vast majority of these writers claim that therapists who refuse to comfort, touch, or hug a patient-in-need is cruel, unloving, and behaving in an anti-therapeutic manner. In contrast, the minority position is that these actions are inappropriately seductive and interfere with analytic work directed towards insight. As we have come to expect, once more the deep unconscious system takes a dim view of these practices and with utmost consistency, sees them as quite unloving and anti-therapeutic.

The Exploration of Countertransferences

The need for therapists to evaluate the loving and unloving qualities of their interventions is linked to the issue of how therapists identify pathological countertransference-based errors in intervening and recognize their unloving mistakes and empathic failures. Here too there is a striking set of differences between the approach to this problem that is adopted by weak as compared to strong adaptive psychotherapists.

In essence, the weak adaptive, conscious system approach relies firstly, on a therapist's ability to consciously recognize a gross error in intervening or an obvious failure to be empathic with the patient. Secondly, attention is paid to patients' conscious objections to an intervention or to blatant regressions in patients' symptomatology which prompt some therapists to search for unloving interventions that they may have made. When a manifest warning signal is detected, therapists are inclined to explore the therapeutic failure directly with the patient, and to thereby elicit the patient's conscious feelings and thoughts about the errant incident. In addition, the therapist may engage in private efforts at self-analysis that also are conducted through explorations of manifest contents and their implications.

These explorations are, as I have suggested, severely limited and quite naïve because they are grounded in the fundamental belief of weak adaptive psychotherapists that their therapeutic ministrations are inherently loving and healing; an attitude that creates strong resistances against the recognition of pathological countertransference-based errors. Because of this approach, many unloving interventions, especially those that are subtly hurtful and uncaring, which are unconsciously perceived and experienced as such by patients are not recognized as non-loving by weak adaptive therapists; they therefore go unanalyzed and unrectified. It is all but impossible, however, for a weak adaptive therapist to discover these problems because their recognition depends on strong adaptive therapeutic methods.

In contrast, strong adaptive therapists work with the basic, empirically derived assumption that their own conscious minds – their therapeutic instrument, if you will – is error-prone because of its natural denial-based defenses and inclinations towards self-punishment. Occasional therapeutic errors are seen as inevitable because of the design of the emotion-processing mind and the strong adaptive therapist is always on the alert for such errors. In so doing, they tend to rely on the deep unconscious wisdom system and its superb love-related sensitivities by continuously monitoring their patients' narrative material for unloving themes and images of harm. They also note of instances in which their interventions do not obtain encoded validation because this too often is a sign of an unloving or falsely loving intervention on their part.

Finally, whenever an unloving intervention has been identified, strong adaptive therapists make use of their patients' encoded narrative imagery to interpret the unconsciously perceived meanings of their unloving comment or behavior. They also use the patients' narrative themes as a guide to rectifying their error and, as often is the case, as a guide on how to resecure an unlovingly modified aspect of the ground rules. In addition, whenever questions about the loving aspects of their interventions arise, strong adaptive therapists engage on their own in adaptation-oriented, narrative-based self-processing to gain access to the deep unconscious motives for their lapses. Given their understanding that death-related issues are a critical factor in their offers of false love, they do not rest until they access the death-related traumas and anxieties that are the most compelling roots of their unloving error. In this way they reach into a powerful realm of deep unconscious experience that goes virtually untouched by weak adaptive therapists.

A Comparative Illustration

To cite one of many representative examples, in the course of present-ing the vignette discussed in Chapter 4, Gabbard (1996) identified and explored a pathological countertransference problem that had affected his therapeutic efforts with his patient, Ms D. He realized that he had been in error in not ending the telephone call from his colleague that had delayed the start of the previous patient's session because it had caused him to expose another patient to Ms D. He saw that he could have arranged to call the colleague back later so he could keep to his time schedule. In exploring the problem, he looked directly at what had happened and came to realize that his patient's view that he had behaved provocatively towards her had an element of truth to it – he had indeed been hostile towards his patient. He therefore decided that her conscious perception of that hostility was valid – an instance in which the patient's so-called transference view of him (the term used here to allude to all conscious feelings patients have towards their ana-lysts) had an element of reality to it. This was as far as he took his self-exploration.

In contrast, a strong adaptive psychotherapist who had modified the ground rule of patients' being given total privacy for their therapeutic experience would immediately view the intervention as pathologically countertransference-based and would quickly engage in private self-processing. He or she understands that every unneeded frame violation is experienced deep unconsciously by patients as both unloving and in error. They would not need to be stirred into self-processing by a patient's negative response to the frame modification, nor would they avoid self-processing simply because the patient had not manifestly complained about the lapse. In addition, an adaptive therapist would pay careful attention to the patient's encoded material and make use of the deep unconsciously gained insights that the patient had garnered in response to the unloving intervention. His or her self-understanding would, then, be derived from two sources: His or her own self-processing activities and the patient's encoded imagery.

Adaptation-oriented self-processing efforts by therapists not only include a conscious exploration of an error, but also involve the search for the deep unconscious meanings of the lapse. This is done by recalling a dream from the night of the lapse – or lacking a dream, by making up a short story. They would then associate to the dream elements with fresh narratives that involve incidents from their lives. Next, they would search for the triggers that had evoked both their lapse and the narrative material that they have now generated. In this regard, they would search for personal death-related traumas in their lives outside of the treatment space that may have evoked their expression of false love. They also would endeavor to identify recent anxiety-provoking, death-related material from and incidents connected with the patient towards whom the falsely loving gesture was made. They would, then, mentally restudy (nothing is recorded by strong adaptive therapists) the material from the patient whom they had injured emotionally to see if they could identify the issues and themes that had evoked their own unresolved death anxieties and unloving lapse.

Once a key triggering event for their error and dream-related imagery has been identified, they would decode the displaced narrative themes in light of the triggering events. They would use the insights so gained to understand the deep unconscious sources of their unloving error and interpret the patient's deep unconscious responses to it, while rectifying whatever aspect of the frame that can be secured. They would privately account for all instances of falsely loving interventions by linking them to their own current and past death-related traumas and anxieties. And finally, they would use these insights to resolve the unconscious conflicts and anxieties that have made them vulnerable to falsely loving expressions in their work with their patients.

This is a far more powerful and deeply effective process than that used by weak adaptive therapists and it reaches into the therapists own death-related anxieties and provide deep insights into their deep unconscious motivations for loving their patients badly. In so doing, these efforts enable them to more consistently be truly loving towards their patients. It also is the best way that a therapist can be truly self-loving and able to work and live his or her life without extremes of deep unconscious guilt caused by unloving interventions.

That said, I turn now to the heart of the problem in trying to be a truly loving patient or therapist in a psychotherapy experience – the spectre of death and the death anxieties that it causes in all human beings.

6

Love is the Puppet, Death the Puppeteer

We come now to a most critical, yet relatively unexamined matter: The role of patient-love and therapist-love in the therapeutic process. I have already discussed the presumed contributions that therapists' love for their patients make to the process of healing. Freud set the tone for thinking on this issue in the previously quoted letter to Jung, written in December of 1906, in which he stated that the psychoanalytic cure is effected by love (McGuire, 1988, pp. 12–13). Both strong and weak adaptive therapists find a measure of validity on this point, but issues arise when it comes to the question of the means by which therapists can or should express this love so that it is truly caring and healing.

Weak adaptive therapists have debated questions like whether seemingly judicious self-revelations and non-sexual physical contact are valid interventions and by implication, expressions of true therapist-love. They also have written about blatant pathological countertransference problems, but have seldom linked them to problems with therapist-loving and have been without specific criteria with which these difficulties can be identified. In addition, they have not been able to develop basic principles as to the precise definition of true versus false therapist-love, nor have they identified the means by which its true form is expressed in the clinical situation.

For strong adaptive therapists, true therapist-love is expressed by means of deep unconsciously validated interventions, that is, by securing the ideal framework of a given psychotherapy and by making interpretations related to the central conflicts, issues, and anxieties that are causing patients' emotional dysfunctions. While loving therapeutic work will proceed slowly towards these issues, its truly loving versions cannot avoid these basic sources of emotional maladaptations, but must, in due course and depending on patients' unfolding material, deal with them in an insightful manner. Short of that, therapists would be invoking forms of avoidance and denial that, however welcome consciously by patients, inevitably will be experienced deep unconsciously as non- or falsely-loving on the part of their therapists.

The key question is then: What is the realm of the fundamental emotional issues that lie at the core of emotional dysfunctions? Is it, as claimed by weak adaptive therapists, love in one or all of its many varieties – oedipal, incestuous, narcissistic, interpersonal, object-related, and such? Should healing in psychotherapy eventually center on the exploration and interpretation of patients' love-related emotions, instinctual drives, and interpersonal and narcissistic needs in light of how they have been affected by early-life experiences and are influenced by the ongoing therapeutic interaction? Or is there some other more profound and compelling concern that humans experience universally that is far more basic to emotional health and ills than problems in loving and being loved? If so, what is it and how does it affect the vicissitudes of love in psychotherapy? These are love-related questions that I shall now endeavor to answer.

The Therapeutic Role of Patient-love

Weak Adaptive Answers

The weak adaptive answer to the question of the role of love-related issues in psychotherapy has several variants, but all of them place problems of loving and being loved at the very center of both neuroses and the therapeutic process. Problems with aggression are seen to play a secondary role and are said to arise mainly when love is not forthcoming, thwarted, or otherwise at issue. Whether referring to basic needs for survival, instinctual drive wishes, the need for caretakers and others, or the quest for mirroring, empathy, merger, and the like, the bottom line is that for weak adaptive therapists love is the central problem in emotional life and resolving love-related conflicts, deprivations, over-gratifications and similar issues are at the heart of the therapeutic endeavor.

Freud (1912a, 1915a) set the tone for this contention. His drive-dominated libido theory posited that problems in loving, based largely on unconscious incestuous wishes and aggressive reactions to their frustration or against competitors for that love, are the core issues in emotional life. These ideas led to the expectation that quite naturally patients would invest their libido in their therapists and that the analysis of the conflicted and disruptive aspects of these love-related investments, including their genetic roots, would be the central pursuit in their psychoanalytic treatments. This is the theoretical basis for the concept of transference-love and for the Freudian proposition, accepted in many quarters to this very day, that the analysis of 'the transference' or of 'transference-love' is the basic pursuit in dynamic psychotherapies. Thus, the insightful resolution of a patient's 'transference neurosis' is at the heart of sound and lasting symptom relief.

Unmistakably, then, Freud put love at the center of psychoanalysis. On this basis, analysts and therapists came to believe that patients inevitably will fall in love with them, consciously and openly and more rarely, unconsciously. The analytic resolution of this so-called transference-love carried out by tracing it to its childhood or infantile sources was and is still seen as the basic vehicle of emotional cure. In one form or another, love pure and simple, and on its own terms, became and still is for many therapists the fundamental problem in emotional life and in the psychotherapy designed to alleviate emotional dysfunctions.

Later-day writers have offered many different variants of Freud's dictum about love in psychotherapy. For example, beginning with the work of Kohut (1971, 1979), self-psychologists have placed patients' narcissistic needs and self-regulatory requirements at the center of psychotherapy and have viewed the correction of previous narcissistic failures by parental figures as the essential healing transaction that takes place within the therapeutic interaction with the psychoanalyst. Here too love is the core problem, albeit in its narcissistic rather than incestuous form. In a similar vein, the various interactional and relational sub-theories of psychoanalysis place problems with relating to or gaining necessary satisfactions from other individuals as the core problem in emotional life. And these therapists also expect that these interactional, mutually created and shared love-related issues will be re-experienced – and revised – in the course of a psychotherapy experience. In one form or another, love in and of itself, including the love-related conflicts and their history for a given patient, stand at the heart of the therapeutic endeavor.

Natterson (2003), who adopted a therapeutic approach that draws on relational, intersubjective, and classical psychoanalytic thinking, sums up the present-day weak adaptive position on the role of love in psychotherapy in the following ways:

Therapy's premier task then consists of gaining access to this heretofore inaccessible love; that is to actualize the love that is already a basic part of the person. Love's actualization in therapy occurs through the mutually loving nature of the therapeutic experience (p. 513).

We may therefore assert that the therapeutic relationship becomes a loving relationship and that the therapeutic dialogue is basically about love and the expansion of its role in a person's life. (p. 514)

For the weak adaptive psychotherapist, then, true therapist-love involves dealing with and resolving patients' conflicts in loving.

The Strong Adaptive Answer

The strong adaptive approach presents a serious challenge to this position. Love-related issues do, of course, arise in the course of a sound psychotherapy experience. And they do need to be fully understood in depth, explored as to their immediate sources and their connections to early-life experiences, and they should be insightfully resolved. But these love-related problems are not the core issue in emotional life. Problems in loving arise from the love matrix that I alluded to in the introduction to this book: The architecture of the emotion-processing mind; the handling of the rules, frames, and boundaries of psychotherapy; and the human awareness of death, the experience of death-related traumas, and the death anxieties that all of this evokes. Importantly, it has been found that this last component is at the heart of the matter because conscious awareness of death has been the major selection factor in the evolution of the emotion-processing mind and also is the major determinant of how the ground rules and boundaries of psychotherapy are managed.

At bottom, then, death and the death anxieties it evokes are the driving forces behind emotional life and consciously, but more so deep unconsciously, they create the issues and needs that guide and account for the vicissitudes of love in psychotherapy.

As Goes Death, So Goes Love

Freud (1915b, p. 300) implied as much in writing:

If you want to preserve peace, arm for war.... If you want to endure life, prepare yourself for death.

The vicissitudes of love in psychotherapy therefore cannot be understood in depth without a full appreciation of the more basic vicissitudes of the death-related issues within the same treatment experience. The mutuality of patients' and therapists' conscious and more often, deep unconscious concerns and experiences with death is the primary subject of emotional life and psychotherapy. The mutuality of their concerns and experiences with love is a secondary, albeit important, issue, but not the heart of the matter. Indeed, confining the explorations of psychotherapy to love-related issues needs to be seen as a defense against and denial of deeper and more critical problems that are death-related.

With this in mind, let's take a fresh look at the role played by the exploration of love in the transactions of psychotherapy.

The Role of Love-related Issues in Psychotherapy

In the mother-child interaction, love, broadly defined in terms of caring, providing narcissistic supplies, offering support for tension and anxiety management, and the like, assures the survival of the infant and supports and helps to build his or her mental and adaptive resources. Love is thus at the center of an individual's needs for care and for other individuals with whom the infant can and needs to interact, be with and share with in a manner that satisfies, soothes, and reassures. Ideally, love ultimately also serves the deep human need to reproduce and extend a person's lineage. There are, then, multiple conscious and unconscious satisfactions in loving and being loved. Clearly, most kinds of adult relationships satisfy only a portion of these love-related needs, with true love between a husband and wife coming closest to being all encompassing in this regard.

What loving satisfactions are, then, appropriate for psychotherapy patients and their therapists? Expressions of true love from therapists provide patients with inherent support and non-sexual caring that enhances their ego functioning and coping capacities, strengthens patients' superegos, supports the healthy satisfaction of id wishes and needs, and facilitates the healing process. For their part, patients' true love for their therapists serves mainly to reassure them that there are people in this world who deserve their love and also comfort them in their seeing that they are capable of truly loving others, especially those who care for and love them.

In like vein, for therapists, the experience of true patient-love also is reassuring and supportive, and it enhances their therapeutic skills and adaptive capabilities. Therapists' ability to truly love their patients and their experiences of their patients' deep unconscious validation of that love similarly reassure them that they are capable of truly loving others in a manner that is appropriate for the conditions under which that love is being offered. This ego- and superego-building experience, which is grounded in the deep unconscious experience of offering patients unconsciously validated interventions, is one of the most basic inherent satisfactions of being a sound, truly loving psychotherapist.

In this light, we can see that there are two ways in which the exploration and resolution of love-related issues tend to enter and need to be dealt with in the therapeutic process:

The first pertains to the vicissitudes of love in the therapeutic interaction itself and mainly to the interpretation of patients' unconscious perceptions of the loving qualities, true and false, of their therapists' interventions.

The second involves the story of the patient's past love relationships as it affects his or her capacity to cope with life's traumas and to effectively take part in insight-oriented psychotherapy.

When a therapist creates an ideal setting and set of ground rules for a patient's psychotherapy, and otherwise intervenes in a manner that obtains deep unconscious validating responses from the patient, true therapist-love prevails and serves as a broad ego-enhancing backdrop to the therapeutic work for the patient – and therapist as well. The only problem that this love poses for the patient pertains to the unconscious anxieties it evokes in patients who are threatened by being truly loved. Strong adaptive explorations do not support the idea that the underlying issue in these cases is a fear of identity-obliterating merger with the therapist. Instead, problems appear to arise primarily because of the existential death anxieties evoked by the entrapping qualities of a lovingly secured set of ground rules for a treatment experience. In addition, under these truly loving conditions, predator death anxieties also are activated in patients who have harmed others and cannot tolerate being loved instead of punished.

It follows, then, the only insightful way to resolve these resistances to effective therapeutic ministrations lies not with exploring the problem of love per se, but with the exploration, as the patient's material permits, of the patient's death-related issues and deep unconscious guilt. It is only after patients have found a deep unconscious means of coming to terms with the finality of personal death and of achieving atonement and self-forgiveness for the harm that they have done to others that they are able to be truly loved by their therapists and others without destroying that love – and are able to truly love others as well.

The principle that death, death-related traumas, and death anxieties are the core issues in psychotherapy, and that loved-related issues are subservient to them, holds true for every aspect of love and love-related conflicts in emotional life and its psychotherapy.

Another reason that love becomes a problem in need of exploration and resolution for patients in psychotherapy is seen when therapists fail to love their patients truly and do so falsely or not at all. Because they engage in manifest-content, conscious system forms of psychotherapy and do not access patients' deep unconscious love-related wisdom, weak adaptive therapists tend to offer their patients many false forms of love as witnessed by their patients' deep unconscious perceptions of their interventions. For their part, strong adaptive therapists also may love their patients falsely from time to time, as seen when they commit therapeutic errors that are in truth – i.e., deep unconsciously perceived as – either unloving or falsely loving interventions. Patients tend to work over these moments of failed love deep unconsciously, although at times, with blatantly loveless or harmful therapists, they may do so openly and consciously. In most instances, however, they do not respond manifestly to being falsely loved, but instead encode clues to this false love that their therapists can detect only by listening for narrative themes and trigger decoding their deep unconscious, love-related meanings. Indeed, patients' deep unconscious minds not only detect their therapists' falsely loving interventions, they also encode correctives and models of rectification. Patients' deep unconscious wisdom even goes so far as to offer encoded insights to errant therapists – deep unconscious interpretations, if you will. The deep unconscious goal evidently is to enable therapists to get to the deeper sources of their failed love and take the necessary corrective measures. Indeed, the deep unconscious wisdom subsystem has an uncanny ability to detect the death-related sources of therapists' errors, especially those that are ground-rule and frame-violating.

All in all, then, when faced with false or failed love from their therapists, patients naturally make extensive deep unconscious efforts to cure their therapists and to help them to resolve their problems in loving (Searles, 1965, 1973). It must be stressed, however, that therapists can benefit from these encoded healing ministrations only if they allow their patients' material to help them to recognize an erroneous intervention and draw insights from the patient's deep unconscious resources by engaging in trigger decoding their narrative material.

These interludes of being unloved by their therapists can be recruited for an insightful healing process because therapists' traumatic interventions deep unconsciously activate patients' early life experiences of being unloved and prompt them to rework these early love-related problems. Paradoxically, experiences of true therapist-love also may evoke past love-related traumas and this too will allow for their working over. In all such cases, resolving patients' love-related conflicts is preparatory for dealing with the underlying death-related issues that stand at the core of their emotional suffering.

True love prepares patients and therapists for their inevitable battle with death.

Enhancing Adaptive Resources

In this connection, it is well to appreciate that there are two basic ways of enhancing an individual's adaptive resources. The first and relatively benign way is by loving that person truly. The second is paradoxical and takes shape as being unloving and as traumatizing individuals in ways that cause them, if they happen to be capable of it, to mobilize their resources to defend themselves against the harm being done to them. It is well known that many highly successful people suffered major death-related traumas in their early lives. These traumas were damaging in some ways, but based on their own inherited capabilities, they also led to a high level of resourcefulness on their part. In less gifted individuals, these traumas would cause lasting damage to their emotion-processing minds and compromise their ability to truly love others.

These principles apply quite strongly to the therapeutic relationship. Therapists can strengthen their patients' coping capacities by either loving them truly or by traumatizing them with unloving or falsely loving frame violations and erroneous interventions. To be clear, however, this second type of enhancement is always damaging to some extent and therefore comes at a high price, even though the detrimental side of this process is often ignored or denied by all concerned. Strong adaptive therapists see this mechanism as the basis for many seemingly successful outcomes of weak adaptive forms of treatment.

In contrast, truly loving psychotherapists inherently enhance their patients' adaptive capacities through both frame-securing efforts that hold patients well and the offer of trigger-decoded insights that provide them with adaptive wisdom. These efforts also promote positive identificatory processes in patients that are both generally strengthening and healing. The resolution of patients' death anxieties play a role in these endeavors because experiences of true therapist-love stir up patients' death-related issues – anxiety-provoking experiences that nevertheless become available for interpretation and working through.

Enabling patients to make deep unconscious peace with those who caused their death-related traumas, be it others or themselves, and to insightfully resolve their residual death anxieties, are the fundamental means through which therapist-love contributes to the healing of patients' emotional dysfunctions.

Love and Death

All in all, then, death is the fundamental subject of psychotherapy. And true therapist-love is the ingredient that best enables patients to cope with the disruptive anxieties that therapeutic efforts designed to resolve their death anxieties cause them. It follows too that therapists must insightfully come to terms with and resolve their own death anxieties in order to be able to tolerate and offer the kind of truly loving therapeutic interventions that enable patients to make peace with these very same universal issues. That said, I shall now sum up how each form of death anxiety can, and often does, play a role in a given psychotherapy experience and how it affects the vicissitudes of love in the therapeutic interaction.

Existential Death Anxiety

This type of death anxiety is aroused when psychotherapy frames are secured to the greatest extent feasible. Much as we are entrapped in a life from which death is the only exit, these ideal conditions of therapy universally evoke secured-frame death anxieties based on patients' – and therapists' – sense of being constrained and entrapped by the ground rules of treatment. As noted earlier, securing this kind of framework for a patient's psychotherapy is a deeply conveyed expression of true therapist-love, but few patients – or the therapists who do so – consciously appreciate the caring nature and holding qualities of this love. Most of the positive effects of these frames are experienced on the deep unconscious level, but they are intense and quite real.

Paradoxically, patients often consciously experience this form of ideal therapist-love as threatening and even unloving. For example, adhering to ground rules related to the day and time of sessions or charging a fee for missed sessions, while validated as truly loving unconsciously, is often consciously seen by patients – and again, often by their therapists as well – as hurtful and unloving. In addition, securing frames and working with death-related, encoded narratives, while welcomed deep unconsciously, is often experienced consciously by all concerned as dangerous and also seemingly unloving.

Under truly loving, secured-frame conditions patients tend to reactivate the memories of, and re-experience deep unconsciously and then consciously, their personal death-related traumas. At other times, these traumas are reactivated when a therapist intervenes in ways that are harmful and unloving because the intervention resembles and therefore reawakens past death-related events. By design, the emotion-processing mind typically seals off from awareness – and from time to time, from encoded expression – the most awful ramifications of severely harmful incidents. It follows then that whichever way this cover is removed, be it through interventions that are either truly or falsely loving, patients tend to consciously feel unloved by therapists who play a role in these upsetting therapeutic interludes. On the one hand, the feeling of being unloved is deep unconsciously confirmed when therapists have intervened in harmful ways, but it is not supported deep unconsciously when therapists have secured frames in a truly loving manner.

All in all, then, the unconscious anticipation and experience of these anxiety-provoking developments may evoke conscious feelings that the therapist is cold and unloving. But when frame-securing is involved, the offer of an ideal set of ground rules is not the cause of these conscious perceptions. Instead, it is the underlying, reactivated trauma and death anxieties that are their source and while the negative image of the therapist is understandable, it is, in terms of the necessities of insightful cure, quite misguided.

Notice too that conscious and deep unconscious appraisals of the loving and unloving attributes of therapists' interventions often are at odds with each other. This is why, as I have been emphasizing, it is essential for therapists to learn how to trigger decode patients' – and their own – trigger-evoked narratives in order to ascertain the patients' deep unconscious appraisal of a particular love-related interlude. It is in that part of their minds that humans experience and know the truth about love in psychotherapy – and in everyday life as well.

Predatory Death Anxieties

The human fear of being harmed by others tends to be evoked deep unconsciously when therapists unnecessarily and in unloving ways modify the ideal ground rules of treatment. Frustrating departures from the ideal frame, such as a sudden increase in a therapist's fee, feel consciously persecutory to patients, but these well-deserved feelings tend to be put aside by patients even as their effects continue to be experienced deep unconsciously. As for frame alterations that are consciously gratifying for patients, such as changing the time of a patient's session at his or her request, they are experienced as persecutory solely on the deep unconscious level. In either case, these harmful, unloving interventions tend to deep unconsciously reactivate patients' past incidents of persecution, broadly defined. Typically, these earlier, unloving events involve ways in which parents and others harmed the patient in his or her early years – e.g., a birth defect, parental abandonment, cumulative incidents of physical and emotional harm, and the like. All of these happenings are experienced deep unconsciously as attempts at murder and therefore as death-related.

In the past, these traumatized patients tend to consciously deny the rage that they feel towards those who have harmed them. Deep unconsciously, however, they have experienced murderous rage at these perpetrators of harm. When traumatized by an unconsciously invalidated verbal or frame-management intervention, this rage is unconsciously directed towards the offending psychotherapist. And these furious reactions, in which the therapist is seen consciously and/or deep unconsciously as both unloving and hurtful, evoke considerable deep unconscious guilt in the patient. Fearful of these feelings and impulses, patients often turn against their hurtful therapists and leave therapy. In some cases, however, there is a paradoxical demand from the patient for some kind of consciously gratifying expression of false love from the therapist that is sought to compensate for the damage that the therapist is causing the patient. The deep unconsciously guilt-ridden therapist often complies with these requests for falsely loving interventions, even though doing so tends to aggravate rather than resolve these situations. Love and death move in tandem during these interludes.

Predator Death Anxiety

Secured frames and narrative forms of psychotherapy also pose the threat of the re-arousal of incidents in which patients caused harm to others. This particular group of reactivated death-related traumas tend to involve giving birth to a damaged child, miscarriages, abortions, and the abandonment of family members, especially children. Here too, in response to the interventions that cause the reawakening of these traumas, patients consciously see their therapists as unloving, while deep unconsciously seeing them in the very opposite way – as truly loving and caring.

As for the specific ways that therapists arouse these particular death anxieties, the most frequent cause involves moments when therapists become seriously ill or injured. This situation may be implied by a therapist's unexpected, sudden and often extended absence from his or her office. The trauma may be compounded if the therapist directly informs the patient as to the cause of these missed sessions, even though this frame-violating revelation may be necessary at times of emergency. At such times, patients' persecutory death anxieties are aroused because they are harmed by the therapist's absence. But para-doxically, patients' predator death anxieties also are aroused by these bouts of illness in the therapist. This is the case because deep uncon-sciously, patients always hold themselves responsible for their thera-pists' illnesses and injuries. This is a universal, archetypal response to illness and injury in those whom we love and are closest, and it holds true even when the therapist simply cancels several scheduled sessions without giving a reason for doing so.

In respect to love, patients tend to react in mixed ways to these trau-matic incidents. Consciously, they often feel concerned for their thera-pists' welfare and experience conscious loving feelings accordingly. These may be expressions of constrained true patient-love, but they also may be falsely loving by motivating efforts to modify the ground rules of treatment, as seen when patients seek personal information from their therapist or offer medical advice to them. Deep uncon-sciously, the reaction to an illness in a therapist also tends to be mixed. There are unconscious feelings of true patient-love, but also experi-ences of being abandoned and harmed that evoke non-loving feelings as well. Patients' deep unconscious beliefs that they have harmed the sick or injured therapist also tend to make them feel that they are unloving and hurtful. Deep unconscious self-condemnations follow and must be traced back to earlier similar events in the life of the patient, and then interpreted and resolved.

As for ill therapists who cancel sessions, they experience predator death anxiety because of the unloving harm that the signs of illness and the missed sessions cause their patients. There is a danger that therapists will try to compensate for this harm in falsely loving ways, such as offering make-up or extra sessions to their offended patients. These are times that try therapists' souls, times when adhering to the secured frame and to truly loving, deep unconsciously validated interventions are most vital in providing compensatory true therapist-love and in sustaining the healing process for the patient – and therapist as well.

The Emotion-processing Mind and Love

The basic, evolved design of the emotion-processing mind has major, natural and fixed or universal effects on the vicissitudes of love in psychotherapy. To enable us to better understand this influence, I shall briefly review the factors in the evolution of this mental model.

The emotion-related conscious mind evidently evolved first and it was invaluable in enhancing the survival of human beings. There was and is evident adaptive value in having an effective conscious mental system that is protected from overload to the greatest extent possible and is available at all times to handle the daily chores of life and deal with immediate physical and emotional threats. In time, as humans were compelled to deal with more and more potentially disruptive emotionally-charged and life-endangering issues and events, it was naturally advantageous for nature to passively favor minds that had mutated a second system that could handle the excesses of stimulation and challenge whenever an immediate response was not called for.

The development of a new system when a particular operating system begins to be overloaded with adaptation-related tasks is not at all unusual in the evolutionary histories of living organisms (De Duve, 1995). For example, there is evidence that RNA was the first chemical replicator and that, as organisms became more complex and RNA was being overwhelmed by the number of chemical reactions needed to copy the blueprint for a new living organism, nature favored organisms who possessed the mutated DNA that could take over many of the tasks that were being carried out by RNA.

The emotion-processing mind has, then, an evolved configuration that was naturally selected to insure that the conscious system is not overly perturbed by an excess of psychological threats or by physical traumas that do not pose immediate dangers to life and limb. The basic means by which this protection is effected is the use of conscious system denial and obliteration, which in essence entails directing incoming stimuli and emotionally-charged meanings to unconscious perception and deep unconscious adaptive processing. This diverting process is carried out by an unconscious intake system – the *message analyzing center* (Langs, 1995, 2004c, 2005b) that perceives incoming emotionally-charged events and their multi-layered meanings without conscious awareness intervening and 'decides' which incidents and meanings may reach awareness and which may not. For convenience, this complex process of blocking anxiety-provoking events and meanings from awareness is thought of as unconscious perception and conscious system denial. It is a mental mechanism that protects the conscious mind from being over-burdened and dysfunctioning, thereby enabling the system to cope with everyday tasks and urgent provocations as they arise.

Natural selection has, then, favored the retention of a second system of the emotion-processing mind that receives non-emergency events and meanings that seriously threaten conscious system functioning. As is the case with the conscious mind, this deep unconscious system has adaptive processing capabilities that are carried out by its three sub-systems which are devoted respectively to wisdom, morality, and danger. In relation to love in psychotherapy, this is the mental system that processes the events and meanings that unconsciously and most powerfully affect the vicissitudes of love in psychotherapy. This means that the deep unconsciously experienced ramifications of patients' death-related traumas and anxieties are the main regulators and motivators of expressions of love, true and false, in the treatment setting. These factors are invisible to the conscious mind and therefore, the critical role of death anxiety for love in psychotherapy can be fathomed only with the identification of the relevant triggers for the loving expression and with the subsequent trigger decoding of the relevant narrative themes.

Only the deep unconscious mind knows the underlying death-related truths about love in psychotherapy.

The Conscious System and Disruptions in Loving

Until now I have been stressing the defensive posture of the conscious system and the unreliability of its view of emotional life in general and love in particular. I turn now to the role played by this system in regard to loving expressions from patients and therapists.

The conscious system is a love-seeking system in that loving and being loved provides humans with essential satisfactions and serves the survival of both the individual and the species. The search for love from, and being loving with, others begins with the newborn in his or her interaction with the mother and other providers, and continues in various forms throughout life. Love initially involves the infant's enticement of caretakers to be lovingly caring and in time, the infant's responsive love for those who provide such care. As called forth by the infant, parental love satisfies a wide range of survival-related needs, such as those related to nurturance, instinctual drives, narcissistic requisites, interpersonal and interactional necessities, and the like. We may think of this kind of search for and offer of love as involving its unencumbered, non-conflicted, healthy, appropriately satisfying, non-defensive, and non-neurotic version. It is the essence of true love and is quite similar to the kinds of patient- and therapist-love that are deep unconsciously validated through displaced, encoded narrative images in psychotherapy.

The newborn is, then, mentally designed to call forth and give expressions of true love. But no newborn or infant is continuously loved in a proper fashion. Frustrations and being unloved or harmed are inevitable. In addition, caretakers with impaired abilities to love tend to disrupt the flow of mutually shared true love and set the infant on a path towards favoring false rather than true expressions of love in their relationships. Falsely loving others is one sign of emotional maladaptations or neuroses and of more severe emotional disturbances.

Many other factors may tear love asunder. A sampling includes over-intense inner neediness; physical illnesses or injuries; being hurt emotionally or physically by others; feeling consciously guilty over having hurt others; the appearance of competitors for someone's love; having one's reasonable or unreasonable needs frustrated; natural and human disasters, including death-related traumas; being victimized by someone or by an unexpected event; a variety of conscious fears including a dread of closeness and intimacy with others; various unconscious fears of which the existential fear of death looms large; and deep unconscious guilt that creates unconscious needs to be punished and thus to be unloving and unloved. To complicate the situation, there also are paradoxical forms of love in which individuals love someone who has harmed them, and alternatively, in which persons hate someone who has been truly loving towards them.

These are matters that are difficult to sort out in everyday life. The deeper nature of love, true or false, is much clearer in the psychotherapy situation because therapists are in a unique position to identify the triggers for their patients' loving expressions and can have available to them narrative material that illuminates the relevant deep unconscious experiences that are involved in these incidents. This is the case because they themselves create most of these triggers, which are constituted by their interventions. Therapists also are in a special position to test out their ideas about love by intervening and studying their patients' responsive material for both conscious and deep unconscious reactions, including the all-important test of encoded, deep unconscious validation.

Strong adaptive investigations along these lines reveal that manifest, conscious reasons for both patient- and therapist-love do not account for the true nature of the loving feelings and impulses experienced by either party to therapy. On the surface, patients often love therapists whom they consciously believe to be caring and loving, and in many cases, they do so despite the absence of palpable signs of emotional healing. Other patients feel love for and readily forgive therapists who are openly hurtful to them, as seen when a therapist misses a session, is blatantly and inappropriately seductive or hostile towards a patient, or is behaving in a clearly exploitative manner. There also is considerable clinical evidence that many therapists whose interventions are validated deep unconsciously and who unmistakably are deeply loving with their patients may be consciously unloved or disliked by these well cared-for patients – as noted, much of this arises from the consciously painful qualities of sound therapeutic efforts.

All in all, according to the criterion of deep unconscious validation, many harmful therapists are consciously loved by patients, while many truly loving and healing therapists go consciously unloved. Thus, conscious reasons for loving and feeling loved do not account for many paradoxical expressions of patient- and therapist-love. This means that unconscious perceptions and deep unconscious motives are critical factors in activating loving feelings and behaviors. To be clear about patient-love in psychotherapy, then, a therapist must identify the trigger for a loving expression – as noted, for patient-love, it most often involves therapists' interventions – and must trigger decode the patient's narrative imagery in light of the trigger's implications and meanings. This brings us to the deep unconscious system and its multiple roles in respect to love in psychotherapy.

The Deep Unconscious System and Love

The strong adaptive approach has identified several classes of very powerful deep unconscious perceptions and motives that promote true patient- and therapist-love, and another set of deep unconscious perceptions and motives that play a role in causing love to run awry, thereby creating falsely loving feelings and enactments. As previously indicated, in all cases, these factors appear to be ultimately death-related. Indeed, each form of unresolved death anxiety contributes to patients' and therapists' falsely loving feelings and enactments, much as the resolution of these death anxieties favors expressions of true patient- and therapist-love.

With death at its center, there is a tightly woven web of contingencies that play a significant role in expressions of love in psychotherapy. In an ongoing therapeutic interaction, issues connected with loving and being loved are played out by patients and therapists around therapists' management of the ground rules of therapy and patients' responses to these efforts. Therapists' frame-related interventions have significant unconscious effects on both patient- and therapist-love. In principle, securing or accepting an ideal set of ground rules expresses true therapist- or patient-love. In addition, secured-frame conditions for a psychotherapy unconsciously motivates the expression of true forms of love by both patients and therapists, while modified frames unconsciously motivate expressions of false forms of love. To extend these ideas, it is well to appreciate that unresolved death anxieties play a role in frame violations and thus in evoking expressions of false love, while coming to terms with and resolving these anxieties play a role in securing the frame and in expressions of true love.

Predatory death anxiety, which arises when one party to therapy harms the other party, tends to evoke true anger and hatred in the victim. Predatory acts also may evoke responses of false love in the unloved recipient of the harm. Patients who love predatory therapists do so largely because they suffer from predator death anxiety and deep unconscious guilt. This kind of loving response to unloving therapists is a generally unrecognized, but common type of false patient-love.

Predator death anxiety and the deep unconscious guilt caused by harming others are major causes of false patient-love directed unconsciously (and at times, consciously) towards hurtful therapists who are loved because they unwittingly and unconsciously are punishing their guilt-ridden patients.

Existential death anxiety is another major source of false love in psychotherapy because patients often falsely love therapists who intervene incorrectly or stay focused on love-related issues and thereby avoid material related to their death-related traumas and anxieties. They similarly love frame-modifying therapists who relieve them of the secured-frame existential death anxieties that they would experience under these conditions.

The three subsystems of the deep unconscious mind play a role in love in psychotherapy in the follow manner:

The wisdom subsystem is the guardian of true patient- and therapist-love in that it perceives all of the relevant triggers and other factors that evoke an expression of love by a patient or therapist and determines whether that love is deserved and true or undeserved and false. Its appraisals, however, do not emerge directly into awareness, but are encoded in displaced narrative communications. Because the subsystem's assessments do not influence conscious system feelings and actions, it is necessary to trigger decode the messages from this subsystem to ascertain and make use of its invaluable and generally valid appraisals of a loving gesture.

The subsystem of morality and ethics, with its pristine, archetypal, universal code of sound morals and ethics, adopts the viewpoint that high levels of morality and true love are expressed in the unconsciously validated interventions of therapists, especially those that involve securing the ideal framework for treatment. The subsystem also finds false love and immorality in therapists who modify the ideal ground rules of therapy. With strong effects on the conscious system, this subsystem unconsciously orchestrates self-punishments for those who have in the past and at present in a therapy love falsely and immorally, and it rewards those who love truly and ethically.

The danger-sensitive subsystem is responsible for many feelings and enacted expressions of false love that serve to deny death and defend against the anxieties it evokes. This subsystem has an enormous influence over conscious system choices and behaviors. It also is the deep unconscious source of the main resistances seen in psychotherapy, especially those that are invoked to deny death. The subsystem is extremely sensitive to the death-related meanings of many seemingly innocuous interventions, and in the face of conscious acceptance, it activates patients' deep unconscious death anxieties. In turn, these anxieties motivate the use of conscious system denial and obliteration of the aroused death-related issues. As noted, these denial-based defenses can motivate the use of a vast array of falsely loving gestures that are unconsciously designed to interfere with therapeutic progress; these obstacles need to be properly analyzed and resolved. The danger-sensitive subsystem also motivates patients and their therapists to avoid or side-step death-related meanings in patients' material and to modify secured frames lest they arouse dreaded existential death anxieties. When these deep unconscious death anxieties are activated, patients often will feel unloved consciously, but will appreciate the therapist's true love deep unconsciously.

Some Paradoxes of Love in Psychotherapy

There is an essential paradox regarding love in psychotherapy in that secured frames foster expressions of true love in both patients and their therapists, while simultaneously evoking secured-frame, existential death anxieties that motivate expressions of false love. Clinical experience indicates, however, that with patients who have not been severely traumatized, the healing aspects of the secured frame generally will prevail so that true patient-love, quietly expressed, is the outcome. On the other hand, with patients who have been overly traumatized and who suffer from severe existential or predator death anxieties, there will tend to be a conscious dislike or hatred of the frame-securing therapist which, nevertheless, is combined with deep unconscious perceptions of him or her as truly loving. In general, even though they are and appreciate being loved by their therapists deep unconsciously, it is difficult to enable these threatened, angry patients to stay in therapy when the frame is secured. This problem arises because of their devastating, existential dread of closed spaces and their deep unconscious need for the denial of death. These patients tend to abandon truly loving therapists because they mistakenly and self-defensively feel unloved by them.

On the other hand, modified frames are expressions of false therapist-love and they tend to evoke false love in patients. Therapists who offer such conditions for treatment therefore are consciously cherished and falsely loved by many of their patients, even as they are experienced deep unconsciously as unloving and harmful. It is striking to see how much false conscious love patients feel towards unloving and hurtful therapists, a finding that emphasizes the extent to which defenses against death anxiety play a role in love in psychotherapy – and in daily life as well. A complementary finding is the extent to which patients unconsciously fear truly loving therapists and seldom experience conscious love towards them, despite the finding that they express much true love towards them deep unconsciously in their encoded images.

As for therapists, most therapists are fearful of truly loving their patients because of the death anxieties evoked by lovingly securing the ground rules of therapy and making unconsciously validated interpretations – efforts that always lead to expressions of a patients' death-related issues in ways that activate therapists' own unresolved death anxieties. Therapists therefore are naturally inclined to be either unloving or falsely loving towards their patients, a situation that has caused

great harm and grief for themselves, their patients, and the entire field
of psychotherapy.

Some Basic Clinical Precepts

With these ideas in mind, we can turn now to the strong adaptive clinical precepts that appear to enhance therapists' handling of their own
and their patients' feelings of love in psychotherapy. As we have seen,
dealing with love in the treatment situation is a challenge that calls for
sound, well-defined principles of technique lest matters go awry.

In muted, neutralized form, both patient- and therapist-love are
necessary ingredients for effective psychotherapy. This kind of unde-
manding love is, as a rule, an expression of true love. Wishes by
patients for anything more than their therapists' implicit, respectful
loving feelings and care are a reflection of a search for false therapist-
love. While these desires arise from within the patient, they also are
triggered by specific interventions of his or her therapist which almost
always are falsely loving in nature.

Therapists who extend their usual repertoire of interventions in the
name of caring for or loving their patients are, as a rule, expressing a
type of false therapist-love. Most expressions of false patient- or
therapist-love involve departures from the ideal ground rules and
boundaries of psychotherapy – i.e., they are frame-deviant in nature
and thus need to be avoided as much as possible.

In psychotherapy, all loving enactments or attempts to directly
satisfy a loving wish or need in an extra-therapeutic manner are expressions of false patient- or therapist-love. Patients' expressions of love
and their requests for special loving satisfactions from their therapists
should be evaluated in light of the following two factors:

The *therapist-created triggers* to which a patient's loving expression
or request for therapist-love is a response. Patient-love and patients'
searches for love are, in the main, adaptive or maladaptive responses
to their therapists' interventions or failures to intervene – and to
frame-related interventions in particular. In general, as noted, frame-
modifying triggers stimulate false patient-love, while frame-securing
efforts stimulate true patient-love. Severely traumatic events outside
of therapy may on rare occasion also trigger patients' love-related
activities in this regard.

The *encoded themes* in the patient's trigger-evoked, displaced narrative images. True love is validated deep unconsciously through encoded

themes that portray an appropriately loving relationship, people receiving helpful care or deserving gifts and the like. In contrast, false love is identified through displaced, encoded stories of inappropriately loving relationships such as those that are incestuous or extra-marital and through themes of harm and damage.

All in all, the form taken by an expression of patient-love is determined by three immediate factors:

First, the patient's personal love- and trauma-related history, the current status of his or her death-related realities and issues, and his or her present inner state of mind.

Second, the overall interaction with the therapist, including the nature of the therapist's interventions.

And third, the status of the ground rules and boundaries of the therapy and recent changes, if any, in these rules – be they towards securing or modifying the ideal frame.

False patient-love almost always is a maladaptive response to therapist-evoked triggers. Because the therapist contributes to expressions of false patient-love, such love is an interactionally evoked gross behavioral resistance and a sign of an emotional dysfunction that requires proper exploration and resolution. This kind of false patient-love has conscious, superficially unconscious, and deep unconscious sources, of which the last are most critical. Among its more superficial sources are patients' unresolved incestuous wishes; desires for unfulfilled interpersonal and relational satisfactions; and wishes for missing narcissistic supplies and gratifications.

False patient-love also has very crucial deep unconscious sources which always are death-related. Patients who are inclined to seek satisfactions of false love typically have suffered significant death-related traumas in both their early and more recent lives. Satisfactions of false love are always frame-violating and operate as a means of denying death in the sense that the frame violator unconsciously believes that he or she is an exception to the existential rule that death follows life.

In a few words, then, false love is death-defying love.

When therapists satisfy their patients' direct or implicit requests for false love they are supporting their patients' resistances against insightful therapeutic work and reinforcing their maladaptive use of denial mechanisms in dealing with death-related issues. The patient's request and the therapist's response appear to be action-based efforts to alleviate the unbearable, unconsciously experienced death anxieties with which they both are suffering. These satisfactions therefore preclude the insightful resolution of these anxieties and the death-related conflicts with which both parties to therapy are attempting to cope.

There are four factors that contribute to therapists' efforts to seek satisfaction of their own falsely loving feelings and needs with their patients:

First, therapists' inner mental conflicts and dysfunctions, which are based on their personality make-up, early life histories of seduction and death-related traumas, and on their present inner mental state and proclivities.

Second, recent death-related traumas in their everyday or professional lives.

Third, therapists' interactions with their patients and in particular, their interactions with the patient or patients towards whom they are directing their falsely loving attempts at enactment. This includes responses to the psychological features of their patients and to the nature of their patients' life histories and current death-related traumas, as well as to the themes and issues patients bring up in their sessions.

And fourth, the status of the ground rules and boundaries within which therapists work with their patients in general and the patient chosen for the enactment in particular – including any recent change in the framework or conditions of treatment. As is true of patients, therapists are more prone to feel and enact false love in modified frames and more inclined towards feelings of constrained, true love in secured frames.

Therapists are well advised to refrain from carrying out any impulse towards enacted love with a patient. Instead, they should either seek proper personal psychotherapy or engage in private self-processing efforts designed to determine the triggers and deep unconscious sources of these pathological countertransference-based wishes. Their own death-related anxieties and issues always play a role in these situations, so they should strive to identify any recent death-related trauma that may be evoking these wishes and intentions and clarify and resolve the adverse consequences of their early-life, death-related traumas as well.

The satisfaction of false love in psychotherapy has severe adverse effects on both parties to therapy. It may lead to symptomatic regressions; psychosomatic symptoms; maladaptive behaviors within and outside of the therapy, so-called acting in or acting out; self-punitive decisions and behaviors; psychotic symptoms and other adverse effects. It also intensifies patients' resistances and therapists' counter-resistances within the therapy, precluding symptom-resolution through insight unless the false love is interpreted and insightfully renounced.

Expressions of Love

In principle, then, feelings of love in patients must be deeply under-stood in light of both the prevailing triggers from the therapist and the patient's encoded, unconscious views of that love. As long as these feelings are subjective and do not move the patient towards efforts at enactment, there is ample time to explore and interpret the sources and meanings of a loving fantasy. If a patient tries to seek satisfaction or to unilaterally enact his or her loving wishes towards a therapist, to the greatest extent possible the therapist should not participate in the enactment and should apply sound techniques to help the patient to pursue the meanings, conscious and deep unconscious, of the wish for direct satisfaction.

Similar principles apply to therapists' feelings of love for a patient. Persistent subjective feelings of love should be dealt with through private efforts at self-processing or through a proper form of personal psychotherapy. Wishes to engage the patient in satisfying these loving desires call for restraint and for keeping these impulses to oneself; they present an urgent need for private, self-directed therapeutic interventions.

With these ideas in mind, let's look now still more closely at the subjects of patient- and therapist-love in psychotherapy.

7

Patients' Loving and Wishing to be Loved

All loving moments in psychotherapy are the interactional creation of both patient and therapist. Whereas weak adaptive therapists generally see the patient as the prime mover, strong adaptive therapists have found that the therapist usually is the one who must accept the greater responsibility for the therapeutic transactions. Even so, in taking a closer look at our subject I shall turn first to patient-love per se. As I have noted, patients' conscious love for their therapists may be either true or false, while encoded, deep unconscious love is almost always true. As a result, consciously expressed patient-love is far more difficult to evaluate and deal with than its deep unconscious counterpart.

Conscious feelings of love in patients for their therapists tend to be direct responses to conscious beliefs that the therapist is behaving and intervening in a caring and helpful manner. Largely because these are conscious system judgments of doubtful validity, there are problems inherent to these opinions. For one, there are many patients who, invoking the unrecognized use of conscious system denial, feel lovingly towards blatantly hurtful therapists. By and large, these patients suffer from intense deep unconscious guilt for having harmed others and have a strong unconscious need to be punished by their therapists who unwittingly comply. In addition, in situations where therapists are not grossly harmful, patients' conscious convictions that they are being helped often are self-deceptive, false, and once more, denial-based. As we have seen, the conscious system of the emotion-processing mind lacks a reliable means of evaluating the deeply affecting qualities of a therapist's interventional efforts. Conscious system needs for denial and self-punishment not only tend to invalidate a large proportion of patients' conscious judgments of their psychotherapists' efforts, they

106

also prompt patients to favor and consciously love therapists who are deep unconsciously experienced as unloving and harmful.

For these reasons, all expressions of conscious patient-love must be tested against the patient's concomitant, displaced encoded narratives. The deep unconscious wisdom subsystem is the arbiter of love in psychotherapy.

Conscious loving feelings in patients towards their therapists tend to arise as conscious adaptive or maladaptive responses to specific interventions. In order to determine the deep nature of a love-evoking intervention and thereby the underlying quality of the patients' feelings of love toward their therapists, the narrative imagery that follows the intervention must be trigger decoded and studied for the presence or absence of deep unconscious validation. In principle, true patient-love is a response to unconsciously validated interventions and false patient-love a response to unconsciously non-validated therapeutic efforts.

By and large, patients' conscious feelings of love tend to follow falsely rather than truly loving therapeutic interventions. In contrast, deep unconscious expressions of love follow the opposite path and almost always are responsive to truly loving, deep unconsciously validated therapeutic efforts. Thus a wide array of interventions accepted and used by weak adaptive psychotherapists evoke conscious feelings of love towards such therapists that prove on deep unconscious exploration to be false forms of patient-love. Strong adaptive clinical studies have shown that on the whole, the only classes of interventions that regularly obtain deep unconscious validation are interpretations and frame-securing efforts that are based on trigger decoding. There is, then, a remarkably narrow range of consistently truly loving interventions by therapists and most other therapeutic efforts, no matter how well-meaning and kindly, tend to be experienced deep unconsciously as unloving and hurtful. Paradoxically, it is efforts of this kind that tend to arouse conscious love in patients towards their therapists.

Most non-interpretive, supposedly supportive and usually frame-modifying interventions by therapists are experienced by patients as deeply unloving even as they evoke conscious feelings of love towards the therapist. Common examples are appreciative and loving patient-responses to interventions like therapists' reassurances, seemingly helpful directives, changes in the time of sessions at patients' requests, offering make-up or emergency sessions, fee reductions for patients suffering from financial hardships, self-revelations by the therapist, and non-sexual physical contact such as hand-holding or hugging the patient.

All such interventions are experienced deep unconsciously as efforts to enact or act out an expression of therapist-love and as such, they are almost always seen as falsely rather than truly loving. Nevertheless, the conscious mind of both patients and therapists tend to relish these widely sought, non-neutral, frame-violating interventions and patients are lovingly disposed towards therapists who offer them. Even so, as I have been emphasizing, the deep unconscious mind consistently generates encoded narratives that speak for their unloving and harmful aspects and their unconsciously mediated, detrimental effects on all concerned.

Along different lines, to some extent true patient-love may be distinguished from false patient-love based on whether a patient attempts to enact or satisfy his or her loving feelings towards the therapist or restricts the expression of love to momentary subjective feelings and constrained fantasies. As a rule, both sexual fantasies about the therapist and efforts by patients to enact or gratify feelings of love for a therapist, no matter how consciously rationalized, are perceived deep unconsciously as instances of false patient-love. On the other hand, true consciously experienced patient-love is non-demanding of the therapist, non-erotic, and appropriately appreciative of the therapists' sound ministrations. Characteristically, it also is expressed in passing rather than with emphasis, elaboration, and repetition – it is a momentary thought or feeling expressed as quiet love, affection, and the like.

Constrained, consciously experienced patient-love must, however, be put to the test of deep unconscious validation as seen with the emergence of narratives with positive, caring and loving themes. In addition, an expression of true patient-love tends to be followed by a shift to threatening imagery related to the patient's exploration of his or her core, death-related traumas and conflicts as evoked by other triggers within the therapy situation. These issues are anxiety-provoking for both patients and their therapists, and are unconsciously experienced as dangerous and threatening. Nevertheless, patients deep unconsciously recognize the necessity of the emergence of such material and their links to past death-related traumas in order to achieve a truly insightful cure. As I have indicated, death is the primary subject of psychotherapy and true therapist-love is the support and balm that helps patients to work over and resolve their death-related issues.

This inevitable shift from loving interludes to anxiety-provoking, death-related material accounts for one more feature of true, conscious patient-love, namely, that its expression is soon followed by gross behavioral and communicative resistances. The absence of such resistances suggests that the patient-love was false in its nature. This kind of resistance-free, inappropriate patient-love tends to be used by patients in two ways: First, as a means of denying and avoiding the death-related issues that have been aroused by death-related triggers in the therapy, and second, as a response to the relief that patients feel when they unconsciously realize that their therapists are not dealing with or exploring the death-related themes and conflicts reflected in their material. Therapists are motivated to do so based on their own unresolved death anxieties, which often are especially intense because patients' death-related imagery almost always is a response to a death-related trigger created by the therapist – e.g., an assaultive verbal intervention, a death-related frame violation, or a sign of illness or injury in the healer.

This brings us to two additional interactional reasons, that is, unconscious motives for the pervasiveness of false patient-love for falsely loving psychotherapists. The first lies with the power and dread inherent to the death-related, deep unconscious traumas and conflicts that lie in the depths of emotional maladaptations. Because of the psychical pain involved working with the narratives and themes that deal with these issues, patients only rarely feel conscious love towards therapists who enable them to communicate and then interpret these anxiety-provoking concerns. It follows then, that therapists who avoid the exceedingly discomforting death-related meanings encoded in patients' narrative imagery, or deal with these problems intellectually and thereby at a great distance, tend to be consciously loved by their patients – i.e., they are loved for their avoidance of death-related imagery and meanings. Nevertheless, these therapists are not loved by patients deep unconsciously because their deep unconscious systems know full well that the therapist-love offered by these healers is false, unduly defensive, and counterfeit.

The second reason for so much false patient-love is reflected in the finding that patients unconsciously dread secured frames because the invocation of a set of ideal, archetypal ground rules evokes very disturbing forms of existential death anxiety. Patients therefore tend to consciously love therapists who express their love falsely through departures from these ideals. In addition, frame modifications often are consciously pleasing and satisfying to patients so they feel conscious love towards their overly-gratifying therapists. In all of these situations, as I have stressed, the deep unconscious response is quite otherwise and negatively-toned narratives prevail throughout.

The Weak Adaptive Approach

Weak adaptive forms of psychotherapy tend to be unconsciously designed to either avoid death-related issues or to limit their exploration to intellectualized conscious discussions without addressing their more compelling deep unconscious meanings as reflected in the encoded narratives that usually accompanies such imagery. A common form of false patient-love arises, then, from the uninsightful or superficially insightful relief, if any, that patients obtain through these therapist-supported, denial-based defenses.

In my work as a psychiatrist offering medication management to patients in psychotherapy with other mental health professionals, I repeatedly see patients who express conscious love for therapists who make clichéd interpretations or do not interpret at all. The interventions made by these therapists as described to me tend to involve blaming chemical dysfunctions for patients' emotional ills, directives of questionable value, other varieties of inappropriate support, and a wide range of comments of no special import whatsoever.

To cite a brief specific example that I came across in the literature while writing this chapter – one among countless others – I turn to a paper by Cohen and Schermer (2004) in which they attempt to define the concept of depth in the intersubjective approach (see also Hoffman, 1998). The authors cite a clinical illustration (pp. 590–591) in which a middle-aged, extremely distraught woman patient begins her session with the self-loathing report that she dreamt that she had killed a baby. The therapist first acknowledges the horror that the patient had felt in experiencing herself as infanticidal and in due course, he offers an alternative construction – that the baby is a version of herself as a barrier to her development as an adult, a version she needed to destroy.

This intervention is seen by the authors of the paper as a creative use of the baby as a metaphor for a disavowed part of the patient's self and it is believed to be empathic and insightful by reassuring the patient about her own aggression. The authors add that some time after the session, the therapist realized that this image was 'concordant with his own, then unconscious self-narrative memory of an earlier period in his life when he had felt the need to smash an aversive image of himself as a porcelain doll yet also someone born with a visible malformation' (p. 591).

To discuss this vignette, we have here a seemingly loving intervention, but there are no criteria with which the author's assessment of its attributes can be evaluated – we are dealing with unvalidated conscious beliefs.

Nevertheless, it seems clear that the intervention is based on the manifest dream image alone, that it is arbitrary, and that the metaphoric meaning is invoked by the therapist in order to deny the existence of murderous impulses within the patient and to by-pass related anxieties within the therapist. We know too from strong adaptive studies that a real, triggering intervention by the therapist must have had evoked the dream. Rather than searching for this interventional trigger and treating the dream image as conveying an encoded, deep unconscious perception of the therapist – i.e., rather than attempting to trigger decode its disguised meanings – the therapist interprets the image as a metaphoric abstraction with virtually no connection to reality or to the violent impulses within the patient – and in all likelihood, in the therapist as well.

Indications are that the patient felt comforted by this intervention and loved by her therapist. Nevertheless, the unconscious basis for this response appears to be the likelihood that her deep unconscious experience of violent harm done to her by her therapist – and her reactive violence against him – were converted into an uplifting personal struggle within the mind of the patient whose supposed goal was to get rid of the interfering infant within herself. Whereas the patient accepted the intervention consciously and felt loved, we may safely conjecture that deep unconsciously, there was neither validation of the intervention nor support for the belief that the intervention had been truly loving. Indeed, the presented material suggests that the therapist had, in his early life, experienced a basic death-related birth trauma of his own and that the intervention probably served to deny and obliterate both his and his patient's activated predatory and predator death anxieties.

The Strong Adaptive Approach

Strong adaptive psychotherapists endeavor to create the conditions under which patients are likely to respond to therapist-related triggering events (interventions) with narrative material – dreams and guided associations to dreams (or stories) – that encode their deep unconscious perceptions of and reactions to these triggers. They base their trigger-decoded interventions on these narratives and deal meaningfully with these realities and their patients' inner-mental responses to these realities as they link to past death-related traumas. Such work is deep unconsciously perceived as truly loving.

We can see now why conscious and deep unconscious forms of true patient-love are not sustained for very long. Loving moments inevitably set the stage for dealing with issues that are death-related and anxiety-provoking – painful but necessary experiences, however unconscious, that evoke momentary resistances followed by interpretable material. In time, after the new material has been properly trigger decoded and deep unconscious insights are offered to the patient, a new, momentary expression of patient-love is likely to arise – only to be followed once more with both gross behavioral and communicative resistances and freshly triggered, anxiety-provoking, death-related material.

In keeping with the above vignette, aside from the strong adaptive approach, virtually every form of psychotherapy offered today appears to be unwittingly and unconsciously designed to avoid accessing the deep unconscious meanings of patients' death-related traumas as they are activated by therapists' interventions. In most instances, the death-related meanings of these efforts are not registered consciously by patients, but are experienced and processed deep unconsciously. Dealing with death-related narrative imagery and the traumas to which they pertain is painful, yet essential to deep unconscious healing. Truly loving, lasting, insightful relief can come solely through securing psychotherapy frames and trigger decoding patients' deep unconscious death-related narratives and illuminating their links to both current triggers and earlier traumatic experiences.

Problems arise largely because conscious minds have evolved and are designed to defend against and avoid these death-related incidents and many of the more unbearable meanings of these events. Thus, once the recognition of the reality of death comes into play, the conscious mind favors denial-based forms of false love over truly loving perceptions and behaviors. While patients pay dearly for this denial through maladaptive behaviors and emotional symptoms, they do so willingly though without knowing the underlying motives – the use of denial is the preferred conscious system approach to death and its encumbrances. As a result, the conscious minds of patients tend to love therapists who consciously and unconsciously support these denial-based defenses by avoiding death-related interventions or by dealing with death-related imagery with intellectualizations and abstractions that move both their patients and themselves far from reality – specifically, from the realities of death and harm. These therapists also tend to create conditions under which patients are discouraged from generating the encoded narrative vehicles that carry death-related meanings. And when dreams and stories do emerge in their patients' material, they are either ignored by the therapist or interpreted using self-evident, clichéd, intellectualized translations of their surface, but not deep unconscious, meanings.

There are, then, countless ways in which falsely loving and falsely loved therapists create the conditions for a psychotherapy experience and intervene in ways that support their patients and their own denial of death. Unconsciously relieved of their own innate pressures to express encoded death-related material and of delving meaningfully into their death-related experiences and conflicts, patients are inclined to love these therapists with great intensity and with repeated expressions of denial-based, false love. While many patients suffer emotionally because of their lack of insight, their false love continues to find means of expression towards their therapists and at times, they spill over into efforts at enactment and satisfaction. False patient-love also may be displaced into the everyday life of the patient, thereby creating major relationship problems. And in therapy, this love persists even in the face of therapeutic failures and the emergence of fresh emotional symptoms. Rare is the patient who, in the face of continued suffering or of strikingly unloving interventions, falls out of false-love with his or her therapist and decides to leave treatment.

A Clinical Illustration

To cite a relevant case example, Ms Gordon, a young woman in her late twenties, is in psychotherapy with Mr Wall, a social worker, for a severe depression that followed a break-up with her boyfriend. She is in treatment for about a year and not doing well so she asks for a referral to a psychiatrist for anti-depressant medication. Mr Wall refers her to Dr Marks and in the course of the consultation, she tells him about her symptoms, her personal life, and her impressions of her psychotherapy and Mr Wall, whom she sees as a very caring therapist. Ms Gordon then mentions that she sleeps poorly. When Dr Marks asks her if she remembers a recent dream, she tells him that earlier that week, the night before her last session with Mr Wall, she dreamt of being in some kind of open or public space where she was in bed with two men who forced her to have sex with them, after which they began to beat her. She had told the dream to Dr Wall who translated the dream to mean that she had a grim view of men and saw them all as rapists, adding that maybe this included her view of him too. He traced it all to her father who was gruff and seductive with her when she was a child.

Ms Gordon tells Dr Marks that she really doesn't see her therapist as a rapist, that in fact, she loves him – he's been kind and helpful to her in so many ways. She then mentions that Mr Wall was her ex-boyfriend's psychotherapist and that her ex-boyfriend actually had taken her to see Mr Wall when his relationship with her ran into difficulties and he wanted to leave her.

Without going further into this session, we can see that Ms Gordon's conscious love for her therapist is belied by her manifest dream whose encoded adaptive meanings can be deciphered in light of the known therapist-evoked triggers. The themes in this associational network – the image of being forced to have sex with, and being beaten by, two men in public – appear to be responsive to the two known frame-deviant triggers for her dream: First, Mr Wall's acceptance of Ms Gordon as a patient even though he was seeing her ex-boyfriend in therapy, and second, Mr Wall's referral of the patient to Dr Marks for medication. Both of these triggers, which were accepted consciously without protest by the patient, are linked to the theme of two men being involved with the patient. Decoding the patient's dream images in light of these triggers shows that both of these supposedly loving interventions by Mr Wall were viewed deep unconsciously by Ms Gordon as flagrant boundary and frame violations in which she was inappropriately exposed to third parties (the public space) and misused sexually – her ex-boyfriend and Mr Wall in the first instance and Dr Marks and Mr Wall in the second. Both of these interventions are departures from the ideal frame which calls for the total privacy and confidentiality of a psychotherapy and for a private, one-to-one relationship between patient and therapist. Frame modifications of this kind usually are accepted consciously by patients as caring and loving interventions, but are validly perceived deep unconsciously as exploitative sexually and as doing violence to the patient who accepted these frame-violating arrangements for deep unconscious reasons of her own. In fact, during her consultation with Dr Marks, he was able to ascertain that Ms Gordon suffered from deep unconscious guilt over the death of a girlfriend when they were teenagers because Ms Gordon had played an indirect role in the friend's fatal car accident. Indications were that Mr Wall was falsely loved by this patient because unwittingly and unconsciously, he was meting out hurtful interventions that she accepted unconsciously as much deserved punishments for her murderous crime.

All in all, it appears that this patient's love for her therapist was a form of false love and that it probably was unconsciously motivated first, by the punishment she was experiencing unconsciously from her therapist and second, by his avoidance of the patient's death-related issues in connection with the death of her girlfriend and possibly other death-related experiences in her family. Finally, it is well to note that Mr Wall's clichéd transference interpretation of this dream pales in light of the complex meanings that were revealed through trigger decoding the thematic imagery in the patient's dream. Once more we see the striking differences between weak and strong adaptive formulations and interpretations.

Summing up: Therapists should be wary of and mistrust conscious feelings of patient-love towards themselves unless they are validated by accompanying encoded images and themes.

Further Comments on Technique

Technically, therapists have tended to deal directly and manifestly with patient-love, often naively viewing it as genuine without an appreciation for its possibly defensive and self-punishing deeper, unconscious meanings and functions for the patient. Often, the exploration of a patient's loving feelings is avoided entirely and little if anything is done to determine why they have emerged at a particular moment in therapy – i.e., the nature of its triggers – and what they mean on the deep unconscious level of experience. If the therapist, based on manifest impressions, believes that the love is being used as a resistance, which is vaguely defined as anything that the therapist considers to be an obstacle to therapeutic progress, some effort at superficial interpretation may be made although in most cases, it will not obtain encoded validation. Supervisory work indicates that the most common reason that a therapist sees an expression of patient-love as a resistance is that the therapist is uncomfortable with and anxious about the patient's loving feelings towards him or her. The interpretation of the love as a resistance is an effort designed unconsciously to direct the patient to stop feeling that way about the therapist.

In contrast, the strong adaptive approach considers and explores the surface and depths of expressions of patient-love. Whenever a patient expresses loving feelings towards a therapist, the effort is made to identify the interventional triggers that have evoked the loving expression. The therapist then waits for the patient to generate narrative themes or, failing that, he or she asks the patient for a recent dream or advises the patient to make up a short story. This *origination narrative* becomes the source of guided associations from the patient because they are, as a rule, more powerful and critical than the images in the manifest dream. In this way, the therapist obtains a pool of compelling and relevant, displaced encoded themes. The therapist then identifies the stimulus or trigger for the expressed love and on this basis, he or she can trigger decode the narrative themes and determine if the patient-love conveys a genuine appreciation for the therapist's helpful efforts or contrariwise, that it is being used to defend against unconsciously experienced therapist-created harm, most often carried out through some type of frame modification.

Once the deep unconscious meanings of the expressed patient-love have been understood by the therapist, he or she needs to decide whether or not to intervene. If the love is conscious and supported by the encoded themes, or is deeply unconscious and reflected solely in encoded imagery involving loving and caring individuals, the therapist probably is dealing with an expression of true patient-love that has emerged in response to an unconsciously perceived loving and caring, validated intervention. In such cases, the encoded loving images may be allowed to go uninterpreted. On the other hand, an interpretation of an encoded expression of true love is called for whenever a patient's subsequent encoded material touches on his or her death anxieties and presents a view of the insight-pursuing therapist as dangerous and anxiety-provoking. Given that the negative images usually are quite striking, trigger decoding and interpreting the patient's truly loving images is carried out to enable the patient to appreciate that he or she is unconsciously experiencing two sets of images of the therapist – one that is threatening and another that is loving. The patient's experience is summed up with the idea that the therapist is expressing a kind of tough love that is bringing the patient in touch with his or her deepest fears. These interventions enable the patient to further pursue the death-related issues at hand.

It should be understood, however, that a manifest, conscious expression of patient-love is not a communication that validates a therapist's prior interventions. These expressions of love are not encoded and do not reflect a deep unconscious appraisal by the patient of the loving or unloving qualities of a therapist's intervention. Indeed, as has been noted, these manifestly loving feelings often surface in response to interventions that are invalidated through deep unconscious, encoded imagery and thereby serve to deny hurt rather than express true love. There is, then, a crucial distinction between conscious-manifest and deep unconscious-encoded expressions of patient-love, in that the former often serve denial, defense and resistance, while the latter typically are non-defensive and affirming –

a special way of unconsciously validating a recent triggering intervention by a loving psychotherapist.

Patients' Requests for Love

Psychotherapy experiences become quite complicated when patients ask therapists for manifestly loving interventions such as non-sexual physical contact, gratifying changes in the ground rules, small favors or gifts, personal self-revelations, and the like. In the extreme and usually with considerable prior build-up, a patient may even seek sexual contact with the therapist. In all of these situations, the stakes are high for all concerned and the manner in which the therapist intervenes is of great consequence for both parties to the therapy.

In principle, studies from the vantage-point of the strong adaptive approach make clear that there is no sound basis for a therapist to accede to any type of request for a deliberate sign of love from his or her patients. This holds true even though in most cases, patients consciously feel gratified and loved when their therapists comply with these solicitations. Nevertheless, the encoded narratives that follow such interludes consistently speak to the harm done when a therapist accedes to these entreaties. The encoded themes also point to a common set of factors that play a role in this kind of request and they also indicate how therapists should respond to them.

The following are typical features of these situations:

Patients' requests for favors tend to be triggered by their therapists' interventions and on rare occasions, by a death-related trauma outside of treatment. Within the therapy, the most common kind of triggering intervention involves a frame modification that is consciously satisfying for the patient. The intervention may have arisen from a prior request from the patient or from the therapist's own needs to invoke it – e.g., a therapist's request to change the time of a session or his or her asking for permission to write a paper about the patient's psychotherapy, however disguised. These prior frame violations usually are self-serving for the therapist and therefore do not express true therapist-love either consciously or unconsciously. On the other hand, they may be seemingly loving and gratifying for the patient who nonetheless deep unconsciously experiences the gesture as harmful, inappropriately seductive, and anti-therapeutic. In either case, the therapist's self-gratifying frame violation becomes a model for the patient who then responds to the death anxieties evoked by the therapist by obtaining falsely loving favors from him or her. Frame violations and false expressions of love then become prominent maladaptive modes of coping with anxiety-provoking issues for the patient who has modeled himself or herself on – i.e., identified with – the therapist's way of coping with comparable problems.

Patients' requests for loving gestures from their therapists also may arise when patients experience a death-related trauma within or outside of therapy. Outside of therapy, the trigger usually is manifestly death-related, but within the treatment situation, the trigger may be either grossly death-related or only implicitly so. Examples of the first type of trigger include the mention by a therapist that he or she, or a member of his or her family, is ill or has been injured; a therapist's unexplained extended absence from sessions; and a visible indication that the therapist is ill or injured. Examples of the second, more indirect type of death-related intervention, include frame-modifying lapses by therapists, such as forgetting an appointment, mistakenly beginning a session late, inadvertently extending the length of a session, accidentally brushing against a patient, and the like. As the deep unconscious wisdom subsystem well knows, these interventions almost always are unconsciously motivated by active death-related issues and anxieties in the therapist.

It is not uncommon for patients to consciously deny and obliterate their therapists' death-related self-revelations and even more so, signs of illness or injury in the therapist. The indirect death-related triggering interventions made by therapists virtually always go consciously unrecognized as such by patients. But they do register deep unconsciously because its wisdom subsystem knows very well that most frame lapses by therapists are the result of active, unresolved death anxieties. This knowledge and the perceptions on which it is based are reflected in patients' displaced, encoded narratives. Death-related triggers of this kind are common precursors and motivators for patients' request for deliberate, unconsciously motivated, death-denying acts of false love from their therapists.

However disturbing to both patients and therapists, these death-related triggers also offer unique opportunities for patients – and their therapists – to unconsciously process and work through their death-related traumas, conflicts, and anxieties with help from sound, deep unconsciously validated interventions. But this kind of insightful therapeutic work can take place only if the therapist, using the patient's displaced encoded imagery and deep unconscious directives, shows the patient that his or her deep unconscious mind is making quite clear that he or she must turn down the patient's request for a deviant sign of love. Therapists can be quite certain that the deep unconscious system universally indicates that patient-therapist boundaries must be sustained clear and frames kept secured. Gratifying patients' frame-violating entreaties precludes therapeutic work directed towards insight and reinforces patients' resistances and use of acting out and denial in facing death-related situations.

There are as well countless indirect ways that therapists unconsciously and unwittingly indicate to their patients that they are either ill or suffering from an acute death-related trauma. These evocative, self-revealing triggers tend to elude conscious registration by either party to a therapy, although they are perceived deep unconsciously and then encoded in patients' displaced, narratives. When faced with a death-related trauma, humans, including psychotherapists, tend to modify rules, frames, and boundaries, a trend that has gone unnoticed by conscious minds for all these years, even as it has been known to the deep unconscious wisdom subsystem all the while (see however, Galatzer-Levy, 2004). This is a prime example of deep unconscious knowledge that is entirely foreign to conscious thinking.

In addition to invoking unnecessary and harmful falsely loving, ground-rule modifications when under death-related pressures, therapists tend to overlook and obliterate death-related images in their patients' material and they also fail to notice and intervene around their patients' active death-related conflicts as conveyed in their encoded narrative themes. Meanwhile, the death-related issues being communicated indirectly by their therapists are detected by patients' deep unconscious wisdom subsystems and without their knowing their unconscious motives, these unconscious perceptions motivate patients to seek deviant kinds of false love from their therapists. They also drive patients to turn to efforts to enact expressions of frame-deviant false love to their unconsciously recognized wounded healers. In addition, patients' own death anxieties are activated but they go unrecognized and uninterpreted by their therapists, to the detriment of both parties to the therapy. The patient suffers because his or her death-related issues remain unresolved and continue to be a source of emotional maladaptation, and the therapist suffers because he or she experiences deep unconscious guilt and needs for punishment for having failed to properly help the patient.

Death-related triggers often lead to expressions of compensatory false love by both members of the therapeutic dyad.

All in all, then, death-related traumas and anxieties that originate in either a patient or therapist, and that arise in connection with their everyday lives or, more often, in connection with their therapeutic interaction, are prime motivating factors in patients' requests for loving gestures from their therapists. If the therapist acquiesces, falsely loving, denial-serving frame modifications become the preferred mode of coping with activated death anxieties for both the patient and the therapist. Insight is precluded unless the frame modification is rectified and the false love interpreted and renounced – i.e., the falsely loving frame deviation corrected and the secured frame restored. On the other hand, if the therapist does not acquiesce to the patient's conscious pleas for extra-therapeutic care and love, the patient will need to cope with his or her death-related issues verbally and affectively by generating narrative material that facilitates the interpretation of the deep unconscious meanings of the death-related incident. The keys to these efforts are, as always, allowing and encouraging patients to generate encoded narratives and identifying the trigger or triggers that have unconsciously motivated the patient to ask for the falsely loving gesture. Also important is establishing the connections between an incident of this kind and death-related incidents in the patient's earlier life. Similar insights are necessary for the therapist as well.

Patients' Conscious Requests for Love

The wish for true love from a therapist is almost never expressed overtly, largely because patients have no conscious idea or representation of the interventions that constitute the expression of such love by their therapists. Indeed, at present, in most cases this lack of knowledge is true of their therapists as well. The conscious mind therefore is quite incapable of knowing just how therapists should express their genuinely loving – and caring – feelings towards their patients. This helps to account for the rarity of true therapist-love and the prevalence of false love in psychotherapy.

In general, patients' conscious requests for loving gestures are quite rare in a well-run strong adaptive psychotherapy, but they are relatively common in weak adaptive treatment situations. The therapist who offers a secured frame is deep unconsciously holding the patient in an ideal, truly loving manner – the secured frame is the most healing form of true love that a therapist can provide for a patient. Trigger-decoded interpretations also are truly loving and it is for this reason that these two classes of interventions are the basic tools of strong adaptive therapists.

On the other hand, weak adaptive therapists tend to work in modified frames and make interventions that do not obtain deep unconscious, encoded validation. As a result, these interventions must be seen – and are seen deep unconsciously – as non-loving or falsely loving. They tend to motivate efforts by patients to enact expressions of false love towards their therapists and to request falsely loving enactments from their healers. Patients do so in part because deep unconsciously they feel quite unloved and are desperate for some sign of love from their therapists, no matter how false or deeply harmful it may be.

Patients ask their therapists for love or for loving gestures in a wide variety of non-sexual (and more rarely, sexual) ways. Almost all of these requests involve frame modifications that are falsely loving. Examples are legion: Requests to change the time or day of a session, asking to be held by the therapist, appealing to the therapist for some type of self-revelation or asking him or her to see a third party, and the like. These requests for love are indirectly expressed, but quite real.

This was the case with all of the 20 former patients whom I interviewed at length for an investigation into how various weak adaptive therapeutic modalities heal or fail to heal (Langs, 1985). On average, each patient had seen three different psychotherapists, most of them working with some kind of insight-oriented therapeutic paradigm. Except for the rare patient who initiated sexual involvement with her therapist (the therapist was the usual prime mover in this regard), these interviewees seldom described themselves as asking their therapists for open expression of love. On the other hand, most of these former patients did describe frequent requests for frame-modifying expressions of false forms of love (here too the therapist often led the way). These love-related solicitations included asking to borrow books, seeking concrete help with job situations, requesting direct advice on a wide range of matters, asking the therapist to see a friend or family member, pressing the therapist to provide extra therapy sessions, asking for rides home from sessions or to borrow money for carfare, and much more.

For their part, these patients showed little inclination to openly tell their therapists that they loved them, but they did indicate to me that they (consciously) loved their therapists, accounting for their love as a response to their therapists' seemingly loving ministrations. The thera-

peutic efforts that they appreciated included openly supportive comments, gifts from their therapists, a wide range of personal revelations,
referrals of patients to those interviewees who were mental health professionals, vague intellectualized efforts at confrontation and interpretation, and the like. The few patients who did ask directly for manifest
loving gestures from their therapists were women who consciously felt
love for their therapists. It was clear, however, that they made these
requests after they had been involved in an escalating series of
mutually agreed-on frame deviations that culminated in engaging their
therapists in some type of physical contact – e.g., kissing, hugging,
hand-holding, and in some cases, sexually as well. Even the patients
who were not involved sexually with their therapists described many
frame-modifying, evidently falsely loving gestures that they had made
towards their therapists. This included lending the therapist a book,
giving the therapist financial advice, referring a friend to the therapist,
and changing the time of a session at the therapist's request.

There were two striking findings that emerged from the interviews
with these patients:

The first is that with only rare exceptions, there were repetitive
instances in which their therapists behaved in ways that were openly
critical, nasty, deceptive, inappropriately seductive, and clearly
harmful. Nevertheless, these patients consistently ignored the implications of these blatantly hurtful interventions and continued to think of
their therapists as loving and as loved by them. The extent of their
denial of harm was remarkable.

The second finding is that in their interviews, the encoded imagery
that accompanied these patients' loving allusions always involved
unloving themes of harm and the like. There was, then, no encoded
support for these patients' conscious beliefs that their therapists were
caring and truly loving.

We see again that the conscious system simply does not know how
true therapist- (and patient)-love is expressed in psychotherapy. And
given the natural bent of the conscious mind towards false-love, this
means that the patients' conscious pressures for love from their therapists almost always entails a search for, and receipt of, false, anti-
therapeutic love. This is all the more reason for therapists to respond
to such requests with great caution and to maintain an exploratory
rather than gratifying position in this regard. In this light, we can see
that therapists are greatly aided in practicing much needed restraint
by pursuing, decoding, and understanding trigger-evoked, narrative
imagery because the patient's deep unconscious system will always

warn them of the dangers of satisfying any love-related request from a patient.

In the therapy, interludes that begin with a request for love from a patient should culminate with a trigger-decoded interpretation of the request for love and a demonstration to the patient that his or her encoded stories speak clearly for the need for the therapist to not gratify the request. The subsequent direct and encoded communications from the patient most likely will pertain to the current and/or earlier death-related traumas with which these therapeutic transactions are linked.

Technically, the patient's request for a deviant, falsely loving gesture from the therapist is a *gross behavioral resistance* or *patient-indicator* – i.e., an indication from the patient of a need for an intervention by the therapist (Langs, 1992a, 2004c). These efforts can be interpreted by the therapist only if he or she does not gratify the resistance and the wishes it contains. Enactment with the patient precludes the development of such insights, while frustrating and therapeutically processing these requests is almost certain to lead to deep understanding for both the patient and the therapist, who is very much involved in these interactions by virtue of his or her prior interventions.

Strong adaptive findings in this regard validate a remarkable piece of conscious wisdom offered in 1934 by James Strachey in his oft-quoted paper on the therapeutic action of psychoanalysis. In the course of exploring the interactional aspects of analytic healing, Strachey wrote that the analyst who tries to behave as a good [i.e., loving] object [person] is inherently behaving as a bad [i.e., falsely loving and actually harmful] object [person]. The deep unconscious system's perceptions of such supposed expressions of love always speaks to the truth of this insight.

Patients' Deep Unconscious Requests for Love

Consciously, patients are unable to ask for true therapist-love; they are, however, deep unconsciously capable of doing just that. Remarkably, on this level of experience and adaptation, patients are capable of indicating to their therapists when this love is needed and how it should be expressed. They tend to encode these directives when they themselves consciously seek a frame-deviant form of false love from their therapists or when their therapists offer them falsely loving interventions for their own reasons. Thus, whenever there is an *anticipated trigger* – i.e., an expected intervention by the therapist – that entails a falsely loving act on his or her part, the patient can be expected to encode a directive that not only tells the therapist to not carry out the false expression of love, but also indicates how the therapist's true love can and should be expressed under the prevailing circumstances.

Therapists who wish to offer truly loving interventions to their patients can do no better than to learn how to do so from the encoded messages that emanate from their patients' deep unconscious wisdom subsystems.

Some Additional Technical Precepts

The strong adaptive approach has developed an unconsciously validated set of technical principles that can serve to guide therapists in dealing with patients' requests for loving satisfactions from them. Having established that conscious system approaches to these issues are likely to be in error and harmful to the patient – and therapist – we must turn to the deep unconscious system for our guidelines. Short of that, patients become victims of predatory acts clothed in seeming kindness and love from their therapists, while therapists become the perpetrators of harm that is consciously denied but unconsciously perceived. These falsely loving interventions are the source of predator death anxiety and deep unconscious guilt based on the unconsciously perceived immorality of the therapist's effort and they call forth unconscious efforts by the therapist to be self-punishing.

Technically, whenever a patient asks for an act of kindness or love from a therapist, the therapist should invoke the fundamental rule of *free association* and ask the patient to continue to say whatever comes to mind. If the patient then discusses his or her request manifestly and proceeds to intellectualize, the therapist should invoke the strong adaptive rule of *guided, narrative associations* and ask the patient to describe a recent dream or make up a brief story. Once the origination narrative has been created, the patient should be asked to associate to its elements by finding incidents in his or her life that they conjure up. This allows for the development of a rich narrative pool of themes that eventually should contain a notable number of power themes – i.e., allusion to death, illness, harm, and the like. This imagery embodies the patient's deep unconscious view of both his or her request for enacted love (the patient-indicator) and of the therapist who might fulfill it (the anticipated trigger). Interpretation, non-gratification, and frame rectification follow as needed so that true love triumphs over the search for false love.

It has been found that patients' conscious requests for love from their therapists are a way of seeking a repetition of the unloving, harmful acts that their parents or caretakers had directed towards them in their childhoods, acts that contributed to the unconscious basis for the patient's emotional problems. In addition, these requests uniformly are motivated by patients' unresolved death-related anxieties and issues, much as satisfying the request is based unconsciously on the therapist's own unresolved death-related issues.

At bottom the turn to false love is a maladaptive attempt to by-pass or deny activated death-related anxieties and issues.

Notice too that by using the patients' encoded directives to not fulfill their request for a falsely loving gesture, therapists are behaving in ways that are truly loving and caring, and appropriately wise and strong. Offering this kind of love also inherently indicates that a therapist does not suffer from an undue fear of death and that he or she has been able to master their personal death anxieties. In this way, the therapist directs the patient to the most adaptive way to deal with their death anxieties and serves as true model of strength and loving kindness for their patients.

A Clinical Illustration

Mr Ridge, a depressed man in his late 30s, is in therapy with Dr Banks, a clinical psychologist. Some months into the therapy, the patient begins a session by asking his therapist to change the time of his session the following week so he can be a chaperone for a picnic that his 15-year-old son's high school class is going on. He recalls that a couple of months back he had agreed to Dr Banks' request for a change in the time of his session and comments that 'Fair is fair'. He recalls that Dr Banks had asked for the change in time because his son was ill and in the hospital. In like manner, Mr Ridge also wants to take care of his son. It would be nasty and uncaring if Dr Banks did not make the change if he could.

After spending considerable time trying to justify his request, Mr Ridge mentions that he had a dream the previous night in which his brother was having sex with a man whom the patient didn't recognize. Associating to the dream, he points out that two years earlier, his brother had died of a drug overdose. On the day of the dream, the patient was told that the brother's son, who is in his teens, had been hit by a car and was in the hospital. That brings to mind a movie in which a man's son is killed in a gang war and the man goes wild; he corners and rapes a woman, as if that would help him to forget his loss. It was a crazy thing for him to do. He got caught and ended up in jail.

In the dream, his brother was wearing a red tie. That reminds him of his boss at work who is partial to red ties. He's been changing everyone's hours at work and driving everyone crazy. He claims that he's doing it so people can have more time off, but it's actually making everyone work harder and longer than before. There are times when a favor is a curse. Meanwhile, the head of the other division of his firm keeps to regular hours and everyone around him feels secure. He knows how to take care of his people.

To discuss the material to this point in the session, we may note first that Dr Banks did not respond immediately to Mr Ridge's request. A premature response to his patient's request, be it a refusal or accommodation, would have shut off exploration of patient's proposal or confined it to a direct discussion between patient and therapist – i.e., to conscious system evaluations and manifest meanings that would be superficial, simplistic, and unreliable. It also would have interfered with the likelihood that the patient would generate encoded narrative imagery that would reveal the deep unconscious meanings of the request and that also would contain an encoded directive as to how the request should be handled.

The therapist's silence was first met by non-narrative, intellectualized efforts by the patient to justify his request. When the therapist continued to listen silently, the patient soon shifted to narrative expressions – his dream and associations to the dream elements – which turned out to be richly complex, powerful, and deeply meaningful. This sequence supports the technical principle that the correct response to patients' appeals for seemingly loving frame changes is for the therapist to remain silent and, if need be, to direct the patient to continue to say whatever comes to mind. If the patient continues to intellectualize and avoids narrating, the therapist can then ask for a recent dream or for a made-up story, along with narrative associations to their elements. This opens the way to deeply insightful therapeutic work and to making use of the patient's own deep unconscious wisdom and advisories as a basis for responding to the entreaty.

There are two evident, consciously recognized triggers that prompted Mr Ridge to ask for this act of love from his therapist. Outside of the therapy, there was his son's picnic which he was asked to chaperone. Within the therapy, there was the therapist's prior request to change the time of a session. This evidently served as a model for the patient – i.e., in time of need, it is appropriate to ask for and get a frame change. Notice too that Dr Banks' request that his patient change the time of his next session entailed a plea for a conscious expression of evidently false patient-love. Many therapists seek deviant forms of love from their patients at times of death-related stress, thereby engaging the patient in helping them to deny the fundamental ground rule of life, namely, that it is followed by death. For their part, personal schedule permitting, most patients will agree to this kind of request and thereby show their falsely loving concern for the plight of their therapists. All the while, however, as I have stressed, the deep unconscious system will voice strong objections to the falsely loving enactments that are shared by both parties to the therapy.

The Search for Active Triggers

Having identified the main consciously recognized interventional trigger for the patient's solicitation – i.e., the therapist's prior request for a time change – let's turn now to the triggers that are in play unconsciously. As a rule, the search for deep unconsciously active triggers is first centered on the treatment situation and the therapist's interventions, especially those that are frame-related. In carrying out this search, therapists should try to directly recall their most compelling recent interventions and in addition, study their patients' material for manifest and encoded allusions to interventions they may have missed. Next, the therapist's attention should turn to the patient's life outside of treatment to see if there are currently active death-related incidents that also may be triggering patients' deep unconscious responses.

Here, because it is so striking, I shall reverse the usual sequence and first identify the most influential, immediate triggering event outside of Mr Ridge's therapy, namely, his nephew's injury and hospitalization. This event undoubtedly reactivated the patient's conflicts and anxieties related to the death of his brother. In all likelihood, at the time of the brother's death, the patient had experienced predator death anxiety created by an unconscious belief that he – the patient – was in some way responsible for the brother's demise. This deep unconscious taking of responsibility for the death of a loved one is a universal, archetypal response. In addition, the loss of the brother would arouse the patient's existential death anxieties in connection with his own mortality. Because his nephew's injury is a significant, death-related triggering event outside of the therapy, the death anxieties it would create and reactivate in the patient are strong enough to play a role in his behavior in the treatment situation.

Turning next to the therapy and therapist, there is a recent, frame-modifying triggering intervention that appears to still be active and unresolved in the therapy. Both are reflected in the therapist's request that the patient change the time of his session because his son was ill and in the hospital. The first ground rule that this alters pertains to the fixed or set time of the patient's sessions and the second altered rule pertains to the therapist's relative anonymity – i.e., to the avoidance of personal self-revelations. To help us understand the patients' deep unconscious experience of these frame modifications, I shall list their main attributes and implications:

The request for the frame-break was death-related and most likely it was made because of unresolved death anxieties in the therapist. It appears to reflect an unconsciously fashioned attempt by the therapist to cope with the predator and existential death anxieties and deep unconscious guilt aroused in him by his son's illness – anxieties structured in a similar way to those that were evoked in the patient by the death of his brother. By attempting to violate two ground rules, the therapist probably was unconsciously trying to establish the unconscious, delusional belief that both he and his son could violate the existential rule that death follows life. In addition, the therapist's request to change the time of the session and his self-revelation were exploitative of and harmful to the patient – i.e., they are predatory acts. The patient most likely would experience these predatory qualities unconsciously and be inclined to punish the therapist for causing him harm and burdening him with his woes and death anxieties.

As for love, the therapist's request appears to be an appeal for false patient-love. This is a common response in both patients and therapists when death traumas and anxieties are activated. The therapist is implicitly offering a model to the patient as to how to deal with death-related traumas through denial-based, falsely loving frame violations. Both the patient and therapist would be unaware consciously of the ramifications of the therapist's request, even though both of them would perceive and process them deep unconsciously.

Suffice it to say that in the session in which the therapist asked for, and the patient willingly complied with, the change in the time of the next session, Mr Ridge told a story about a man who had been kidnapped and used by a terrorist as a shield against gunfire from troops who were trying to kill the terrorist. This narrative evidently reflected the patient's valid deep unconscious perception that in enacting the two frame violations, Dr Banks was trapping the patient into becoming the therapist's shield against the threat of the death of his son (and the therapist himself as a consequence), and doing it in a way that greatly endangered the patient. It seems evident that patients' conscious reactions to appeals for love from their therapists – Mr Ridge consciously felt pleased that he could be of help to Dr Banks in his time of need – are dramatically different from their deep unconscious reactions.

As for Dr Banks, he believed that he was making a simple, uncomplicated request of his patient that would make matters easier for himself. He interpreted the story about the terrorist and his prisoner as a reflection of Mr Ridge's fear of closeness with men, including himself 'in the transference'. The therapist traced this so-called unconscious transference imagery back to the beatings that the patient had suffered at the hands of his father during his formative years. Important here is the realization that interpretations of these kinds of psychodynamic factors, while true to a limited extent, serve more critically to avoid another, more immediate level of meaning embodied in patients' material that is active, reality-based, extremely significant, and grim, and therefore has far greater effects on the patient – and therapist. Under these conditions, therapists' dynamic interpretations of patients' narratives as reflections of inner fantasies and wishes tend to be used by therapists to deny and avoid the implications and meanings of their own interventions, most of them death-related and harmful to their patients. Much the same applies to therapists' actual appeals for patient-love, explicit or implicit: They too serve on the deepest level as a call for support for the therapist's denial-based defenses against death and the awful anxieties it arouses.

Trigger Decoding the Encoded Themes

Returning to the session at hand, Mr Ridge has asked Dr Banks for a show of therapist-love in the form of a change in the time of his next session. Let's look now at the narratives that the patient generated when his therapist did not immediately respond to his request. First, there is the dream in which the patient's brother is engaged in a homosexual liaison. The patient's initial associations to the dream include an allusion to the brother's death through a drug overdose; the accidental injury of the brother's son; the death of another man's son; and the bereaved father's reaction by raping a woman, which was a crazy, compensatory criminal act that led to his arrest.

The power of this imagery stands in striking contrast to the patient's initial intellectualizations, which were commonplace and unempowered. The narrative themes attest to the importance and deeper ramification of this solicitation. The patient's seemingly reasonable conscious plea for a change in the time of his session and thus, for loving affirmation has multiple deep unconscious undercurrents that stagger the ever-avoidant conscious mind. The patient's deep unconscious system is dealing here with what is called an anticipated trigger, the expectation that the therapist will comply with the patient's request. The narratives encode the patient's unconscious perceptions of the meanings and consequences of this expected intervention, including whether doing so is called for and whether that would be an expression of true or false therapist-love.

Consciously, the patient is convinced that the therapist's compliance with his request would be a sign of the therapist's genuine loving concern and care. But the stories told by the patient, which convey his deep unconscious perceptions of the same anticipated trigger, tell a very different story. First, there is the dream itself, dreamt in anticipation of asking the therapist for the change in time. Trigger decoding the dream imagery we find that the therapist's changing the time of the next session would be experienced deep unconsciously as allowing the patient to seduce him homosexually and as seducing the patient homosexually in return. This is a striking image and immediately reveals the difference between naïve, conscious system approaches to love in psychotherapy and those that stem from the deep unconscious mind. The latter views are far more jaundiced and realistic than those we conjure up consciously.

Next, there is the allusion to the death of the patient's brother and to his son having been hit by a car and hospitalized. These images allude to traumas in the patient's personal life, but as part of the dream-associational network, they also must be treated as encoded themes from the deep unconscious system. They too have multiple meanings. One set is connected to the therapist's prior frame modification and the other to the anticipated frame change. Indeed, because the past and anticipated triggers are similar, the themes can be decoded in almost identical ways for both interventions.

Focusing on the anticipated trigger, the themes indicate that were Dr Banks to change the time of the next session, it would be a way of seriously injuring the patient and that it also would be tantamount to killing him by over-gratifying him in an illegal manner – the allusion to the brother's death through an overdose of drugs. Loving gifts of this kind always are experienced deep unconsciously as destructive over-gratifications and therefore as falsely loving gestures.

The next theme alludes to a murdered son and the father's consequent rape of a woman. These encoded narrative images convey the patient's valid deep unconscious view that changing the time of the next session would be a murderous assault on the patient even though the patient had requested the change. It also would be seen as a rape that is carried out in a rage set off by the therapist's predatory, predator, and existential death anxieties. Thus, the patient's deep unconscious mind is suggesting that were the therapist to agree to the change, he would be assaulting the patient because of his rage and guilt over the life-threatening illness of his son.

Finally, the allusions to the illegality of the grieving father's rape and his being jailed reflects the patient's deep unconscious perceptions of the illegal and immoral qualities of violating the frame under these circumstances – and the unconscious guilt and need for punishment that the change would evoke in both the patient and the therapist. That is, these themes apply to the patient because he asked for the falsely loving frame change, and to the therapist, were he to accede. To help the patient to avoid unconsciously arranging to punish himself for his request, the therapist would have to use these images as a basis for turning down the patient's entreaty and interpret these themes not only as the patient's perceptions of himself (the therapist) but as self-perceptions (of the patient) as well. Failing that, the patient is likely to act out in a self-harmful manner without having any conscious idea as to the deep unconscious reasons that he has done so.

These deep unconscious perceptions are valid, but they also are *selective*. Thus, among the many meanings of a particular frame change, patients experience and work over deep unconsciously those that are selected on the basis of the universal meanings of the frame violation and the patient's particular sensitivities as determined by his past emotional history and present-day death-related emotional issues. Even so, when it comes to love, these personally selected encoded themes clearly indicate that a change in time by Dr Banks would be experienced as an expression of false rather than true love – a valid view that is the very opposite of the patient's conscious picture of his request. Each patient would have his or her own way of encoding the falsity of the loving gesture in question.

Next, the patient offered an addendum to his dream, to the effect that his brother was wearing a red tie. This image led to job-related associations and to a boss who is driving everyone crazy with time changes, a favor that is more like a curse. This boss is contrasted with another division head who holds to steady hours and offers his workers security instead of chaos; he is a good caretaker.

These narrative associations can be decoded in light of the antici-pated trigger as indicating that the time change would destabilize the therapy and upset the patient, and drive him crazy in some undefined manner. The encoded themes also indicate that it would be a serious mistake to change the time, that the therapist's seeming gift of love actually would be a curse – an expression of false love that would create more work for the patient in his therapy. The patient holds up the other boss at work as someone who is truly loving and caring – a love that is expressed by holding the time frame secured. This imagery conveys the patient's deep unconscious offer of a *model of rectification and advisory* to the effect that the time of his next session should not be changed and that true therapist-love would be expressed by the therapist's holding the frame secured.

Continuing the Vignette

At this point in the session, Dr Banks, who recently had begun supervi-sion with a strong adaptive psychotherapist, decides to intervene. He interprets that the patient's dream and associations seem to be address-ing his proposal that he – Dr Banks – change the time of the next session. Consciously, the patient feels justified in making the request because he – the therapist – had done something similar a few weeks back. And while that's quite understandable consciously, his – the patient's – unconscious mind seems to have a very different view of the situation. The themes in his dream and his associations to the dream indicate that unconsciously, he would experience his – the therapist's – changing the hour as allowing himself to be seduced homosexually by the patient and as being homosexually seductive in return. The images indicate that he – the patient – also would feel assaulted physically as if he'd been hit by a car and worse still, he'd experience the change as an act of both murder and rape. The associations to his job situation indi-cate that the change would drive him – the patient – crazy and would be a misguided gift that was more like a curse. His – Mr Ridge's – unconscious recommendation, which is conveyed in the story of the boss who keeps his workers to a single set schedule, is that the time of the session should be held firm and that is what he – Dr Banks – will do. After pausing a moment, Dr Banks adds that the patient's imagery also indicates that his own earlier request to change the time of a session was in error and assaultive and rapacious of the patient – that it had all of the qualities that would accrue to his making a time change now. He – Dr Banks – will bear this in mind and refrain from making such requests in the future.

This intervention is based on trigger decoding the patient's narrative themes in light of the anticipated trigger of the time change – with an addendum that pertains to the therapist's earlier frame break.

Technically, when entirely verbalized expressions of patient-love are expressed in passing without attempts at fulfillment or when wishes for therapist-love are confined to fantasized expressions, the therapist may allow them to pass without interpretation in light of active triggers. But in situations where a frame change is at issue and where death-related issues have activated the request, interventional efforts are a necessity. Thus, whenever a patient or therapist asks for a loving or caring action within treatment, be it through an enactment of extra-therapeutic satisfactions or modifications in the ideal ground rules, the triggers must be identified and a trigger-decoded interpretation and efforts to secure or keep the ideal frame secured must be offered to the patient. In intervening, Dr Banks carried out both of these tasks.

Completing the Vignette

In the session, Mr Ridge pauses and then says that he really wanted to be at the picnic, but maybe he is being frivolous. He then goes back to his dream and to the image of the two men in bed. This time the image brings to mind a newspaper story about a man who had rescued another man who was drowning in the ocean. He had to give the victim mouth-to-mouth resuscitation and the article said that he hated kissing the guy, but he did it to save the man's life.

After intervening in any active manner, a therapist should listen to the patient's responses, especially those that are encoded in subsequent narratives. Conscious acceptance of an intervention simply indicates the absence of conscious objections, but it is open to influence from unconscious needs for both defensive denial and self-punishment so it is not a reliable gauge of the validity of an intervention. On the other hand, conscious refutation of an intervention suggests that the therapist has done so erroneously. Nevertheless, it too is fraught with uncertainties because it may reflect conscious anxieties about renouncing a false form of love and being exposed to very disturbing death-related material and issues. Before deciding on the validity of an intervention, then, the therapist must wait for or solicit encoded narratives. The validity and loving qualities, true or false, of therapists' interventions are matters that can be reliably judged solely by decoding the assessment of an intervention that is made by the patient's deep unconscious wisdom subsystem.

In this case, Mr Ridge responded consciously with a mixture of mild objections and weak acceptance. But his encoded narrative – his fresh association to the dream – is clearly an unconsciously validating tale. It has a strikingly positive image of care-taking and implicit true love in the rescue of the drowning man which is as well a triumph over death and death anxiety. Present here are indications of the two basic forms of deep unconscious validation. The interpersonal form is reflected in saving a man's life, while the cognitive form entails an extension of the intervention made by the therapist to the effect that unconsciously, the lives of both the patient and therapist were in some sense at stake here. Thus, the story of saving a dying man's life seems to decode around the therapist's frame-securing and interpretive interventions as reflecting the patient's unconscious perception that the time change would have seriously endangered the life of the patient; deciding to forego that change was seen as a life-saving act. The therapist's frame-sustaining intervention also indicated deep unconsciously to the patient that the therapist had managed to resolve some of his recent death anxieties and that in some way, the patient himself had been unconsciously helpful to the therapist in this regard.

There is much to be pondered in the realization that a therapist's decision to hold to a ground rule of psychotherapy, which was based on his patient's encoded narrative material, is experienced deep unconsciously by the patient as a death-defying, life-saving intervention. The world of deep unconscious experience is far richer and far more compelling than the world of conscious experience. The enormous importance of patients' deep unconscious experiences for emotional life and the therapeutic process makes it vital that therapists trigger decode patients' narratives so as to enter this awesome, anxiety-provoking unconscious domain and intervene according to the eminently wise adaptive precepts and moral guidelines offered by its wisdom and moral subsystems. This is the essence of true therapist-love and it almost always will evoke true love in patients towards their truly loving and deeply healing psychotherapists.

8

Love and the Psychotherapist

There is, as noted, a strikingly narrow range of interventions available to psychotherapists through which they may express their true love to and for their patients. Problems tend to arise in this regard in two basic, inter-related ways. The first involves therapists' needs to offer falsely loving interventions to their patients, while the second has to do with their related needs to be falsely loved by them.

Because the human mind has evolved under pressures from the three forms of death anxiety that favor conscious system denial and self-punishment, there are natural, unconsciously mediated tendencies in psychotherapists to seek false gifts of love from their patients and to offer false love in return. This means that a critical task along the path to becoming a sound and effective psychotherapist lies with the mastery of these disruptive inclinations and the death anxieties that motivate them. Being able to heal patients through truly loving, deep unconsciously validated interpretations and frame-securing interventions depends on such efforts.

There are at present two major resources available to psychotherapists for this purpose. The first entails working with patients using strong adaptive principles and testing interventions for encoded validation – and directing one's therapeutic work accordingly. Patients' deep unconscious minds know almost everything a therapist needs to know in order to be a sound, truly loving healer. The art of this work lies with learning how to identify critical triggers and in developing an ear for the trigger-related meanings in patients' encoded images and themes. This requires an ability to trigger decode narrative imagery, that is, to make translations that involve transposing a theme from its manifest context – e.g., the dream as dreamt – into its trigger-related context – usually the therapeutic arena – where it takes on new meaning.

The second resource available to therapists for learning how to truly love their patients also depends on developing the craft needed to do strong adaptive psychotherapy. But in this case, these skills are applied to the therapist himself or herself by engaging in personal efforts at self-processing, which is the strong adaptive version of self-analysis (Langs, 1993). In brief, this process is carried out alone in a quiet setting with a set frequency per week and for a set duration of time, usually 30 to 45 minutes. The self-processing therapist begins by remembering a dream from the previous night and then taking the elements or images in the dream and finding incidents and stories from his or her therapeutic work and personal life that these elements bring to mind. It is essential to find incidents with power, that is, that touch on death, illness, injury, harm, and the like. The deep unconscious mind perceives and deals with the most dreaded, anxiety-provoking implications and meanings of events that are excluded from conscious awareness – disturbing encoded power themes are its métier.

After generating an ample pool of themes with notable power, the therapist shifts to searching for their evocative triggers. As is done in working with patients, the search tends to be focused on frame issues, moments in which a ground rule has been secured or modified. While a dramatic triggering event in a therapist's everyday life may evoke deep unconscious responses, for an active psychotherapist, the main triggers processed by his or her deep unconscious mind tend to arise in his or her therapeutic work with patients. These triggers are largely frame-related and unconsciously death-related as well. In general, the clearest indications that the self-processing therapist is on the right track are the generation of a powerful pool of themes, the identification of a compelling frame-related trigger drawn from his or her work with a particular patient, and the appearance of themes that bridge over to or link to the trigger and its most compelling implications.

For example, if a patient has asked for a fee reduction and the therapist has agreed to it, monetary themes and themes of indulgence or sacrifice, as well as seduction, are likely to emerge – even if the fee reduction is a dire necessity for the patient at the moment. In addition, the unresolved death-related issues that deep unconsciously motivated the frame modification by the therapist are likely to emerge. On the other hand, if the therapist has not complied, encoded themes of setting reasonable and necessary limits can be expected to materialize. In that case, secured frame, existential death anxieties are almost certain to follow.

In principle, the evocative triggers and the bridging narrative themes are both likely to be frame-related because the deep unconscious system is focused on the ground rules of therapy – and of life in general. The deep unconscious wisdom subsystem advocates that frames be secured because it knows that secured frames are ideally adaptive and that they offer both patients and therapists the optimal conditions for therapy (and daily life) – i.e., that they are loving, ego-enhancing, and healing. The deep unconscious subsystem of morality and ethics similarly advocates secured frames because therapists' handling of the ground rules of therapy expresses their moral positions. Thus, securing an archetypal ground rule or a set of rules is loving because it also reflects a high level of morality in a psychotherapist, while modifying these rules is deep unconsciously perceived as unethical and immoral – and punishable and unloving as well.

The Role of Death Anxiety

Death anxiety tends to play a major role in therapists' choice of profession and in their day-to-day work with patients. The danger-sensitive subsystem of the deep unconscious mind is concerned with ground rules in a way that is very different from the two other deep unconscious subsystems. It perceives death-related dangers and generates intense unconsciously mediated signals of death anxiety in the presence of manifest and non-manifest, consciously and deep unconsciously perceived, death-related threats and their most anxiety-provoking meanings. This means that the system is sensitive to death-related aspects of events about which the conscious mind has no idea whatsoever. It also means that when someone in the life of a therapist dies, this subsystem will perceive and respond to the more unbearable, consciously obliterated aspects of the event – for example, the conviction in a mourner that he or she has caused or contributed to the individual's death, even when this is not the case in reality.

Existential Death Anxiety

The danger-sensitive subsystem also creates death anxieties in therapists when they secure the framework of therapy with a particular patient. There is no manifest death-related threat in securing an ideal, healing frame, but the danger-sensitive subsystem perceives an entrapping existential threat under such conditions. On this level of experience, the secured frame is a closed space with major restrictions that are experienced as dangerous and this ensnared experience is felt to be comparable to being born to die – that is, being born into a closed world-space from which the only exit is through personal demise.

The danger-sensitive subsystem also is especially wary of other experiences that are unconsciously perceived as death-related and its basic approach to these issues tends to be anxiety-based, maladaptive, and costly. The subsystem signals the conscious system with unconsciously experienced anxieties that evoke conscious system, denial-based defenses. This causes major counter-resistances in therapists who fail to properly secure the frames of their treatment situations. Unconsciously experienced existential death anxiety is, then, a major cause of pathological countertransferences in psychotherapists and the main basis for their unloving or falsely loving frame-violating interventions.

This type of death anxiety is, for example, overly- intense in therapists who are seriously ill or injured, or dying (Galatzer-Levy, 2004) and it also intensifies when therapists' family members and close friends are in similar predicaments. These situations create enormous pressures in therapists to give to, and receive from, their patients (and others in their lives) false forms of love.

The pervasiveness of frame-violating interventions by psychotherapists speak for major unresolved death anxieties in mental health professionals. It follows too that these are deep unconsciously experienced anxieties that must be accessed and resolved through a therapist's self-processing efforts if he or she is to become truly loving with patients – and with those in their everyday lives as well.

Predatory Death Anxiety

Therapists often are required to deal with triggers constituted as comments from and behaviors of patients who act in a predatory manner towards them. Patients may do this by being verbally abusive and argumentative, by being trenchantly resistant, or through hurtful frame violations like missing or being late to sessions, abruptly terminating treatment, or offering falsely loving gifts to their therapists. In instances of this kind, which always are interactionally created, it is incumbent on the therapist to find the interventions that they have made to trigger the patient's predatory behavior, which are likely to have predatory qualities of their own. Understanding these triggers and the predatory death anxieties that they arouse in patients is critical lest the therapist participate with the patient in a vicious circle in which a therapist's predatory interventions are followed by predatory acts against the therapist by the patient, which evokes vengeance in the therapist – ad infinitum.

Therapists who are victimized by their patients should engage in self-processing in order to find their contribution to this harm and resolve the unconscious motives that prompted the therapist to behave in an unloving, errant manner. It is important too for therapists to realize that they may respond to predatory acts from their patients by paradoxically offering them gestures of false love – e.g., an extra session, the extension of an hour, a fee reduction, and the like. Deep unconsciously, therapists who act in this manner are trying to deny the harm being caused to them by, and rage against, the offending patient. This response also tends to set up a vicious cycle of patient-assaults and therapist's falsely loving gestures that does damage to all concerned.

In regard to therapists' personal lives, a history of having been seriously harmed early and even later in life should alert them to their likely need to give and receive false love as a means of compensating for the damage that had been done to them. Therapists who were born with a congenital disorder, abandoned by their caretakers, physically beaten or severely damaged emotionally, and otherwise victimized by their caretakers need to be on the alert for biases towards falsely loving frame modifications that unconsciously damage patients as the therapist had been damaged. They also should strive to discover and resolve the deep unconscious genetic sources of their falsely loving and unloving interventions, which are often motivated by unconscious wishes to deny the inevitable murderous rage that these therapists feel towards those who had harmed them earlier in their lives.

Predator Death Anxiety

Finally, therapists' predator death anxieties are triggered most often in response to their own deep unconscious perceptions of their harmful interventions to their patients. While many of these interventions are consciously sanctioned by their colleagues and mentors, therapists' deep unconscious wisdom subsystems deftly perceive the harm that they are perpetrating against their patients. In these instances, the therapist's subsystem of morality and ethics becomes active and perceives the immoral qualities of damaging, falsely loving or non-loving interventions. The subsystem then arranges unconsciously for the therapist to make a variety of self-defeating decisions whose guilt-ridden deep unconscious sources go unrecognized. Here too, intense efforts at self-processing are called for to set matters straight.

In their personal lives, therapists who have caused significant harm to others, as happens with miscarriages, abortions, having children with congenital abnormalities, abandoning spouses and children, and the like, tend to be strongly inclined to violate ground rules and boundaries because of deep unconscious needs to provoke patients and others into enacting punitive actions against them. These therapists also tend to over-gratify and falsely love their patients in unconscious efforts to compensate for the damage that they have caused others. As we can see, death-related traumas and the three forms of death anxiety experienced by psychotherapists can make it extremely difficult for them to consistently offer their patients true forms of healing love.

Self-processing

In doing self-processing in response to a therapeutic problem, a therapist should search for and identify two critical factors: First, the triggering communication from or action by the patient that has evoked the therapist's maladaptive behavior. And second, when present (as is likely the case), the predatory interventions on his or her part that triggered the patient's predatory behavior. The goal is to gain deep unconscious insight into the underlying issues that have prompted an erroneous unloving intervention and to enable the therapist to work in a truly loving manner with his or her patients. Therapists often behave in falsely loving ways with their patients because of their own existential and predator death anxieties and deep unconscious guilt. The falsely loving act is a maladaptive attempt to undo the unconsciously perceived harm that is being done by the therapist to the patient, but it also is a way of seeking to be punished by the patient who will, as a rule, unconsciously perceive the falsity of the loving gesture and react by becoming hostile towards the therapist in a subtle or blatant manner. Effective self-processing is a therapist's ultimate gift of true self-love, one that enables him or her to be truly loving towards his or her patients in a satisfyingly consistent fashion.

Therapists' Searches for False Patient-love

Drawing on my extensive work as a supervisor of various forms of psychotherapy, my own experiences early in my career as a psychoanalyst and psychotherapist, and my readings of the psychodynamic literature, it is abundantly clear that psychotherapists offer far more false love to their patients than their patients offer to or request from them. Most of this deceptive love is offered through departures from the ideal frame, a class of interventions that can be devastatingly unloving because they usually serve the therapist's needs far more than those of their patients. A common sequence begins with a therapist offering a gesture of false love to a patient, who then responds with an expression of false love of his or her own, creating a vicious circle and misalliance (Langs, 1975, 1978a,b) that may go around and around over months and years of therapy. Much the same holds for the frequency with which therapists openly or more subtly ask patients for expressions of false patient-love towards themselves and obtain comparable requests from their patients in return (Searles, 1973; Langs, 1985).

There are countless generally unrecognized frame-modifying ways in which therapists ask their patients for, and provide their patients with, enactments of false love as perceived by the deep unconscious system. Many of these expressions are taken for granted by weak adaptive psychotherapists and go unexamined for deep unconscious meanings and effects. Common examples include therapists asking patients to change the agreed-on time of their session; asking patients for fee increases; informing patients of their own or a family member's impairments, illnesses or injuries, or making other kinds of self-revelations; asking for assistance with, or favors regarding, personal events, concerns, and problems that are outside of the therapeutic endeavor; making a barter agreement with the patient instead of the usual fee arrangement; asking the patient for any type of non-sexual or sexual physical or social contact; requesting patients' permission to use material from his or her sessions in writing a journal paper, book chapter, or book (using the patient in this manner without the patient's knowledge is predatory and distinctly exploitative of the patient); and making queries that are in the service of therapists' personal or professional gain, as seen in obtaining advice regarding financial investments.

A therapist's satisfaction in doing psychotherapy should be confined to receiving an appropriate fee and helping patients to heal their emotional wounds and resolve their emotional maladaptations. The deep unconscious minds of both patients and therapists ask this of therapists and thereby impose a variety of frustrations, limits, and boundaries that therapists need to learn to accept and endure in order to be truly loving and to consistently intervene in the service of the patient's therapeutic goals and needs for genuine, muted forms of true therapist-love. Here too, biology and the evolution of the emotion-processing mind play a role in that, with the introduction of the awareness of death and the anxieties that it evokes, therapists are inclined to seek falsely loving satisfactions that maladaptively enable them to deny death or to be punished for having harmed others. Constraints on intervening therefore are not easily accepted by psychotherapists and falsely loving interventions are strongly, but self-deceptively, rationalized. It is only with intense efforts at self-processing that therapists can come to terms with these restrictions, resolve their natural unconscious needs to falsely love their patients, and be comfortable doing psychotherapy based on truly loving interventions.

Therapists' Offers of False Love

There is as well a related list – and it too is quite long – that touches on ways in which therapists quite naturally tend to offer false love to their patients. Here too we may consider some common, but generally unappreciated examples. They include interventions like giving advice and making other kinds of supposedly supportive but deeply unloving gratuitous comments related to patients' emotional problems and outside lives; lending or giving patients books, magazines, and personal possessions; introducing patients to other individuals, arranging for social contacts of any kind, and providing patients with job and educational possibilities; referring clients to therapist-patients; reducing fees unnecessarily; offering extra sessions; seeing third parties in the absence of a life-threatening emergency; trying to be empathic by being personally self-revealing; touching patients reassuringly or sexually; holding the patient's hand or giving the patient a kiss or a hug; providing the patient with food, drink, or other forms of nourishment; expressing any kind of open loving feelings towards the patient; giving patients their home or vacation telephone number or address; speaking to or seeing the patient between scheduled sessions; keeping in touch with the patient during absences and vacations, by snail mail, email, or telephone; and continuing to have contact with patients after their therapy has ended.

This list goes on and on. Many of these supposedly loving acts are subject to controversy among weak adaptive psychotherapists. In contrast, based on trigger decoding and accessing the views of the deep unconscious system on these matters, strong adaptive psychotherapists have found that without exception, behaviors of this kind are unconsciously experienced as predatory, harmful, seductive, exploitative, self-serving, maladaptive, anti-therapeutic, and pathological – and distinctly unloving. We see then the extent to which, in psychotherapy, surface appearances often are deceiving. Many seemingly supportive and deliberately caring acts by therapists are deep unconsciously experienced as exceedingly destructive – and patients respond accordingly (Strachey, 1934).

By and large, most patients consciously accept and favor these falsely loving, frame-deviant acts. It is only when these behaviors reach an ill-defined extreme or become sexual in nature that some, but not all, patients will object. In general, the conscious minds of both patients and therapists conspire to create therapeutic misalliances in which a therapist's expression of false love leads to a similar expression from the patient in a sequence that is the beginning of another type of increasingly harmful, mutually unloving vicious circle that is harmful to all concerned.

Most of the detrimental consequences of these falsely loving acts by therapist are mediated deep unconsciously. We therefore need to be clear that unconscious transmission does not imply an absence of effects. Indeed, these unconsciously mediated influences are ever-present, universal, and extremely powerful. They can be highly destructive for both patients and therapists. Furthermore, they tend to persist because the true sources of the resultant dysfunctions in both the patient and therapist are not recognized consciously as such by either party to therapy. The connection between symptomatic regressions and other untoward problems that arise in patients and their therapists' offers of false love is denied consciously by both parties to the therapy situation. Instead, therapists tend to hold their patients' and their psychopathology fully accountable for the suffering that patients have had to endure largely because of their therapists' misguided acts of false love. Only the consistent use of trigger decoding can put therapists on the right track, so they can begin to recognize the dire effects of the generally well-meaning but truly ill-conceived, falsely loving comments and behaviors that they have been taught to use and that are unwittingly supported by both their patients and colleagues for anything but sound reasons.

Clinical Illustrations

As I said, examples of expressions of therapists' false love of their patients are legion. While there are important differences in repercussions when a falsely loving act is non-sexual as compared to sexual, and when it is inadvertent as compared to deliberate, there also are important similarities to the meanings, implications, and ramifications of all of these misguided acts. To illustrate, I turn again to clinical examples drawn from the 20 interviews with former psychotherapy patients that I carried out in the 1980's (Langs, 1985). This material shows something of the range of what therapists will do – and patients will accept – when it comes to false ways of loving their patients and it also demonstrates some of the many adverse effects of these enactments.

An Act of Sexual Seduction

Ms Sangino was a woman in her early 20s when she went to Dr Nardone, an elderly male psychiatrist, because she was depressed and inhibited with men. Several months into her therapy, Dr Nardone told the patient that he had loving feelings towards her but it was clear to him that she was afraid of being a woman as testified by the fact that she was a virgin and hadn't made a single sexual advance towards him. In little time, the patient was performing fellatio on her therapist. Soon after this began, she started to pick up men at bars and she became promiscuous sexually.

In time, Ms Sangino began to feel that this wasn't how therapy should be done and she left treatment. Her next psychiatrist, a woman whom she found through her priest, told the patient that she knew Dr Nardone and that, in light of what he said and did, he must have loved the patient. Confused and disillusioned, Ms Sangino began to feel that she was a sinner in the eyes of God and soon left this psychiatrist as well. As a last resort, she went to a psychiatrist who specialized in treating patients with disturbing religious feelings, but he was abusive and would keep her waiting while he saw other patients during the time scheduled for her sessions. Again she left treatment – if we may call it that.

A few months later, still filled with conscious guilt and self-condemnations over her loss of control sexually and entertaining suicidal thoughts, Ms Sangino traveled to Italy. It was there, while walking alone on an isolated country dirt road, that she saw Christ descend from heaven, enter her body, and purify her soul. She has been stable and not promiscuous ever since.

It seems fair to say that Dr Nardone's act of self-serving, desperate, and inexcusable false love with Ms Sangino drove the patient crazy – there were no indication of prior psychotic symptoms – and prompted an unconscious identification with the therapist that led to her sexual promiscuity. Her behavior also can be understood as an external enactment or acting out of the patient's conscious and unconscious perceptions of the therapist in light of his seductive interventions which can be thought of as his projectively identifying into his patient his sexual

madness and his underlying death anxieties. Dr Nardone had suffered a
heart attack several months before he saw Ms Sangino. Thus, there
were indications that he was suffering from severe existential death
anxieties and that these anxieties had unconsciously motivated his
falsely loving, frame-violating behavior. Left to her own devices, after
her next therapist madly defended Dr Nardone and her last therapist
abused her, Ms Sangino found an effective, albeit delusional way to
cure herself through a self-loving hallucinatory experience that she was
able to keep isolated in her mind so that she was free to function well
in her daily life.

While extreme, this vignette is archetypal: False forms of love can be
understood as expressions of therapist-madness that, by means of conscious and unconscious perception and projective identification, drive
patients mad. Yet even though the enactment here was a frame-violating
sexual act, the underlying anxieties and issues were death-related. We
may speculate that Dr Nardone's unmastered existential death anxieties
unconsciously played a major role in his misusing his patient to enact a
sexual form of the denial of death in which his sexual prowess and his
being able to violate the ground rules of therapy were used to create the
delusion or illusion that he was an exception to the existential rule that
death follows life. Support for this thesis is found in the patient's suicidal
fantasies which on the conscious level are based on her conscious guilt
for having become involved sexually with her therapist and other men
chosen randomly. But on the deep unconscious level, her suicidal
thoughts may have been based on her deep unconscious perceptions and
processing of the non-manifest implications of her psychiatrist's behavior – he seems to have been trying to save himself from killing himself or
dying, and yet was doing so by acting in a blatantly self-destructive
manner. As recently reviewed by Galatzer-Levy (2004), therapists are
inclined to engage in a multiplicity of serious frame violations when they
are faced with serious or fatal illnesses.

Non-sexual Physical Contact

Mr Edwards, who was a psychotherapist, was in psychotherapy with a
social worker who worked in his agency, Ms Elton, who saw him for
therapy in the basement of her home-office. Consciously, Mr Edwards
was convinced that his therapist loved and cared for him and that she was
there for him in his times of need. He recalled being upset in a session a
few months into his therapy when Ms Elton told him that she knew what
his problem was – he was a child! He began to sob uncontrollably and

the therapist shared with him the revelation that she had once been deeply hurt by a break-up with a former lover and that she had cried then like the patient was crying at the moment. She then took the patient's hand in hers and stroked it warmly again and again. Consciously, the patient found these interventions very loving and quite reassuring.

That night he had a dream. He was in a cavern. Two white hands came up through the floor of the cavern, grabbed hold of his hand, and tried to pull him down through the floor of the cavern in order to destroy him.

There are two bridging themes in the patient's dream that support the thesis that the encoded aspects of Mr Edwards' dream are about his therapist. The first is the cavern, which represents the therapist's basement home-office, and the second are the hands that reached out to pull the patient through the floor of the cavern – a representation of the hand-holding, falsely loving, triggering intervention. On this basis, we again find that there is a dramatic difference between a patient's conscious perceptions of a therapist's seemingly loving interventions and his unconscious perceptions of the same acts. A pair of frame-violating interventions – a self-revelation that violates the ground rule of therapists' relative anonymity and holding the patient's hand which violates the ground rule that precludes physical contact between patient and therapist – that are consciously experienced as expressions of genuine love are deep unconsciously experienced as an unloving attempt at murder. We can be quite sure that the deep unconscious experience is the more accurate and far more influential of the two versions of this intervention.

With the single exception of Ms Sangino, all of the patients I interviewed had been subjected to supposedly loving interventions that were accepted and cherished consciously but decried deep unconsciously. Expressions of false love appear to be one of the staples of psychotherapy, counseling, and psychoanalysis as practiced today. Patients suffer badly as a result even though they often recruit their therapists' falsely loving interventions for self-punishment and for denial-based defenses against death anxieties that sometimes bring them relief on the surface while they continue to suffer in other ways whose deep unconscious but real sources are not appreciated. The denial of death offered by these interventions promotes a related denial of the dire consequences of these falsely loving interventions. This was seen in this study in the finding that all but one of these former patients suffered some type of new emotional symptom after terminating their last and well-liked therapy experience, but none of them saw these symptoms as a result of some failure in their therapy and therapist. The encoded voice of the deep unconscious wisdom subsystem speaks to these failures and fights fiercely against this way of doing psychotherapy, only to go unheard for want of the use of trigger decoding.

Further Illustrations

Dr Freed was able to rationalize a series of escalating, falsely loving frame violations that his patient, Mrs Frank, accepted as signs of his love for her. Early in the therapy, after an upsetting session, he called the patient at her home to see if she was all right – a practice he then continued for some time. There followed in relatively short succession an exchange of gifts with Mrs Frank at holiday time, giving her rides home after sessions, holding hands with her, feeding her bottles of milk supposedly to satisfy her frustrated oral cravings, allowing her to lie with him on his couch, and finally, allowing her to perform fellatio on him.

Mrs Frank, who was trained as a psychotherapist, consciously felt loved by her therapist and was attracted to him. She believed that he was trying to gratify her long-frustrated emotional needs and was attempting to break through her inhibitions and sexual problems.

Nevertheless, in her interview with me, she generated a series of encoded images that contradicted these beliefs. In addition to these negative encoded perceptions, however, this patient endured a mini-psychotic experience after one of her sexual encounters with her therapist. She hallucinated the presence of dangerous animals and evil people in her bedroom and became fearful that she was about to be attacked or murdered. This is telling symptomatic encoded portrayal of the invasive violence of her therapist's falsely loving acts. It dramatically shows the kind of dangerous madness that these acts can create in patients and while the situation was extreme, the lesson is not: Therapists need to be forewarned about the dire consequences of false love and they need to learn to do therapy in ways that are truly loving so as to be truly healing for their patients.

Once again, death anxiety played a significant, unconscious role in what happened here. Mrs Frank's son had attempted suicide months before she began her therapy. Her predator death anxiety, and her conscious and deep unconscious guilt, undoubtedly played a significant role in her acceptance of her therapist's falsely loving, clearly damaging and exploitative frame-violating actions which evidently served to punish her for the harm she believed that she had done – and probably did – to her son. Dr Freed provided her with punishments that appear to have brought her a measure of ill-gotten relief from her guilt, but they also evoked an episode of psychosis.

Possibly because she had been punished enough, the patient left therapy after this episode. Some time later, when a fresh opportunity for further sexual contact with Dr Freed presented itself, Mrs Frank refused to go that route. As happened with Ms Sangino, Mrs Frank's experience with madness may well have been in part a self-curative happening that brought her relief at the expense of risking a fully psychotic break with reality.

Dr Artis gave his patient, Mrs Young, a copy of his autobiography, a gift that made her feel special in his eyes. Nevertheless, she then dreamt that Dr Artis was examining her vagina with a tongue depressor and says: 'Well, it's very rusty, like it's out of use.'

The dream was interpreted by the therapist as the patient's perception of herself, based on the fact that she had not had sex with her husband in some time. The patient's associations to the dream, however, were about Dr Artis and the self-revelations that he had made in his book, including his marital and sexual difficulties. It appears, then, that the dream-associational network is speaking for the patient's encoded perceptions of the seductive and penetrating qualities of the therapist's falsely loving gift of his book and of the revelations that he made in it. They also show how a non-sexual gift of false love can be – and often is – experienced deep unconsciously as a sexual transgression.

In her interview with me, the patient unconsciously validated these formulations with an association about how, on reading the therapist's book, she realized that she had no idea how to have a good sexual relationship and that it was pretty crazy for her not to know how to be intimate with a man. As so often is the case, a patient's allusion to her own failings and madness evidently encodes her valid unconscious perceptions of these very same difficulties in her therapist.

Ms Muncey was faced with a different kind of love-related issue, that of her therapist for another patient – a form of love that surfaced several times in my interview study. This situation arose when, six months into her therapy, Ms Muncey arrived for a session to find another woman in the waiting room. Her therapist, Dr Norman, explained that the woman had the hour prior to Ms Muncey's, but her car had broken down. He asked Ms Muncey if she would mind waiting to see him until the following hour which was free. In a show of false patient-love, Ms Muncey willingly agreed.

At the beginning of this changed hour, the therapist asked directly if it bothered the patient that he had changed the time of her session.

When she said that she hadn't minded at first but then felt resentful, the therapist told her that she not only was resentful, but was angry. Ms Muncey then recalled that as a child, she was put down and punished if she expressed her feelings. There were times that her mother favored her brother to such an extent that she actually took the food off the patient's plate and gave it to him.

This almost transparent encoded unconscious perception of the therapist's frame-violating intervention was interpreted in her session as the genetic source of the patient's irrational anger at the therapist. It is noteworthy too that despite the therapist's efforts to keep the discussion of his unloving frame violation to the manifest, unencoded level of communication, the patient managed to find the means to encode some of her unconscious perceptions of the therapist in light of his unloving, frame-deviant intervention. Nevertheless, the therapist did not connect these themes to his behavior, but invoked a so-called genetic transference interpretation to deny his patient's disguised condemnation of what he had done.

In the following session, the patient reported a dream in which she is in a car in which her mother seems to be in the driver's seat, while she herself is in the back seat. She suddenly realizes that nobody is driving the car. In desperation, she gets into the driver's seat herself.

Such are the dreams of patients whose encoded messages go unrecognized and uninterpreted by their therapists. The risk to her life that the patient was experiencing in this driverless psychotherapy are clearly portrayed. Other material indicated that Ms Muncey suffered many other forms of manifest and implicit unloving punishments from Dr Norman. Indications are that she stayed in therapy with him because of deep unconscious predator death anxiety and guilt over the death of her father whom she unconsciously believed she had killed. This is a common fate for guilt-ridden patients who turn to falsely loving and unloving psychotherapists for the unconscious satisfaction of their self-punitive needs.

An Extended Vignette

Ms Brown, a young woman in her mid-20s, was in once-weekly psychotherapy with Dr Boyd because of episodes of depression. The therapy, which was in its second year, had a psychodynamic cast and the therapist endeavored to explore the superficial unconscious reasons for his patient's depression in light of past events. In all, this was a weak adaptive, conscious system form of treatment with efforts to extract meaning from manifest contents; there was no sense of deep unconscious adaptation and no use of trigger decoding.

The therapy centered around the divorce of Ms Brown's parents when she was 12 years old. Their disputes had intensified that year when the patient's older sister, Mary, had died suddenly of meningitis. Dr Boyd had repeatedly interpreted his patient's guilt for wishing that her sister were dead and he loosely connected it to her unresolved issues with abandonment, her inability to be by herself for any length of time, and her anger with her parents because they did not stay together.

Dr Boyd was flexible in managing the ground rules of the therapy. He requested changes in the time of the patients' sessions when he had a professional meeting to attend and he offered alternative times for the patient's sessions when business commitments interfered with her making sessions as scheduled. He had reduced his fee when the patient was temporarily out of work and had accepted a gift of a scarf from the patient the previous Christmas, justifying the intervention as necessary in light of the patient's fragile ego and her vulnerability to rejection. He also did so on the basis of his empathy for his patient: He felt that he understood her especially well because he too had lost a sibling in his teenage years, a brother who had been killed in a skiing accident. This was not, however, something that he had shared with his patient.

Shortly before the sessions I shall present, Ms Brown's closest friend, Emily, attempted suicide with some sleeping pills that she had received from her internist. The attempt, which followed a break-up with her boyfriend who had become involved with another woman, was more a gesture than a serious effort to kill herself because she had taken only six pills. She was briefly hospitalized and then released.

In the patient's therapy session after this had happened, Ms Brown, who manifestly loved working with Dr Boyd, asked him if he would see Emily in consultation and possibly take her on as a patient. She went on to say that she felt that he would be the perfect therapist for her, adding that she was asking for this favor as a way of showing how much she trusted and appreciated him. She had already mentioned the idea to Emily, who knew how much she loves Dr Boyd, and Emily was all for it – she'd be really hurt if he refused to see her. Dr Boyd brought up the possibility that she would be jealous of Emily if he were to see her in therapy and Ms Brown dismissed the idea as ridiculous. The discussion then centered on the patient's worries about her friend and her reiterating that she would feel a lot better about her if Dr Boyd were to see her.

The patient then recalled a dream from the previous night in which she is in her bedroom with Emily. A man with a knife comes in through the bedroom window which abuts onto a fire escape and he threatens to murder both of them. In associating to the dream, Ms Brown commented that both she and Emily were in danger and added that they both needed someone to protect them, someone like Dr Boyd.

After interpreting the dream as reflecting Ms Brown's jaundiced view of men and her fear of the penis, the therapist told her that he would see her friend Emily in consultation because, as her dream indicated, the patient did indeed see both herself and her friend in danger of being harmed. He left open the question of taking her into therapy with him.

To comment on the love-related issues in this session to this point, we may think of this situation as one in which a patient is offering her therapist a gift of patient-love through the referral of a friend. The therapist, in accepting the gift, is, in return, offering his loving care to his patient. While we must decode the narrative imagery from the patient in this and subsequent sessions to decide whether these expressions of love are true or false, healing or harmful, we have good reason based on strong adaptive findings to hypothesize that the love here is false on both sides. We even have a clue to this contention in that we can trigger decode Ms Brown's dream as an unconscious perception of Dr Boyd in light of the anticipated trigger that he would see her friend, Emily, in consultation. The dream indicates that the therapist would be perceived as an intruder who intends to murder rather than help or love both Ms Brown and her friend. This reading of the deep unconscious meaning of his expected acceptance of the referral-love-gift is exactly the opposite of the conscious spin that both the patient and therapist have given to this potential intervention – i.e., their conscious belief that he would be playing the role of a loving rescuer and savior for the two women. That said, lacking narrative associations to the patient's dream – itself a sign that meaning is being concealed – we must await the material of the following session in hope of obtaining storied images that will more clearly define the deep unconscious meanings that are accruing to the therapist's now agreeing to see Emily.

As a perspective, we should identify the many ideal, archetypal ground rules that this intended intervention violates. They include the total confidentiality of Ms Brown's psychotherapy – and of Emily's therapy as well; the one-to-one privacy of both therapies; the implicit ground rule that the therapist's satisfactions in the therapy are restricted to his receiving his fee from, and being helpful to, the patient; the implicit ground rule that precludes patients' providing their therapists with extra-therapeutic gratifications – i.e., that forbids patient's falsely loving enactments; the relative anonymity of the therapist in that he is participating in the revelation to Emily that he is seeing Ms Brown in psychotherapy and to Ms Brown that he will be seeing Emily in consultation. Even as she seems to calmly and happily accept this intervention consciously, we can see that there are a lot of symptom-causing issues for Ms Brown to work over deep unconsciously and a call for her to help her therapist find the means of resolving them.

In general, falsely loving, frame-modifying proposals by patients to their therapists almost never come up in secured-frame treatment situations. They arise, as they did in this vignette, almost entirely in psychotherapies in which the ground rules and interpersonal boundaries between patient and therapist are loosely drawn in a falsely loving manner. As we have seen, frame modifications tend to beget frame modifications, much as false love tends to beget false love, often with mounting intensity in regard to the flagrancy of the frame violation and the extent of the impact it has on both parties to the therapy.

In this case, for example, the patient's unexplored frame-deviant gift – the scarf – appears to have begotten another unprocessed frame-deviant gift – Emily – whose consequences we shall soon have a chance to observe. Stated in terms of love, it seems fair to say that the patient's expression of false love – her gift of the scarf – was accepted by the therapist as a falsely loving gesture on his part and that this exchange of falsely loving acts set the stage for a more powerful exchange of falsely loving gifts in which another human being was being used by both patient and therapist as the largess – and as the predated victim of both of them. As a result, both patient and therapist are likely to suffer from predator death anxiety and deep unconscious guilt.

Lastly, it is well to note that unresolved death anxiety lurks behind the behavior of both Ms Brown and Dr Boyd. Both have lost a sibling and both are likely to believe deep unconsciously that they are accountable for their deaths. The predator death anxiety that this evokes undoubtedly haunts their lives and this psychotherapy, and motivates them to engage in frame-violating acts that symbolically defy the rule that death follows life. In addition, because frame violations are inherently harmful to all concerned, they repeat on some level the imagined murderous predatory act for which they continue to suffer with deep unconscious guilt and they set the stage for being further punished by the other party as well. In this light, the empathy that the therapist feels for his patient actually serves unconsciously to promote a harmful, unloving therapeutic misalliance (Langs, 1975, 1978a,b) in which both patient and therapist make use of frame violations as an extremely costly way of trying to cope with their death-related traumas and unresolved death anxieties. Indeed, Dr Boyd's laxity in handling the ground rules of his psychotherapies and his avoidance of death-related material in working with his patients appear to have been deep unconsciously motivated to a significant extent by the loss of his brother and his unconscious efforts to deny his role in the loss.

Dr Boyd saw Emily in consultation prior to Ms Brown's next session, which she began by thanking him profusely for agreeing to see her friend in therapy (as she evidently had learned from Emily). She then mentioned that she's thinking of buying an apartment because a real bargain has come her way through a friend at work. She's hesitant to do it because it would mean ending her therapy because she couldn't afford both therapy and an apartment, but it may be a necessary decision.

She paused and then said that she wasn't sure if she should mention it, but Emily had a great dream the night after her session with Dr Boyd. In the dream Emily's father cornered her in his bedroom and tried to rape her. Ms Brown commented that if Dr Boyd thinks that she – Ms Brown – has problems with men, Emily has even worse problems. A week ago Emily had agreed to go out on a date with her boss at work – he's a married man – and when she took him back to her apartment for a drink, he tried to date-rape her.

Dr Boyd responded by asking Ms Brown if she had had a dream of her own and the patient said that she actually had had two dreams the previous night. In the first dream, Dr Boyd was telling her that he's dropping her as a patient because he found out that she had murdered one of her friends. In the second dream, she was with her dead sister who had come back to life as her twin.

Dr Boyd intervened and asked the patient a series of questions about the details of the dream. When this seemed to lead nowhere, he suggested that in bringing up Emily's dream, Ms Brown was revealing a wish that Emily be his patient rather than herself. As her first dream showed, she'd like to project her own problems onto her friend and deny them as her own. As for Ms Brown's second dream, it seemed to indicate that she still has unresolved issues with the death of her sister. A direct discussion of these problems ensued.

Suffice it to say that in the following session, Ms Brown announced plans to leave her therapy within the month because she was planning to buy the apartment she had been offered. In a session soon after the hour I have just excerpted, she reported another dream in which the world was coming to an end because a woman saboteur had infiltrated an unguarded American arsenal of atomic weapons. The woman stole an atomic bomb and set it off, starting a chain reaction and holocaust. The patient awoke from this nightmare in a panic and had been having panic attacks ever since. The therapist tried to fathom where his patient's anxieties were coming from and with little to go on, he tried linking them to the patient's thoughts of stopping treatment and genetically, to the divorce of her parents and the death of her sister in the patient's childhood. When these interventions were met with conscious skepticism, he decided to put the patient on Xanax to alleviate her episodes of panic.

To comment, we may first note the sparseness of narrative material and the absence of narrative associations to the patient's dreams. Motivated by the anxieties created by their own deep unconscious danger-sensitive subsystems, weak adaptive therapists intuitively sense that narrative imagery is likely to carry increasingly devastating indictments of their interventions and more and more malignant pictures of themselves in light of the violence that lies beneath their falsely loving and non-adaptive, unconsciously invalidated, conscious-system interventions.

This contention was supported by a mathematically-grounded, formal science research study of recorded consultations and psychotherapy sessions conducted by a variety of psychoanalysts and psychotherapists. It was found through quantitative measures that during these sessions, as the themes in their patients' encoded narratives grew in power and became more grim and unconsciously critical of the therapist, these therapists tended to intervene intellectually in ways that shut down the patient's narrative communications – and with it their encoded indictments of their therapists' efforts. Even though they had no conscious idea as to the unconscious perceptions that were being conveyed to them by their patients and also were quite unaware of the deep unconscious guilt that they were experiencing for harming them – recording patients' therapy sessions, while vital for psychotherapy research, nonetheless is predatory of the patient – these therapists intervened to protect themselves from their patients' mounting deep unconscious criticisms and condemnations (Langs *et al.*, 1996). They made similarly disruptive interventions when death-related material emerged as well. This kind of sequence is quite common in weak adaptive psychotherapies of all kinds.

As for the session at hand, the main triggering intervention evidently is Dr Boyd's decision to accept this patient-referral and seeming gift of love from his patient, Ms Brown. His patient's response – I shall be alluding to Ms Brown as his patient and will refer to Emily by name – begins with a direct show of appreciation for the intervention. Consciously, then, Ms Brown feels loved by her therapist and loves him in return – according to her conscious appraisal, he had carried out a loving act.

Next, the patient brings up a situation that may cause her to terminate her therapy – a possibility that she carried out soon after this session. In light of the prevailing trigger, it appears that the therapist's consciously appreciated seeming act of love contributed to a severe gross behavioral resistance in the patient – i.e., her thoughts of terminating treatment, which she soon uninsightfully enacted. This unconsciously mediated result of therapists' acceptance of falsely loving gifts from patients is quite common. Gross behavioral resistances such as absences, late-nesses, offers of additional frame-deviant forms of false patient-love, and premature terminations of therapy are high among the consequences of this class of falsely loving triggers. In addition, communicative resis-tances – e.g., the shutting down of narrative expressions – also frequently appear under these circumstances.

The patient's report of Emily's dream comes next. This is an unusual resistance in that it offers someone else's dream for therapeutic pro-cessing rather than a dream of the patient's. The content of the dream suggests that Emily seems to be experiencing beginning therapy with Dr Boyd as a situation in which she is a predatory victim of an horren-dous frame violation – an incestuous rape. This image is not primarily an encoded reflection of a fantasy derived from past seductions by her father, but is a valid deep unconscious perception of an actual meaning of the prevailing frame-violating trigger. The therapist has in reality repeated on some level the predatory sexual assaults that Emily once had experienced with her father. Her guilt over being stimulated by her father's seductiveness and over his recent death were among the critical deep unconscious motives that prompted Emily to accept Ms Brown's referral to Dr Boyd. Indeed, for unconscious reasons of their own, patients are all too willing to be victims of their therapists' falsely loving, errant interventions and the harm that they eventually cause both parties to therapy.

Technically, it is advisable that a therapist avoid commenting on or inter-preting a dream from someone other than the patient. Emily's dream does, of course, convey some of Ms Brown's own unconscious perceptions of the therapist in light of the prevailing triggers. Nevertheless, the likely meanings of the material should be appreciated by the therapist without comment to the patient, lest he actively participate in a therapeutic misalliance in which Ms Brown's therapy is turned over to Emily and is no longer her own. To comment on the dream also would bring Emily into Ms Brown's sessions, thereby further compromising the one-to-one ground rule of her psychotherapy.

The importance of the question of whose therapy this is – a problem created by the trigger of Dr Boyd's seeing Emily in consultation – is emphasized by the fact that the patient began this session with Emily's dream. In itself, the patient's reporting the dream carries the implicit message that, now that the therapist has accepted Emily into treatment, Ms Brown is no longer his patient. At the same time, the dream report indicates that the patient no longer knows who is in therapy with the therapist, nor is she able to keep intact the boundary between herself and Emily – it is as if they have, because of the trigger, merged with one another. This quandary is projected onto or projectively identified into the therapist who became unsure as to how to handle the dream – should he interpret it as belonging to Emily, to the patient, or what? Here too necessary boundaries have been made porous, including those between the therapist and his patients and between the therapist's patients themselves.

The same dilemma applies to the patient's sole association to Emily's dream – the story of Emily's dating a married man at work and being date-raped. Whose deep unconscious perception of the therapist is this? Emily's? The patient's? Both? How is the therapist to know?

The ideal ground rules of the work place call for an absence of social contact between a boss and his employees, while dating a married man also is forbidden by the deep unconscious subsystem of morality and ethics. The frame-violating aspects of this narrative reflect Emily's – and Ms Brown's – deep unconscious perceptions of one of the critical meanings of the trigger: It is a forbidden, forced seduction that entails being unfaithful to a third party – i.e., the boss' wife is a disguised representation of the patient who was betrayed by the therapist by his seeing Emily.

Dr Boyd's discomfort with this material arose manifestly because he was confused about what to do with it and because he was beginning to have doubts about his decision to see Emily in therapy. In addition, the confusion was the result of his own deep unconscious perceptions of the meanings of these narratives. Therapists suffer from deep unconscious guilt when they are confronted through their patients' unconscious communications with the predatory impact and meanings of their interventions. In the absence of conscious awareness of the ramifications of what they have done, they are prone to punish themselves accordingly.

Therapists who trigger decode material of this kind in light of their own interventions – and they seldom intervene in this kind of falsely loving, frame-deviant manner – are likely to experience conscious guilt, but they can then process the sources of this guilt and make amends so as to reduce or negate their need to punish themselves unduly. In contrast, therapists who are consciously unaware of these issues have no way to make amends because they have no idea as to what needs to be amended. As a result, they are prone to cause further harm to their patients and are likely to continue to punish themselves for their unconsciously perceived misdeeds for long periods of time.

Returning to the vignette, at her therapist's request, the patient eventually reported two dreams of her own. In the first dream, Dr Boyd drops her as a patient because she has murdered one of her friends. Strong adaptive clinical studies indicate that patients' manifest dreams of their therapists are almost always triggered by blatantly frame-violating and falsely loving interventions. These dreams tend to be negatively toned because of the harmful nature of the frame violation through which the therapist has imposed his or her extra-therapeutic needs onto the patient. Even though the therapist saw Emily at the request of his patient, this principle holds true because the therapist's own pathological needs played a significant role in his agreeing to do so. As the expert, the therapist must bear the greater responsibility for the consequences of misguided, falsely loving misalliances between himself and his patients.

Here too, the image of being dropped as a patient by the therapist is not primarily a fantasy or wish, but is a portrayal of one of the actual implications of the therapist's decision to see Emily in therapy. In the conscious mind, the therapist can see both of these friends on equal terms and the ramifications of this decision can be discussed and interpreted superficially when themes of rivalry and the like arise in either treatment situation. This kind of conscious system thinking has led weak adaptive psychotherapists to mistakenly believe that they can do almost anything deviant with a patient and then analyze away the detrimental effects of these false expressions of love. Few ideas could be further from the truth. Indeed, this is a conscious system form of denial that is not shared by the deep unconscious wisdom subsystem. There, accepting Emily as a patient is equated with dismissing Ms Brown from treatment. This unconsciously perceived implication of the trigger also is reflected in the patient's thoughts of terminating her therapy and as noted, in her bringing up Emily's dream in her session. In the deep unconscious mind, there can be only one patient per therapist among friends and relatives – it is an implied archetypal ground rule that exists, it would appear, to insure the much-needed privacy and confidentiality of psychotherapy and to prevent therapists from exploiting their patients.

The allusion to Ms Brown's having murdered a friend is a powerful, composite image that can be decoded in light of the trigger in at least five different ways:

First, as a thinly disguised deep unconscious realization that in referring Emily to Dr Boyd, the patient has not expressed her love and concern for her friend, but has instead, irretrievably harmed her.

Second, as an unconscious perception that by asking the therapist to see Emily, the patient was trying to harm and destroy Dr Boyd.

Third, as an unconscious perception of the harm that Dr Boyd is doing to Emily by seeing her in therapy under these conditions.

Fourth, as a reflection of the irretrievable harm that the therapist is causing Ms Brown by seeing her friend.

And fifth and last, as the patient's deep unconscious perception of the serious harm that Dr Boyd was doing to himself.

These trigger-decoded meanings strongly suggest that the therapist's supposedly loving acceptance of this patient-referral had multiple unloving ramifications, all valid and affecting, that were causing terrible harm to all concerned.

Beware of patients bearing gifts.

The patient's second dream is about her sister's coming back to life as her twin. In light of the triggering event, this image conveys the idea that by bringing Emily into therapy with Dr Boyd, the patient had resurrected her dead sister. By violating several archetypal ground rules, the patient and therapist have defied that aspect of the existential ground rule that states that death is loss for all eternity. Thus, these frame violations deep unconsciously are an effort to deny the finality of death – Emily is the patient's sister returned to life. We may suppose that this same deep unconscious dynamic was operating in Dr Boyd – accepting Emily into therapy under the prevailing conditions was for him a restoration of his dead brother. This is a thesis that he would have to be tested out through his own, private efforts at self-processing. In similar fashion, entering therapy in this way probably was for Emily a way of bringing her dead father back to life. These are all costly, potentially disruptive ways to try to magically deny loss and death. Left unanalyzed and unrectified, they are certain to lead to further maladaptive, harmful falsely loving acts, within and outside of therapy by all three participants in this misalliance.

The image of twin sisters leads to another unconscious delusion that is probably being played out here. Clinical studies indicate that patients who arrange for a friend or relative to see their therapists are acting out the unconscious belief that if one member of the trio dies, the other two will live on, thereby negating the sense of loss involved in the death. Human beings – patients and therapists – often go to mad extremes to deny death and to try to alleviate the death anxieties it arouses. Joining their patients in enacting such madness certainly is not a constructive way for therapists to help their patients resolve their death anxieties and heal their madness.

As for the postscript to this session, the panic attacks that the patient was experiencing speak for the failure of her – and the therapist's – desperate efforts to gain relief from their death anxieties through this major frame violation. The attacks also seem to stem from the therapist's failure to properly interpret and rectify this frame violation and from the anxieties that the patient was experiencing in response to the frame violation itself – her destructive view of the therapist in light of what he had done. The therapist also appears to have projectively identified his own unresolved death anxieties into the patient who was unable to contain and metabolize them and suffered accordingly.

The patient's dream of the end of the world speaks to her deep unconscious realization that her therapy was in effect destroyed by this frame deviation, even though the treatment continued consciously for a while longer, after which it did indeed end. The image of the unguarded door seems to be a corrective that speaks for the need for the therapist to have properly guarded the door to his office – i.e., that he should not have allowed Emily to enter the therapeutic space. Emily's presence is seen unconsciously as having destroyed everything and everyone, but the deadly woman also represents the two patients and the therapist as well – all three parties have colluded to destroy the viable therapeutic world in which the patient was seeing her therapist.

Once more we see that the conscious mind cannot be trusted to fairly judge the meanings and ramifications of therapists' interventions, including those that seem on the surface to be caring and loving. It also seems fair to say that the conscious mind is bathed in ignorance about, and is self-defeating and self-destructive in, matters of love in psychotherapy.

Issues of Technique

There are a set of sound principles of technique that can serve therapists quite well in dealing with their own inclinations to be loving towards their patients, especially in response to requests from their patients. As I have tried to show, most of these proposals from patients entail requests for false rather than true therapist-love so the precepts that follow are designed to enable the therapist to determine which type of love is involved and to intervene accordingly.

Because I have already alluded to many of these precepts, I will describe them in succinct fashion. Whenever a patient asks a therapist for a deliberate expression of care and love, the therapist should not immediately agree to or reject the request. Instead, the patient should be encouraged to generate narrative imagery so as to reveal his or her deep unconscious views of the situation. Two triggers also must be taken into account: The prior intervention that has set the stage for the request and the anticipated trigger of the therapist complying with the request. Trigger-decoding interpretations and sustaining the secured frame by not agreeing to the satisfy the entreaty should then be carried out in light of both of these triggers.

In intervening, the role played by death-related issues must eventually be an aspect of the interpretive process. The therapist also must acknowledge his or her contribution to the patient's proposed falsely loving action, doing so entirely on the basis of the patient's encoded imagery. There is no room in these situations for holding the patient alone accountable for his or her falsely loving proposal. The patient's encoded imagery generally will provide the therapist with all that he or she needs to insightfully resolve the patient's wish for a falsely loving enactment by the therapist. The net result can be an interlude that begins with false love and ends with love that is true and healing.

True Therapist-love

As I have been indicating, there are a limited number of ways that therapists can express true love for their patients. There are, then, strong constraints on expressions of this love which is not self-proclaimed like much of false therapist-love, but it is quietly satisfying for the therapist-giver and the patient-receiver. As we have seen, true therapist-love essentially is expressed through frame-securing and unconsciously validated trigger-decoded interventions. Patients tend to receive such love unconsciously and reveal their sense of being truly loved through encoded dreams and stories that touch on moments of genuine caring and love between two people.

The claim that only deep unconsciously validated frame-securing and properly trigger-decoded interventions are expressions of true therapist-love is founded on extremely consistent strong adaptive findings. Given that the deep unconscious mind operates on the basis of archetypes – evolved universal needs and ways of perceiving and coping with the emotional world and its traumas that are not found in the conscious mind – these consistencies are not at all surprising.

Because of the evolved design of the emotion-processing mind, therapists need to renounce their many natural pathological and maladaptive emotional needs and defenses in order to forego turning to expressions of false love. In so doing, they are likely to gain the satisfaction of loving patients in true fashion and in having that love appreciated unconsciously and at times, consciously – by their patients and themselves as well. By confining themselves to true love they also benefit because they are trying to heal their patients in a truly loving manner. In making use of unconsciously validated, truly loving interventions therapists also spare their patients much harm, while they spare themselves a great deal of predator death anxiety and deep unconscious guilt with needs for self-punishment.

In addition to the satisfactions that accrue to truly loving therapists for the love that they inherently (and not deliberately) convey to their patients, there are special satisfactions that come only from these kinds of therapeutic efforts. Encoded imagery is the poetry and magic of human communication. Decoding an encoded image and experiencing the wonders of the human capacity to unconsciously perceive and disguise allusions to grim and affecting realities is an awesome encounter for a psychotherapist. Much the same applies to taking in the miraculous wisdom of the deep unconscious mind and in viewing the power and innocence of how the emotional world is experienced on this level. Entering this world is both a privilege and a truly unique if not somewhat frightening source of gratification for all concerned. Then too there are the seemingly endless discoveries that a working in this vein leads to – the conscious mind is forever unprepared for, and in awe of, what the deep unconscious mind sees, experiences, and knows. This exciting and awesome experience of learning new and surprising things about the human mind, and about patients and oneself, is part of the reward of doing psychotherapy in a truly loving fashion. The culmination of this kind of therapeutic work in the insightful cure of the patient and the personal growth of the therapist is the last but not least of the rewards that come to truly loving psychotherapists.

A Loving Therapeutic Interlude

Dr Pike, a male therapist, overslept and missed his scheduled early morning session with Mrs Meade. He did not call the patient nor did she call him. She begins the following session by telling Dr Pike that she had waited for him to arrive for the session and had wondered what had happened to him. When the therapist remains silent, she tells him that she had imagined several possibilities: That he had had an emergency with a patient that took him out of his office, that he'd been stuck in traffic, or that someone in his family was ill. She was sure he had a good reason for not being here.

She had had a dream the night he didn't show for her session in which she is looking at a wrecked car that has a dead man inside of it, slumped at the wheel. Associating to the dream, she recalls that as a teenager she saw a highway accident in which the driver, who was a middle-aged man, appeared to be dead. She remembers thinking about his family and how he wasn't going to come home as expected, and wondering how they would find out that he had died. She also recalls a movie she saw a year ago in which a woman's lover disappeared from sight. She tried to find him, but couldn't; she was convinced that he was dead. Eventually, she found out that he wasn't dead but was living with another woman, and in a rage, she killed him by running over him with a car.

Dr Pike intervenes and suggests that the patient's dream and her associations to the dream must convey her reactions to his absence the previous week. The images of the lost lover and dead man indicate that unconsciously, if not consciously, Mrs Meade felt that he had abandoned her and that she was convinced that he had died. Now that she knew that he was alive, she evidently wanted to murder him for what he did last week, largely because she felt that he no longer loved her and had spent the time with someone else, perhaps another woman.

Mrs Meade is silent for a while and then says that another association to the dream is coming to mind. She remembers driving in the family car with her father as a child. She'd been crying because he had spanked her because she had teased and hit her younger brother. She'd been upset because her grandmother had died that week and it was her first experience with death. She had apologized profusely to her father and had promised to stop teasing her brother. Her father seemed to accept her promise and also to have felt guilty for having hit her because he was taking her to a mall to buy a new dress. He could be nasty, but he also could be a love. She missed him a lot these days.

I chose this vignette because it begins with a traumatic, distinctly unloving frame violation by the therapist and ends with a clear expression of true therapist-love. The patient's conscious reaction to her therapist's absence was to believe that he had had a good reason for not being at the session and to speculate as to its cause – albeit without consciously thinking that he might be dead or that death played a role in his absence. Her dream-associational network indicated, however, that deep unconsciously, the thought that he might have died was a major concern. So too was her experience that she'd been abandoned by a lover – a probable allusion to previous truly loving interventions that the therapist had made – and of wanting to murder him for being with another woman, which is another fantasy about why the therapist had missed the session.

In this regard, we should be clear that the triggering event here is the therapist's absence and that it had evoked a variety of unconscious perceptions that had, in turn, stirred up a variety of unconscious beliefs or fantasies as to the reason for his unloving, frame-violating intervention. These fantasies are not genetically-based distortions or misperceptions of what the therapist has done, as implied by the concept of transference, but are natural speculations as to why he did what he did. A similar understanding applies to the link to the death of the patient's grandmother – it is a natural and appropriate connection to the trigger and not a source of misperceptions of the therapist.

The therapist did not explain the cause of his absence but instead, correctly allowed the patient to begin, and continue to speak in, the session. Faced with a highly traumatic trigger and buttressed by her therapist's decision to not engage with her in a manifest discussion of her feelings and fantasies about his absence, the patient soon began to generate narrative imagery through her dream and associations to the dream. Expressing encoded, deep unconscious reactions to triggers of this kind is a natural adaptive response to a therapist-evoked trauma – all the therapist needs to do at first is to not get in the way of the patient's need to narrate. On this basis, the therapist will then be able to interpret and trigger decode the patient's encoded deep unconscious perceptions of the more forbidding meanings of the traumatic trigger. As needed, frame rectification at the behest of the patient's encoded directives comes next, after which the therapist listens for encoded validation – or its lack. This is the only known means by which an unloving act by a therapist can be the basis for a reparative response that is truly loving. Conscious excuses or explanations, and other types of non-adaptive, self-generated interventions, simply extend the unloving harm being done to the patient by the therapist.

In the session, Dr Pike did offer Mrs Meade a trigger-decoded inter-pretation of her deep unconscious perceptions of, and reactions to, his absence. The patient unconsciously validated the intervention with the story of her father's shift from punishing her for causing harm to her brother to rewarding her for her renouncing her need to harm him – from the father's hating her to loving her. While the theme of being hit by her father shows that the patient experienced real harm from the therapist's absence, the theme of the father's giving her a gift of love shows that the therapist's reparative intervention also had a real and positive impact on the patient. True therapist-love is, as I have been saying, hard to express, but quite rewarding for all concerned when a therapist understands exactly how to convey it.

As a final note, I would propose that the patient's allusion to the death of her grandmother as the source of her violence against her brother is a deep unconscious interpretation to the therapist, to the effect that a death-related trauma had triggered his lapse. The deep unconscious wisdom subsystem knows full well that this almost always is the case with frame-violating lapses. As it turned out, death anxiety had indeed been a significant unconscious motive that prompted Dr Pike to oversleep and miss his patient's session. At the time – and quite unknown to the patient – his sister was seriously ill with a tumor of the lungs. Dr Pike's absence was an unconscious effort to undo the threat of death by enacting a drama in which the absent person who is believed to be dead – i.e., he himself – is not dead but quite alive and able to reappear. It also was unconsciously motivated by Dr Pike's predator death anxiety and deep unconscious guilt because of uncon-scious beliefs that he had contributed to his sister's illness. The uncon-scious goal in this regard was to be punished by his patient because of his neglecting her.

Love trumpets itself in psychotherapy for all to hear and see, while death lurks in the shadows actually telling love what it must do.

9

The Search for True Love

As we have seen, the main problem with love in psychotherapy is not so much about giving and receiving true love as it is about not giving and receiving love that is false and ultimately – and often secretly – harmful. Throughout the book, I have alluded to various reasons why present-day psychotherapists offer so much false love to their patients and seek so much false love in return. In like manner, I have touched on many reasons why patients prefer to receive false rather than true love from their therapists and why they tend so often to falsely love their therapists for, as they say, 'all the wrong reasons'. In bringing this book to a close, I shall now gather together the main reasons for the prevalence of false rather than true love in psychotherapy – and in much of everyday life – and sum up what therapists can do to change this most troubling situation.

The Evolved Mind

We begin as we must with the evolution of the emotion-processing mind and its present design, perhaps the most flawed and costly outcome of natural selection in the history of the human species (Langs, 1992b, 1996, 2004c). The story begins with the acquisition of language which brought with it many advancements in adaptive resources and in human creativity. But language also brought with it the unique ability of humans to represent and process events intrapsychically. In the emotional domain, where resources that favor survival are involved, this feature of the mind eventually contributed to the development of the emotion-processing mind with its dual processing systems, one linked – or capable of being linked – to awareness (the conscious system) and the other entirely without such a connection (the deep unconscious system). The conscious system evidently evolved first and when the system's resources became overwhelmed in having to process an ever-increasing number of emotionally-charged traumas and their emotionally assaultive meanings, minds capable of perception without awareness and deep unconscious adaptive activities were naturally favored because they could handle the emotional overload and reduce the incidence of conscious system dysfunctions.

Language acquisition also gave humans the capacity to recognize themselves as distinct from others and the ability to foresee future events. These developments led, in turn, to the realization that all humans eventually must die, a uniquely human conscious insight with enormous after-effects, largely because it became a major source of potentially disruptive existential death anxieties. These anxieties were joined by newly formed versions of predatory death anxiety and by the development of another distinctly human trait, the capability to develop predator death anxiety and deep unconscious guilt. This trio of death anxieties was in all likelihood among the most powerful of the many selection factors that shaped the design of the emotion-processing mind.

Especially noteworthy is the finding that human existential death anxieties were dealt with most successfully by minds that were capable of intensive use of denial and obliteration – of unawareness, if you will. Despite the enormous cost that comes from not being aware of emotionally significant information, individuals with these capacities evidently survived better than those with minds with lesser capabilities for denial. The latter minds apparently suffered from relatively more moments of intense death anxiety that interfered with conscious abilities to cope with danger and survive. Minds with a strong capacity for predator death anxiety and deep unconscious guilt also faired better than those with weaker versions of these features. This seems to have been the case because the capacity for deep unconscious guilt tends to diminish, however insufficiently, the human inclination to unnecessarily harm others, which carries with it the risk of retaliatory responses from those who are harmed.

There are elaborate connections between these evolutionary developments and expressions of love in psychotherapy. The role of a psychotherapist is to help patients alter and resolve their maladaptive emotional symptoms and behavior patterns. As I have been emphasizing, therapists who do this through trigger-decoded interpretations and frame-securing efforts are, by deep unconscious standards, truly loving of their patients. But this kind of love is expressed by bringing into awareness the denied and repressed meanings of patients' death-related traumas and by interpreting the nature and sources of patients' death anxieties as they are once again mobilized in the immediate psychotherapy situation by interventions of the therapist, and less often, by events in patients' everyday lives.

The prototypical situation is this: A current death-related trauma in the psychotherapy – i.e., an intervention that arouses a patient's death anxieties by either securing or modifying the frame – intensifies a patient's current death anxieties and reactivates the patient's past death-related traumas and the anxieties and conflicts associated with them. As concerns the psychological and/or physical damage that is being perpetrated in both the present situation and the past, the patient may have been a victim, a perpetrator, or an affected observer. Added to the death anxieties evoked by these incidents is the patient's ever-present, background existential death anxieties. The result is a constellation of anxiety-provoking incidents and expectations that on the one hand are the deepest roots of the patient's maladaptive dysfunctions, and on the other, the substance of the issues that inevitably must be triggered, represented narratively, worked through, and insightfully resolved to allow for lasting emotional relief and optimal functioning in the future.

We can see, then, that true therapist-love is tough love offered by therapists strong enough to endure a shared journey through the realm of death and helplessness to which loving interventions bring their patients and themselves. True therapist-love is a genuinely caring love that is painful to administer and painful to receive, yet ultimately uplifting for all concerned. It is a love that also is an essential part of a deep healing process designed to resolve the patient's raw, death-related emotional wounds. This traumatic yet caring therapeutic work needs to be carried out lovingly at a measured pace that depends on the triggers created by the therapist and what the patient is able to express and tolerate at any given moment as reflected in his or her responsive encoded narratives. It is, then, a love that rings true even as it activates the deepest and most intense dread and fears experienced by human beings, including both patients and therapists.

We need to be clear, however, that as much as one part of patients' emotion-processing minds wish, both consciously and deep unconsciously, to be truly loved and healed, there are other parts of their emotion-processing minds that consciously wish to be falsely loved and that oppose the healing process. Clinical observations make clear that these opposing forces have an enormous influence over a patient's conscious system and his or her conscious attitudes and consciously orchestrated behaviors. Despite their consistent deep unconscious search for true therapist-love and cure, patients repeatedly alternate between seeking true and false love from their therapists. Similarly, they go back and forth between moments of insight and forgiveness – of others and themselves – and moments in which their unresolved guilt prompts them unconsciously to condemn and punish death-related offenders, especially themselves.

Love, truly expressed, is healing, but it heals in the face of strong opposition in both patients and their therapists. These resistances directed against a truly loving cure are grounded in the evolved tendency of the conscious system to use various forms of denial in dealing with each type of death-related threat. In response to psychological predatory threats from individuals on whom one is dependent, the conscious mind will deny that the other person intends to be, or actually is, being harmful. Confronted with predator death anxiety, the conscious system will deny having harmed others, while in dealing with the eventual certainty of personal death, the conscious mind will find countless ways in both thought and action to deny its vulnerability and helplessness in regard to the inevitable end of a life and convince itself that life lives on after death (Langs, 1997).

True therapist-love entails undoing each of these forms of death-related denial. This is a painful surrender of defenses for the therapists and their conscious systems, and patients often manifestly show either indifference or dislike for therapists who love them in this manner. Whatever love patients do feel is expressed through encoded images derived from their deep unconscious systems. Open feelings of patient-love for therapists who carry out this kind of truly loving therapeutic work therefore are quite rare. Indeed, it is only the deep unconscious mind with its archetypal, truly healing wisdom that deeply appreciates the love offered by therapists of this ilk.

This kind of therapeutic work is arduous for psychotherapists because it runs counter to the natural inclinations of their evolved conscious minds. It therefore takes a great deal of self-processing and years of doing therapy as guided by deep unconscious validation for therapists to sufficiently master their existential and other forms of death anxiety so as to be truly loving of their patients. Beyond that, complete mastery is all but impossible and lapses into false expressions of therapist-love are inevitable. Nevertheless, as we saw in the previous chapter, such interludes can be turned into moments of true love if their deep nature is recognized and the responsive encoded narrative themes are used to offer deep unconsciously validated interpretations and frame-securing interventions.

To offer a final perspective on the role of evolution in the natural selection of emotion-processing minds and the effects of these minds on expressions of love in psychotherapy, it is well to note that while genes have a powerful influence on the behavior and choices of living beings, there also is much evidence that humans in particular are not slaves to their genes (Langs, 1996, 2004b; Rose, 1997). Indeed, one of the evolved capabilities that genes have engineered for humans is the ability to overcome or decide to act in opposition to genetically pro-grammed tendencies. That is, the selfish gene (Dawkins, 1976; Slavin and Kriegman, 1992) does not autocratically run human life – the gene itself has seen to that. It follows then that even though there are fixed, inherited archetypes for the design, operations, and preferences of emotion-processing minds, humans do have the capacity to overcome the detrimental effects of these universal propensities. It does, however, take a great deal of effort and insight to do so.

The Role of Deep Unconscious Guilt

A second and extremely powerful, natural source of opposition to true love in psychotherapy – and again, in much of everyday life – derives from patients' and therapists' deep unconscious guilt for having harmed others. For example, patients' encoded responses to interpreta-tions that activate moments when they damaged others reveal that the deep unconscious subsystem of morality and ethics has evolved in a manner that is inordinately unforgiving in response to acts of harm. It takes an enormous amount of working through for lasting deep uncon-scious atonement, repentance, reparation, and forgiveness to appear in patients' encoded imagery. In the meantime, these patients seek false rather than true love from their therapists because they unconsciously believe that they do not deserve to be truly loved and because false love is inherently punitive. They also offer their therapists harmful ver-sions of false love of their own, motivated by their deep unconscious need to be punished by the therapist for their deceptiveness.

Therapists' predator death anxieties and deep unconscious guilt inter-fere with their expressing true love for and to their patients because ther-apists' deep unconscious guilt moves them towards interventions that are unconsciously designed to have their patients punish them for their unloving errant ways. In many ways, then, the evolved design of the emotion-processing mind conspires against true love in psychotherapy. Therapists need to summon up – i.e., trigger decode – the wisdom of the deep unconscious mind to combat their own and their patients' misleading and self-defeating natural inclinations. The odds are stacked against success because the death-sensitive and moral subsystems of the deep unconscious system have an enormous unconscious influence on the conscious mind, while their opponent in these matters – the deep unconscious wisdom subsystem which knows the shape of true love – has only the slightest effect on conscious choices and behaviors.

The Role of Ground Rules and Frames

The responsibility for the prevalence of false love in psychotherapy falls more to psychotherapists than their patients (Langs, 1998b). Therapists decide on and arrange the basic framework and ground rules of therapy. If they secure the most ideal frame of therapy possible for their patients, they are expressing true love; if not, false therapist-love prevails. And the choices that they make become models for how patients express their love for their therapists. This runs counter to the weak adaptive belief that patients, in their need to recreate their past life experiences and to express their transferences, are the prime movers for resistances, misalliances and pathological reenactments in psychotherapy. To the contrary, in subtle and blatant ways that often operate outside of their awareness, therapists are the prime movers in the therapy situation; it is they who first and foremost orchestrate reenactments of past pathological relationships with their patients. This principle applies quite strongly to the nature of the loving exchanges that take place between themselves and their patients in the course of a psychotherapy experience.

In addition to their own inherently loving or unloving qualities, the ground rules of psychotherapy also define the conditions under which love, true or false, will be expressed by both patients and therapists. The secured frame creates a setting in which it is safe to express both conscious and unconscious feelings of love and as we saw, it also exerts little or no pressure on the parties to therapy to love falsely and unwisely. In addition, because of their truly loving qualities, secured frames also implicitly unconsciously motivate expressions of true love by both parties to treatment.

On the other hand, the deviant frame creates conditions under which it is unsafe for a patient to express true love consciously – if there is an occasion to feel it – because there are no assurances that this love will not be exploited by the frame-violating therapist and a strong likelihood that it will. Furthermore, there can be no true therapist-love within a deviant frame unless it is expressed by securing a deviant ground rule that is open to rectification – even truly loving interpretations must be grounded in truly loving, frame-securing efforts.

The Preference for False Love

With this understanding in hand, let's turn again to the question of why, with few exceptions, therapists evidently are unable or reluctant to offer true love to their patients and why for their part, most patients are willing to accept such love or offer it to their therapists as well. An initial clue to this situation comes from the clinical finding that many patients who suddenly leave truly loving forms of psychotherapy have suffered from extremely traumatic death-related experiences or are dealing at the time of their flight with significant, unbearable death-related issues. For example, they may have a history of a hereditary illness or malformation, have been party to an abortion or miscarriage, be suffering from a fatal or potentially fatal illness, or have a relative or close friend who is suffering in this way, or they may be related to someone who has committed suicide. With a handful of as yet unexplained exceptions, most of these patients refuse to enter therapy or remain with a therapist who is truly loving and frame-securing. Indications are that unbearable degrees of death anxiety and deep unconscious guilt account for their flight from these truly loving therapists. Much the same can be inferred regarding therapists' reluctance to offer their patients secured frames.

As for other factors in the scarcity of truly loving psychotherapists, there may well be a tendency for individuals with unresolved death-related issues to become psychotherapists. This trend would account for their aversion to working in secured frames and to offering the death-related interpretations that characterize truly loving interventions – such efforts arouse too much unresolved death anxiety within themselves to be tolerable. Therapists also suffer from the universal human tendency to avoid situations that activate existential death anxieties.

Another important source of threat to therapists arises when death-related events that touch closely on similar traumas of their own occur in their patients' lives. At such times, their patients' death-related associations and behaviors are experienced deep unconsciously by these therapists as predatory acts and they activate the therapist's use of denial to combat the aroused death anxieties. Therapists are inclined to construct treatment in unloving ways to protect themselves from these emotional dangers and they also tend to respond to patients' unloving attacks with retaliatory unloving interventions of their own. Along different lines, therapists who are suffering from deep unconscious guilt tend to create falsely loving settings and make falsely loving interventions as ways of unconsciously inviting their patients to punish them for their misdeeds. Finally, therapists who are facing serious illnesses or injuries, or the prospect of dying, are strongly inclined to engage in serious frame violations based on evident efforts to deny their personal mortality (Galatzer-Levy, 2004).

The death-related realities of a therapist's life, past and present, have profound effects on how he or she frames, conducts, and loves within a psychotherapy experience.

Predatory and Predator Death Anxiety

This leads me to take a final look at the effects of predatory and predator death anxiety on therapists' preferences for love in psychotherapy. As I have said, by and large, predatory death anxiety prompts the mobilization of both physical and mental resources, and sharpens conscious and unconscious perceptions and efforts at coping with the danger at hand. As a result, humans generally tend to be angry with and experience hatred for those who harm them and love those who offer them care and support. There are, however, at least two sets of conditions in which these principles do not hold forth and both are relevant to the psychotherapy situation.

In the first, the harm takes the form of emotional or minimal physical damage and the predator is someone on whom the individual must rely on. In these cases, the victim often consciously feels loved even though that love is experienced deep unconsciously as damaging and false. This neediness and paradoxical response is not uncommon in patients' relationships with their therapists and it is another factor that promotes many unrecognized expressions of false therapist- and patient-love in the course of a treatment experience.

In the second type of situation, the individual is suffering from predator death anxiety and unconsciously seeks false love from others who mete out the love in forms that are in fact, unconsciously mediated forms of punishment. This kind of punitive false love is the unwitting métier of many present-day psychotherapists and patients falsely love them for it consciously even as they recognize the harm that is being done to them deep unconsciously.

Many of the needs for false love in psychotherapy also arise because of the lack of influence of deep unconscious wisdom on the conscious mind and its choices. This arises because deep unconscious wisdom is always linked to death-related traumas and issues that are unbearable to awareness. As a result, the wisdom subsystem speaks to the surface of the mind solely through encoded narratives that the conscious mind is afraid of and reluctant to trigger decode. Because of this, deep unconscious wisdom is a voice of adaptive reason and sensibility whose messages and advisories usually go unheard and unheeded by the conscious minds of both patients and therapists.

Some Lesser Reasons for False Therapist-love

There are several other lesser, superficially unconscious reasons for therapists' avoidance of true love in psychotherapy. Among these are objections to and difficulties with the necessary restraints and renunciations that are required in order to offer patients true love and the anxieties that must be endured to do so. Another factor lies with therapists' identifications with falsely loving individuals, like their parents or psychotherapists. There also is the need in therapists to conform to prevailing practices in order to be part of a peer group of therapists, to be asked to teach in psychotherapy training programs, or to receive referrals from colleagues. Psychotherapy and psychoanalysis are conformist disciplines and therapists' offers of false love to their patients is an aspect of this conformity.

As for psychotherapy patients, seeking and obtaining false therapist-love enables them to forgive their falsely loving, harmful parents for the wrongs that they did to them. The unconscious idea behind this mechanism is that forgiving a falsely loving psychotherapist implies forgiving the falsely loving parent. The acceptance of false love from a therapist also is an ill-gotten way that patients come to accept their own ways of falsely loving others – including their therapists. Therapists' who love in this manner motivate and sanction patients' inclinations to behave in similar fashion. Indeed, one of the more dire consequences of patients' seeking and obtaining false therapist-love is that they are then more strongly motivated to seek versions of false love in their everyday lives. As I found in my interview study (Langs, 1985), many failed personal love relationships that patients suffer during and after their psychotherapies stem from the intensification of unconscious needs of this kind. In another love-related vicious cycle, patients enter treatment seeking false love, receive that love from their therapists, and subsequently, seek – and give – more of this kind of love in their lives outside of treatment. Only true therapist-love conveyed solely through deep unconsciously validated interventions can break these cycles of exchanges of false love for both parties to therapy.

Patients also search for and accept false therapist-love because of superficially unconscious needs for immediate gratification, however pathological or inappropriate it may be. On this level, frustrations are experienced as dangerous and annihilating, while satisfactions of needs, including those that are pathological, are seen as life-giving. This simplistic, conscious system belief accounts for many rationalizations made by patients to the effect that their falsely loving therapists are truly empathic and supportive. To the contrary, deep unconsciously, these therapists are seen as quite unempathic and distinctly unsupportive.

Along similar lines, the necessary boundaries and limits that are inherent to receiving true therapist-love often are consciously experienced as dangerously restrictive and unloving, even though deep unconsciously, they are experienced as enormously loving and healing. False therapist-love tends to be almost boundariless or entails behaviors that involve highly permeable or porous interpersonal boundaries. This seeming limitlessness creates the conscious illusion or delusion of love in both patients and their therapists and it helps to set a pattern for loving falsely that is harmful for all concerned.

A Clinical Example

To cite another example from my interview study (Langs, 1985), the first therapist to see Dr King, a male psychologist, was Dr Bass, who was a psychologist and professor at the university where Dr King was attending classes. Dr Bass saw the patient for a reduced fee. Consciously, the patient felt that this was a sign that the therapist cared about him and was concerned for his welfare. Nevertheless, his associations in his interview with me immediately went to Dr Bass' colleague, Michael, who had made the referral. As Dr King saw it, Michael had a crush on him and was probably homosexual; there was no way he should have come on to a student – i.e., Dr King – like that. His next image in the interview was that of his first adolescent dream in which he was having intercourse with his sister.

Here, a seemingly loving decision by a therapist to see a student-patient for a low fee is consciously seen as caring and loving, but deep unconsciously, is viewed as homosexually seductive and incestuous, and entirely inappropriate. The comment that there was no way that Michael should have behaved as he did is an unconscious model of rectification to the effect that the therapist should not have seductively reduced his fee. Notice too that while the conscious mind has a single view of the situation, the deep unconscious mind harbors two simultaneous views and both appear to be valid and true.

Dr King later saw Dr Land for further therapy. Because the patient was sexually promiscuous and had engaged in frequent, compulsive masturbation, the therapist mandated that the patient not have sex with a woman for one year. This was presented to him as a means of helping him to learn self-control and justified by the therapist because someone had to offer tough love to Dr King. The patient was delighted that someone finally understood him and cared enough to not indulge him.

After telling me about this intervention, Dr King thought of his mother who was psychotic when he was a child and of a sister whom he had seduced. He then recalled that his mother had weaned him at a late age by lying to him about the contents of the second bottle that she offered him after his first bottle was finished. The night after the therapist's injunction had been invoked, the patient dreamt that he was in the water swimming with a woman. A shark attacks him and bites off his leg.

Once more the encoded images of the therapist in light of his supposedly loving intervention contradicts the patient's conscious picture. The deep unconscious view is that the intervention was an unloving act of madness, that, like the patient's mother, the therapist's injunction was a psychotic intervention and his advice to the patient to avoid sex was like trying to wean him from the bottle in a lying, deceptive manner. Finally, the patient's dream speaks to the violence, bodily harm, sense of being castrated, and death anxiety that the therapist's predatory directive caused him.

Therapists' Motives for Loving Falsely

The need in psychotherapists to love their patients in false and harmful ways is extremely strong. I have already discussed the death-related factors in this preference and shall now offer some further insights into the sources of this predilection. While the basic driving forces empowering this tendency are comparable to those that prevail in patients, there are as well additional factors that account for this bent in therapists.

One such determinant lies with the particular nature of some therapists' psychopathology. For example, therapists who are blatantly unloving and who have had sexual relations with their patients have been found to be severely depressed or to have borderline or psychopathic personality disorders (Celenza, 1991, 1998; Celenza and Gabbard, 2003; Gabbard and Lester, 1995). In a similar vein, therapists with strikingly exploitative and sadistic needs, and those who suffer with corrupt superegos and who have impaired deep unconscious subsystems of morality and ethics, also are inclined to be falsely loving with their patients. In addition, these falsely loving behaviors may stem from impairments in judgment and reality testing, fears of setting limits and maintaining appropriate boundaries, and an inability to tolerate frustration and to reasonably and necessarily frustrate their patients as well.

Unloving therapists tend to gain pleasure by being overly indulgent and overly gratifying with their patients, with whom they secretly identify as they try to drown them in falsely loving satisfactions. When they have suffered from poor care-taking themselves, these therapists also tend unconsciously to be enraged over having to care for their patients and they are unable to sacrifice their own pathological needs in the service of providing for the healthy needs of those who are entrusted to their care. Another problem lies with their fear of intimacy with their patients – an experience that they unconsciously see as dangerous and engulfing. Often, they were harmed or seduced by a parent in their early years and in striving to be different from them, they are, in their own way, as destructive towards their patients as their parents were towards them. Other unresolved problems that contribute to this propensity for false love include a therapist's strikingly unhappy home life and unsatisfying relationships with significant others, past and/or present. These problems prompt therapists to turn to their patients in falsely loving ways in the hope of obtaining these satisfactions from them in return – a search that harms all concerned.

We have seen too that a wide range of death-related traumas can motivate therapists to exploit their patients. In these situations, both sexual and non-sexual offers of false love, almost always in the form of frame-violating comments or actions, serve therapists as ways of denying the threat of death and obliterating their activated existential death anxieties. Nevertheless, these behaviors are predatory of the patient and evoke deep unconscious guilt and predator death anxiety in the therapist who thereby trades one form of death anxiety for another, more self-punitive form. In this connection, it is of note that as therapists grow older and pass into middle age, they often experience a need to intensify expressions of false love in order to reduce the mounting existential and persecutory death anxieties that they are experiencing. When faced with a serious or fatal illness, they tend to turn to boundary violations and other frame violations in an effort to deny their vulnerability to death and to convince themselves that they are exceptions to the existential rule that death follows life (Galatzer-Levy, 2004).

Another type of experience that often magnifies therapists' use of falsely loving, frame-violating interventions involves experiences of false love and inappropriate seduction in the their early or later lives. An all too common source of incidents of this kind lies with a therapist's own psychotherapy experience. Many psychotherapists are over-invested in their work with patients who are mental health professionals and they tend to be overly seductive or especially aggressive with them, and falsely loving in a variety of ways, to the often unnoticed harm to both parties to the therapy.

It is well for us as therapists to recognize that we are especially vulnerable to death-related traumas in our daily lives and that these traumas exert profound effects on how we love and do not love our patients. As therapists, we need to be forever on the alert for such incidents and for the likelihood that they will motivate us to love our patients far more falsely than truly.

A Truly Loving Exchange

To offer a final illustration of true therapist-love, I turn to the psychotherapy of Mrs Abbott, a woman in her forties, who was in psychotherapy with Dr Webb, a male psychotherapist with a strong adaptive orientation. She was being seen in therapy because of periodic episodes of intense anxiety. Several months into the treatment, at the end of the session prior to the hour I will briefly excerpt, the therapist, who was trailing the patient as she left in order to close the door to his consultation room behind her, inadvertently brushed his hand against her back.

Mrs Abbott begins the next session by saying that she had almost forgotten to come to her session today. She had a dream the night of the last session in which a man was fondling her breasts. Associating, she says that the man looked a lot like a therapist she had seen on a television talk show. Her thoughts then go to a dentist named Dr Beck whom she had gone to some years earlier. One day, he made a pass at her by bending over and kissing her on the lips. She had been aroused, but had put him off and stopped going to him. What made it so awful was that sometime earlier he had told her that his wife had died and she had felt a lot of sympathy for him. Her thoughts then shift to having seen a play on television in which a father sexually molested his teenage daughter and was caught and sent to jail.

Dr Webb intervenes and points out that the imagery must in some way reflect Mrs Abbott's perceptions of him as having been seductive with her. The question is: What has he done to provoke these images? Mrs Abbott thinks for a while and says she has no idea what it could be. Maybe she is having fantasies of seducing Dr Webb and is projecting her wishes onto him. She ruminates intellectually for a while and the therapist asks her to go back to her dream for more associations. [This is an effort to help the patient develop more encoded clues to the missing (unidentified) trigger.] When the patient draws a blank, he suggests that she go over the themes in her imagery to see if they brought to mind something that he had done that could be evoking these images. After denying that Dr Webb had ever fondled her breasts, Mrs Abbott suddenly remembers that she had the vague feeling that he had brushed against her back as she left his consultation room at the end of the previous session. She hadn't mentioned it because she was sure it was her imagination.

Dr Webb intervenes and suggests that her unconscious mind appears to be quite certain that he had in fact touched her and he adds that she evidently had experienced the physical contact as incestuous and as sexually molesting. Mrs Abbott falls silent for a while and then says that she's embarrassed to tell Dr Webb that the thought that she loved him had just intruded into her mind.

After a brief pause, Mrs Abbott goes back to her dream and comes up with another guided association that involved the same former dentist. She recalls that she had gone to see him because she had had an impacted wisdom tooth that had been extracted by another dentist who had botched up the surgery. She had been suffering from a severe infection which had started to spread to her jaw and Dr Beck had virtually saved her life by curing her of the disease.

To comment on the vignette, this is a situation in which a therapist inadvertently had intervened by expressing a physical form of what appears to have been deep unconsciously perceived by the patient as incestuous, false love. The patient did not in this instance respond with false love of her own, but reacted adaptively by bringing her dream and associations to the dream into her session. After the therapist had trigger decoded and interpreted her dream-associational network of themes, the patient experienced a passing feeling of love for her therapist. In order to decide whether this love was true or false we must look at the activating trigger for the experience. The narrative material from the patient indicates that it followed an interpretive intervention that eventually obtained deep unconscious, encoded validation through the allusion to the healing efforts of the otherwise seductive dentist. Thus the patient's conscious feeling of love for her therapist appears to have been an expression of true patient-love in that it was evanescent and it followed an unconsciously validated, truly loving intervention on the part of the therapist.

In regard to love, then, the sequence was:

An inadvertent expression of false therapist-love when the therapist brushed against the patient.

An unconscious, implicit expression of true patient-love when the patient came to the following session and engaged meaningfully in the therapeutic process. This response also inherently offered the therapist an invitation and opportunity to become truly loving himself.

An unconscious, implicit expression of true therapist-love when the therapist made his trigger-decoded, deep unconsciously validated interpretation.

An explicit, conscious feeling of true patient-love when the patient experienced momentary conscious loving feelings towards the therapist.

And an implicit, unconscious expression of patient-love when the patient went on to associate further to her dream and to unconsciously validate the therapist's interpretation.

This is an example, then, of a situation in which a therapist, with the unconscious help of his patient (Searles, 1973), was able to turn a moment of inadvertent false love on his part into a moment of true love shared by both parties to therapy. And much as false cycles of love are generally initiated by therapists, in this instance the therapist was responsible for a cycling of true love between himself and his patient.

Therapists do indeed almost always point to the pathways of love, true or false, down which they and their patients traverse.

Two final comments about this vignette:

First, it is well to note that deep unconsciously, the patient experienced her therapist's non-sexual physical contact with her as having sexual and incestuous qualities – meanings that, left uninterpreted, would have had adverse affects on both the patient and the therapist. The patient was a victim of an accidental predatory act by the therapist and she was likely to experience predatory death anxiety, while the therapist, as the perpetrator of the act, was likely to experience predator death anxiety and deep unconscious guilt with needs for self-punishment.

Second, the patient's allusion to the death of the dentist's wife is another example of deep unconscious wisdom and knowledge. This is another likely example of an *encoded, deep unconscious interpretation* by the patient to the therapist (Langs, 2004c) – essentially, to the effect that death anxiety had caused him to have his lapse. As noted, the deep unconscious wisdom subsystem appreciates that most inadvertent frame violations by therapists are motivated by unresolved death anxieties. In this case, although the patient had no way of knowing, the therapist's brother, who had lived in another city, had died recently. Dr Webb was suffering from existential and predator death anxieties and his frame-violating, accidental contact with the patient unconsciously was designed to deny his own vulnerability to the existential rule that death follows life and to evoke a punitive response from his patient.

The more wisdom that therapists accumulate from their patients' deep unconscious wisdom subsystems and from their own efforts at self-processing, the more truly loving and effective as therapists they will be.

Some Final Thoughts on Love

At the heart of this book lies the realization that the resolution of death-related deep unconscious needs for false love is the key to making true therapist- and patient-love the medium within which deeply effective psychotherapy is carried forward. To effect this change, therapists must learn how to distinguish true from false expressions of love from both themselves and their patients. For too long now, therapists have been misled in these efforts by their poorly designed and ineffective conscious minds.

In the course of the book I have tried to stress that the evolved design of the emotion-processing mind has made therapists easy victims of their own misguided conscious tendencies in the emotional realm, inclinations that derail their efforts to be truly loving mental healers. There are an overwhelming number of factors that unconsciously press therapists towards loving their patients falsely and badly. In the face of these pressures, therapists need to recruit every aide they

can find to turn the tide towards consistent expressions of true therapist-love and towards the creation of truly loving, sound therapeutic
settings and interpretations that are consistently validated by the always
wise and reliable deep unconscious wisdom subsystem.

Being a truly loving parent to an infant or child is a natural biological process, but being a loving psychotherapist to an emotionally ill
patient who is suffering from inordinate amounts of death anxiety is,
by contrast, an unnatural pursuit. At the moment, the deep unconscious
wisdom subsystems of their patients – and themselves – offer the only
reliable guidelines as to how therapists can defy nature and be truly
loving and caring for their patients. Given that the core of this wisdom
is linked with death and our most dreaded death anxieties, this is no
easy task.

In the world of human emotions where conscious system denial and
paradoxical responses prevail, it is humbling to realize that in the psychotherapy consultation room, it is the narrating patient rather than the
intellectually-oriented therapist who expresses the greater wisdom. The
truly wise therapist takes full advantage of this truth. In this sense,
then, therapists are simply mediators between their patients' deep
unconscious wisdom subsystems and their overly defensive conscious
minds. Patients truly heal themselves, but they need their therapists to
tell them how they are doing it.

Much the same applies to my writing this book. I had only to listen
to the love-related, encoded images of my patients – and of the patients
of my supervisees – to discover what needed to be said about love in
psychotherapy. I have, then, been their conduit, for they have, with
their gifted, deep unconscious wisdom subsystems, structured this
book for me. It is my fervent hope that I have heard and translated their
encoded messages correctly and that I have properly conveyed the
shrewdness and true love that they contain. To the extent that I have
succeeded, both you, my reader, and I, your author, will from this day
forward be in a position to love our patients more truly and wisely – a
most satisfying prospect indeed.

Bibliography

Arlow, J. and Brenner, C. (1964) *Psychoanalytic Concepts and the Structural Theory* (New York: International Universities Press).

Aron, L. (1990) 'One-person and two-person psychologies and the method of Psychoanalysis', *Psychoanalytic Psychology*, 7, pp. 475–485.

Atwood, G. and Stolorow, R. (1984) *Structures of Subjectivity: Explorations in Psychoanalytic Phenomenology* (Hillsdale, NJ: The Analytic Press).

Bacal, H. and Newman, K. (1990) *Theories of Object Relations: Bridges to Self Psychology* (New York: Columbia University Press).

Blum, H. (1973) 'The Concept of Erotized Transference', *Journal of the American Psychoanalytic Association*, 21, pp. 61–76.

Blum, H. (2004) 'The Wise Baby and the Wild Analyst', *Psychoanalytic Psychology*, 21, pp. 3–15.

Bolognini, S. (1994) 'Transference: Erotized, Erotic, Loving, Affectionate', *International Journal of Psycho-Analysis*, 75, pp. 73–86.

Breckenridge, K. (2000) Physical Touch in Psychoanalysis: A Closet Phenomenon?, *Psychoanalytic Inquiry*, 20, pp. 2–20.

Breuer, J. and Freud, S. (1893–1895) *Studies on Hysteria, Standard Edition*, Vol. II (London: Hogarth Press).

Carotenuto, A. (1982) *A Secret Symmetry: Sabina Spielrein Between Jung and Freud* (New York: Pantheon Books).

Casement, P. (1982) 'Some Pressures on the Analyst for Physical Contact During the Re-living of an Early Trauma', *International Review of Psycho-Analysis*, 9, pp. 279–286.

Casement, P. (2000) 'The Issue of Touch: A Retrospective Overview, *Psychoanalytic Inquiry*, 20, pp. 160–184.

Celenza, A. (1991) 'The Misuse of Countertransference Love in Sexual Intimacies Between Therapists and Patients', *Psychoanalytic Psychology*, 8, pp. 501–509.

Celenza, A. (1998) 'Precursors to Sexual Misconduct: Preliminary Findings', *Psychoanalytic Psychology*, 15, pp. 378–395.

Celenza, A. and Gabbard, G. (2003) 'Analysts Who Commit Sexual Boundary Violations: A Lost Cause?', *Journal of the American Psychoanalytic Association*, 51, pp. 636.

Celenza, A. and Hilsenroth, M. (1997) 'Personality Characteristics of Mental Health Professionals Who Have Engaged in Sexual Dual Relationships: A Rorschach Investigation', *Bulletin of the Menninger Clinic*, 61, pp. 90–107.

Chertok, L. (1968) 'The Discovery of the Transference: Toward an Epistemological Interpretation', *International Journal of Psycho-Analysis*, 49, pp. 560–576.

Cohen, B. and Schermer, V. (2004) 'Self-Transformation and the Unconscious in Contemporary Psychoanalytic Therapy: The Problem of "Depth" Within a Relational and Intersubjective Frame of Reference', *Psychoanalytic Psychology*, 21, pp. 580–600.

Cooper, S. (1998a) 'Analyst-Subjectivity, Analyst-Disclosure, and the Aims of Psychoanalysis', *Psychoanalytic Quarterly*, 67, pp. 379–406.

Cooper, S. (1998b) 'Countertransference Disclosure and the Conceptualization of Psychoanalytic Technique', *Psychoanalytic Quarterly*, 67, pp. 128–156.

Davies, J. (1994) 'Love in the Afternoon: A Relational Consideration of Desire and Dread in the Countertransference', *Psychoanalytic Dialogues*, 4, pp. 153–170.

Davies, J. (1998) 'Between the Disclosure and Foreclosure of Erotic Transference-Countertransference', *Psychoanalytic Dialogues*, 8, pp. 747–766.

Dawkins, R. (1976) *The Selfish Gene* (New York: Oxford University Press).

De Duve, C. (1995) *Vital Dust: The Origin And Evolution Of Life On Earth* (New York: Basic Books).

Donn, L. (1988) *Freud and Jung: Years of Friendship, Years of Loss* (New York: Collier Books).

Ferenczi, S. (1950 [1909]) *Sex in Psychoanalysis* (New York: Brunner).

Ferenczi, S. (1955 [1928]) 'The Elasticity of Psycho-Analytic Technique', in M. Balint (ed.) *Final Contributions to the Problems and Methods of Psycho-Analysis* (London: Hogarth Press) p. 97.

Fosshage, J. (2000) 'The Meanings of Touch in Psychoanalysis: A Time for Reassessment', *Psychoanalytic Inquiry*, 20, pp. 21–43.

Fox, R. (1984) 'The Principle of Abstinence Reconsidered', *International Review of Psycho-Analysis*, 11, pp. 227–236.

Freud, S. (1900) *The Interpretation of Dreams, Standard Edition*: 4 and 5 (London: Hogarth Press).

Freud, S. (1909) 'Notes Upon a Case of Obessional Neurosis', *Standard Edition*, Vol. X, pp. 153–318 (London: Hogarth Press).

Freud, S. (1910) 'The Future Prospects of Psycho-Analytic Therapy', *Standard Edition*, Vol. XI, pp. 139–151 (London: Hogarth Press).

Freud, S. (1912a) 'The Dynamics of Transference', *Standard Edition*, Vol. XII, pp. 97–108 (London: Hogarth Press).

Freud, S. (1912b) 'Recommendations to Physicians Practising Psycho-Analysis', *Standard Edition*, Vol. XII, pp. 109–120 (London: Hogarth Press).

Freud, S. (1913) 'On Beginning the Treatment (Further Recommendations on the Technique of Psycho-Analysis I)' *Standard Edition*, Vol. XII, pp. 121–144 (London: Hogarth Press).

Freud, S. (1915a) 'Observations on Transference Love (Further Recommendations on the Technique of Psycho-Analysis III)' *Standard Edition*, Vol. XII, pp. 157–171 (London: Hogarth Press).

Freud, S. (1915b) 'Thoughts for the Times on War and Death', *Standard Edition*, Vol. XIV, pp. 273–300 (London: Hogarth Press).

Freud, S. (1918) 'From the History of an Infantile Neurosis', *Standard Edition*, Vol. XVIII, pp. 1–122 (London: Hogarth Press).

Freud, S. (1923) *The Ego and the Id, Standard Edition*, Vol. XIX, pp. 3–66 (London: Hogarth Press).

Friedman, L. (2005) 'Is There a Special Psychoanalytic Love?', *Journal of the American Psychoanalytic Association*, 53, pp. 349–375.

Gabbard, G. (1994) 'Commentaries on Papers by Tansey, Davies and Hirsh', *Psychoanalytic Dialogues*, 4, pp. 193–213.

Gabbard, G. (1996) *Love and Hate in the Analytic Setting* (Lanham, MD: Rowman & Littlefield).

Gabbard, G. (1998) Commentaries on Paper by Jody Messler Davies', *Psychoanalytic Dialogues*, 8, pp. 781–189.

Gabbard, G. and Lester, E. (1995) *Boundaries and Boundary Violations in Psychoanalysis* (New York: Basic Books).

Galatzer-Levy, R. (2004) 'The Death of the Analyst', *Journal of the American Psychoanalytic Association*, 52, pp. 999–1024.

Gay, P. (1988) *Freud: A Life For Our Time* (New York: Anchor Books-Doubleday).

Goodman, M. and Teicher, A. (1988) 'To Touch or Not to Touch', *Psychotherapy*, 25, pp. 492–500.

Gordon, R., Aron, L., Mitchell, S. and Davies, J. (1998) 'Relational Psychoanalysis', in R. Langs (ed.), *Current Theories of Psychoanalysis* (Madison, CT: International Universities Press), pp. 31–58.

Gorkin, M. (1987) *The Uses of Countertransference* (Northvale, NJ: Aronson).

Green, M. (1999) *Otto Gross: Freudian Psychoanalyst, 1877–1920* (Lampeter, UK: The Edwin Mellen Press).

Greenberg, J. (1991) 'Countertransference and Reality', *Psychoanalytic Dialogues*, 1, pp. 52–73.

Greenberg, J, (1995) 'Self-Disclosure: Is it Psychoanalytic?', *Contemporary Psychoanalysis*, 31, pp. 193–205.

Grosskurth, P. (1991) *The Secret Ring: Freud's Inner Circle and the Politics of Psychoanalysis* (Reading, MA: Addison-Wesley).

Hannah, B. (1997) *Jung: His Life and Work* (Wilmette, IL: Chiron).

Hoffman, I. (1983) 'The Patient as Interpreter of the Analyst's Experience', *Contemporary Psychoanalysis*, 19, pp. 389–422.

Hoffman, I. (1991) 'Discussion: Toward a Social Constructivist View of the Psychoanalytic Situation', *Psychoanalytic Dialogues*, 1, pp. 74–105.

Hoffman, I. (1992) 'Some Practical Considerations of a Social-Constructivist View of the Psychoanalytic Situation', *Psychoanalytic Dialogues*, 2, pp. 287–304.

Hoffman, I. (1998) 'Poetic Transformation of Erotic Experience', *Psychoanalytic Dialogues*, 8, pp. 791–804.

Holder, A. (2000) 'To Touch or Not to Touch: That is the Question', *Psychoanalytic Inquiry*, 20, pp. 44–64.

Kerr, J. (1993) *A Most Dangerous Method: The Story of Jung, Freud, and Sabina Spielrein* (New York: Knopf).

Kohut, H. (1971) *The Analysis of the Self* (New York: International Universities Press).

Kohut, H. (1977) *The Restoration of the Self* (New York: International Universities Press).

Langs, R. (1975) 'Therapeutic Misalliances', *International Journal of Psychoanalytic Psychotherapy*, 4, pp. 77–105.

Langs, R. (1976) *The Bipersonal Field* (New York: Jason Aronson).

Langs, R. (1978a) 'Misalliance and Framework in the Case of the Rat Man', in R. Langs (ed.), *Technique in Transition* (New York: Jason Aronson) pp. 253–273.

Langs, R. (1978b) 'Misalliance and Framework in the Case of the Wolf Man', in R. Langs (ed.), *Technique in Transition* (New York: Jason Aronson) pp. 177–293.

Langs, R. (1985) *Madness and Cure* (Lake Worth, FL: Gardner Press).

Langs, R. (1988) *Decoding Your Dreams* (New York: Henry Holt).

Langs, R. (1992a) '1923: The Advance That Retreated From the Architecture of the Mind', *International Journal of Communicative Psychoanalysis and Psychotherapy*, 7, pp. 3–15.

Langs, R. (1992b) *Science, Systems, and Psychoanalysis* (London: Karnac Books).

Langs, R. (1993) *Empowered Psychotherapy* (London: Karnac Books).

Langs, R. (1995) *Clinical Practice and the Architecture of the Mind* (London: Karnac Books).

Langs, R. (1996) *The Evolution of the Emotion-Processing Mind, With an Introduction to Mental Darwinism* (London: Karnac Books).

Langs, R., Badalamenti, A. and Thomson, L. (1996) *The Cosmic Circle: The Unification of Mind, Matter and Energy* (Brooklyn, NY: Alliance Publishing).

Langs, R. (1997) *Death Anxiety and Clinical Practice* (London: Karnac Books).

Langs, R. (ed.) (1998a) *Current Theories of Psychoanalysis* (Madison, CT: International Universities Press).

Langs, R. (1998b) *Ground Rules in Psychotherapy and Counselling* (London: Karnac Books).

Langs, R. (1999) *Dreams and Emotional Adaptation* (Phoenix, AZ: Zeig, Tucker).

Langs, R. (2002) 'Three Forms of Death Anxiety', in D. Leichty (ed.), *Death and Denial: Interdisciplinary Perspectives on the Legacy of Ernest Becker* (Westport, CT: Greenwood), pp. 73–84.

Langs, R. (2003) 'Adaptive Insights into Death Anxiety', *The Psychoanalytic Review*, 90, pp. 565–582.

Langs, R. (2004a) 'Adaptive Insights into Death Anxiety', in J. Piven (ed.), *The Psychology of Death in Fantasy and History* (Westport, CT: Praeger), pp. 275–290.

Langs, R. (2004b) 'Death Anxiety and the Emotion-processing Mind', *Psychoanalytic Psychology*, 21, pp. 31–53.

Langs, R. (2004c) *Fundamentals of Adaptive Psychotherapy and Counseling* (London: Palgrave-Macmillan).

Langs, R. (2005a) 'Hallmarks of the Adaptive Approach: Reply to Bornstein (2005) and Goodheart (2005)', *Psychoanalytic Psychology*, 22, pp. 78–85.

Langs, R. (2005b) 'The Challenge of the Strong Adaptive Approach', *Psychoanalytic Psychology*, 22, pp 49–68.

Langs, R. (2005c) 'Relational perspectives and the strong adaptive paradigm of communicative psychoanalysis', in J. Mills (ed.), *Relational and Intersubjective Perspectives in Psychoanalysis* (Lanham, MD: Jason Aronson), pp. 223–254.

Lester, E. (1985) 'The Female Analyst and the Erotized Transference', *International Journal of Psycho-Analysis*, 66, pp. 283–293.

Lindon, J. (1994) 'Gratification and Provision in Psychoanalysis: Should We Get Rid of "The Rule of Abstinence"?', *Psychoanalytic Dialogues*, 4, pp. 549–582.

Little, M. (1951) 'Counter-Transference and the Patient's Response to it', *International Journal of Psycho-Analysis*, 32, pp. 32–40.

Loewis, R. (1998) 'Constructivist Accounts of Psychoanalysis', in R. Langs (ed.), *Current Theories of Psychoanalysis* (Madison, CT: International Universities Press), pp. 103–124.

Mann, D. (ed.) (1999) *Erotic Transference and Countertransference: Clinical Practice in Psychotherapy* (London: Routledge).

McGuire, W. (ed.) (1988) *The Freud/Jung Letters: The Correspondence Between Sigmund Freud and C. G. Jung* (Cambridge, MA: Harvard University Press).

McLaughlin, J. (1995) 'Touching Limits in the Analytic Dyad', *Psychoanalytic Quarterly*, 64, pp. 433–465.

McLaughlin, J. (2000) 'The Problem and Place of Physical Contact in Analytic Work: Some Reflections on Handholding in the Analytic Situation', *Psychoanalytic Inquiry*, 20, pp. 65–81.

McLynn, F. (1996) *Carl Gustav Jung* (New York: St. Martin's Press).

Miller, M. and Dorpat, T. (1998) 'Interactional psychoanalytic Theory', in R. Langs (ed.), *Current Theories of Psychoanalysis* (Madison, CT: International Universities Press), pp. 1–29.

Mitchell, S. (1988) *Relational Concepts in Psychoanalysis* (Cambridge, MA: Harvard University Press).

Mitchell, S. (1993) *Hope and Dread in Psychoanalysis* (New York: Basic Books).

Mitchell, S. (2000) *Relationality: From Attachment to Intersubjectivity* (Hillsdale, NJ: Analytic Press).

Natterson, J. (2003) 'Love in Psychotherapy', *Psychoanalytic Psychology*, 20, pp. 509–521.

Orange, D. (1998) 'Intersubjective Theory', in R. Langs (ed.), *Current Theories of Psychoanalysis* (Madison, CT: International Universities Press), pp. 59–72.

Orange, D., Atwood, G. and Stolorow, R. (1997) *Working Intersubjectively: Contextualism in Psychoanalytic Practice* (Hillsdale, NJ: The Analytic Press).

Pizer, B. (2000) 'Negotiating Analytic Holding: Discussion of Patrick Casement's *Learning from the Patient*', *Psychoanalytic Inquiry*, 20, pp. 82–107.

Rabin, H. (1995) 'The Liberating Effect on the Analyst of the Paradigm Shift in Psychoanalysis', *Psychoanalytic Psychology*, 12, pp. 467–495.

Rabin, H. (2003) 'Love in the Countertransference: Controversies and Questions', *Psychoanalytic Psychology*, 20, pp. 677–690.

Raney, J. (1984) 'Narcissistic Defensiveness and the Communicative Approach, in J. Raney (ed.), *Listening and Interpreting* (New York: Aronson), pp. 465–490.

Renik, O. (1993) 'Analytic Interaction: Conceptualizing Technique in Light of the Analyst's Irreducible Subjectivity', *Psychoanalytic Quarterly*, 62, pp. 553–571.

Renik, O. (1995) 'The Ideal of the Anonymous Analyst and the Problem of Self-Disclosure', *Psychoanalytic Quarterly*, 64, pp. 466–495.

Renik, O. (1999) 'Playing One's Cards Face Up in Analysis: An Approach to the Problem of Self-Disclosure', *Psychoanalytic Quarterly*, 68, pp. 521–539.

Rose, S. (1997) *Lifelines: Biology Beyond Determinism* (New York: Oxford University Press).

Ruderman, E. (2000) 'Intimate Communications: The Values and Boundaries of Touch in the Psychoanalytic Setting', *Psychoanalytic Inquiry*, 20, pp. 108–123.

Schlesinger, H. and Appelbaum, A. (2000) 'When Words are not Enough', *Psychoanalytic Inquiry*, 20, pp. 124–143.

Searles, H. (1965) 'Oedipal Love in the Countertransference', in H. Searles (ed.), *Collected Papers on Schizophrenia and Related Subjects* (New York: International Universities Press), pp. 284–203.

Searles, H. (1973) 'The Patient as Therapist to his Analyst', in P. Giovacchini (ed.), *Tactics and Techniques in Psychoanalytic Therapy, Vol 2: Countertransference* (New York: Aronson), pp. 95–151.

Singer, E. (1998) 'The Interpersonal Approach to Psychoanalysis', in R. Langs (ed.), *Current Theories of Psychoanalysis* (Madison, CT: International Universities Press), pp. 73–101.

Slavin, J. (2002) 'The Innocence of Sexuality', *Psychoanalytic Quarterly*, 71, pp. 51–80.

Slavin, J., Rahmani, M. and Pollack, L. (1998) 'Reality and Danger in Psychoanalytic Treatment', *Psychoanalytic Quarterly*, 67, pp. 191–217.

Slavin, M. and Kriegman, D. (1992) *The Adaptive Design of the Human Psyche* (New York: Guilford Press).

Smith, D. (1991) *Hidden Conversations: An Introduction to Communicative Psychoanalysis* (London: Routledge).

Strachey, J. (1934) 'The Nature of the Therapeutic Action of Psychoanalysis', *International Journal of Psycho-Analysis*, 15, pp. 127–159.

Stolorow, R., Brandchaft, B. and Atwood, G. (1987) *Psychoanalytic Treatment: An Intersubjective Approach* (Hillsdale, NJ: The Analytic Press).

Szasz, T. (1963) 'The Concept of Transference', *International Journal of Psycho-Analysis*, 44, pp. 432–43.

Toronto, E. (2001) 'The Human Touch: An Exploration of the Role and Meaning of Physical Touch in Psychoanalysis', *Psychoanalytic Psychology*, 18, pp. 37–54.

Trop, J. (1988) 'Erotic and Erotized Transference: A Self-psychological Perspective', *Psychoanalytic Psychology*, 5, pp. 269–284.

Woodmansey, A. (1988) 'Are Psychotherapists Out of Touch?', *British Journal of Psychotherapy*, 5, pp. 57–65.

Glossary of Terms

The Strong Adaptive Approach
Synonyms:
The Communicative Approach
The Adaptive Approach
The Adaptational-interactional Approach

Adaptation – The attempt to effectively cope with and survive environmental challenges. Adaptation is the prime function of all living beings, including humans.

Adaptive context – Synonymous with 'trigger,' the term alludes to an emotionally charged event to which an individual is coping, consciously and/or deep unconsciously.

Anxiety, death-related – The anxieties caused by events that are linked to death in some manner. These links may be manifest and self-evident or non-manifest and the implications of events that are unconsciously experienced as causing harm to individuals. In psychotherapy, many seemingly innocuous interventions of therapists cause this kind of unconsciously experienced harm to patients and therefore are death-related. See also: death anxiety.

Approach, strong adaptive – See strong adaptive approach, the.

Approach, weak adaptive – See weak adaptive approach, the.

Archetype – A term used to characterize relatively fixed, universal, inherited mental propensities such as ways of perceiving oneself and the external world, adaptive preferences, moral values, and the like. The deep unconscious mind is strongly archetypal in its design and operations.

Associations, free – Unencumbered communications from patients who are saying whatever is coming to their minds without censorship.

Associations, guided – A technique used in strong adaptive psychotherapy in which patients are advised to associate to the elements of a dream or original story with fresh narratives that touch on their lives or known events. These associations are, then, evoked by the images and actions contained in an origination narrative which thereby serve as the patient's guide.

Bipersonal field – A term used to characterize the theoretical interpersonal, psychodynamically charged therapeutic space defined by the setting, ground rules, and boundaries of psychotherapy. The concept speaks for the systemic aspects of the patient-therapist relationship and for shared interactions between patients and their therapists. From this perspective, both parties to therapy contribute to all of the happenings in a treatment experience, behavioral and subjective, in both patients and therapists.

Coincidental narrative – see narrative, coincidental.

Conscious system – see system, conscious.

Counter-resistances – Obstacles to therapeutic progress that come from therapists as reflected in their undue silences and erroneous active interventions. These impediments are seen as products of the bipersonal field with contributions from both patients and therapists. Unresolved death anxieties are the core source of these misguided therapeutic efforts. See also resistances.

Countertransference – A term currently used to refer to all of a therapist's feelings and thoughts about, and reactions to, his or her patients, be they appropriate, intuitive, empathic, and healthy – or inappropriate, unintuitive, unempathic, and pathological.

Danger-sensitive subsystem, of the deep unconscious mind – A postulated adaptive subsystem of the deep unconscious mind that operates without conscious awareness and is extremely sensitive to both blatant and implied death-related threats and dangers. In response to these traumatic triggering events, the subsystem activates one or more of the three forms of death anxiety.

Danger situation – An event or relationship that is traumatic or has traumatic potential and is likely to arouse an individual's death anxieties. See also death-related event.

Death anxiety – A broad term used to describe the various forms of anxiety, conscious and deep unconscious, caused by the awareness of death and the experience of death-related traumas.

Death anxiety, existential – The universal, entrapping, claustrum-related anxiety evoked in humans, including patients and therapists, by the realization of their ultimate demise. This type of anxiety mobilizes various defensive denial and obliterating activities, both mentally and behaviorally. In psychotherapy, this dreaded anxiety is a response to secured frames and it characteristically prompts frame violation by the one or both participants to treatment.

Death anxiety, predator – The anxiety that's activated when an individual harms others psychologically and/or physically. This type of anxiety evokes conscious, and especially deep unconscious, guilt and activates deep unconscious needs for punishment that tend to lead to guilt-motivated acts of self-harm. Unconscious guilt is a major problem for humankind in general and errant psychotherapists in particular.

Death anxiety, predatory – The anxiety caused by threats of harm and death, psychological and/or physical, from other living beings, especially humans, and from natural disasters. This type of anxiety evokes a mobilization of mental and physical resources in preparation for fight or flight. Exceptions to this response are seen when the perpetrator of harm is someone on whom the victim is dependent, such as patients with their therapists.

Death-related event – An incident that arouses one or another form of death anxiety. The traumatic evocative event is connected with death directly or indirectly and experienced consciously or deep unconsciously.

Decoding, trigger – The strong adaptive method of deciphering encoded narrative themes by using their evocative triggers as decoding keys.

Deep unconscious system – See system, deep unconscious.

Denial – A psychological mechanism through which many unbearable incoming environmental events and meanings are barred from conscious registration. Because adaptation to external events is the primary function of the emotion-processing mind, denial is the basic human psychological defense and repression is a secondary defensive mental mechanism. Denial is the primary human defense against existential death anxiety and in psychotherapy, it is effected by perception-obliterating actions such as ground rule violations and mentally, through perceptual blindness and a shut down of encoded narrative communications.

Denial, conscious system – The primary defense, obliterating in nature, that is automatically invoked by the conscious mind in order to protect itself from experiencing overwhelming events and meanings of events that could cause the system to be overloaded with disruptive inputs and malfunction as a result.

Denial, deep unconscious – A rare form of denial that may occur in psychotherapy patients in response to overwhelmingly traumatic interventions by their therapists, most of them involving frame violations. Its hallmark is the generation by patients of positive encoded themes in response to a blatantly harmful intervention by their therapists. As a rule, this kind of denial quickly gives way to damaging themes that reflect the actual nature of the trigger.

Derivative – An encoded theme in a manifest dream or narrative that is representative of, and thereby serves to disguise, an unconscious perception or a meaning of such a perception.

Dream-associational network – A collection of encoded narrative themes constituted by the themes in a manifest dream and in guided associations to the dream elements.

Emotion-processing mind, the – The organ of adaptation – i.e., the mental module – that has evolved in humans to cope with environmental threats from living beings, especially other humans, and to physical disasters and their meanings. The module is meaning sensitive and it has two basic components: The conscious and deep unconscious systems. See also module, mental.

Emotional-related mind – Those components of the human mind that are involved in the production of affects, emotions, and feelings. This mental module has strong links to the body and regulates the expression or discharge of affects and emotions. It is to be distinguished from the emotion-processing mind, whose outputs are adaptive plans and reactions in response to emotionally-charged, traumatic events or triggers.

Empowered psychotherapy – See psychotherapy, self-processing.

Encoded messages – see messages, encoded.

Evolutionary biology – The most fundamental of the biological sub-sciences, one that deals with both the nature of organismic adaptations and their long term histories, including the forces or selection factors that have led to changes in adaptive structures, functions, and strategies in response to environmental threats.

Existential death anxiety – See death anxiety, existential.

Frame, framework, of psychotherapy – A term that embraces the ground rules and boundaries, as well as the physical setting, established for a psychotherapy experience.

Frame, ideal, archetypal – The set of universally sought and deep unconsciously validated ground rules, setting, and boundaries for a psychotherapy experience. This includes a set fee, frequency, time and length of sessions; total privacy and confidentiality; the relative anonymity of the therapist; the absence of physical contact between patient and therapist; and the therapist's use of neutral interventions, defined as those that obtain deep unconscious validation. See also frame, secured.

Frame, modified – A set of ground rules for psychotherapy in which one or more of the ideal, unconsciously validated ground rules is either not invoked or is altered. This type of frame evokes predatory death anxieties in patients and predator death anxieties in offending therapists. Therapists who create such frames also are deep unconsciously experienced by their patients as falsely loving or unloving and their patients tend to respond with false forms of love themselves.

Frame, secured – The ideal, soundly holding set of archetypal ground rules that universally are supported and validated by patients' deep unconscious system as seen through its encoded, narrative imagery. These frames are the source of notable existential death anxieties that often cause an unconscious dread of the optimal conditions for a psychotherapy experience. In addition, therapists who offer and sustain secured frames are deep unconsciously experienced by their patients as truly loving and patients tend to respond to this love deep unconsciously with loving expressions of their own. See also frame, ideal, archetypal.

Frame, therapeutic – The ground rules and setting of a psychotherapy which serve as an influential context for the ongoing therapeutic interaction.

Fundamental rule of free association, the – See associations, free.

Ground rules, of therapy – See frame, framework, of psychotherapy.

Indicators – Signs of emotional disturbance in patients that are characterized by unilateral frame modifications, gross behavioral and communicative resistances, emotional-related symptoms, and interpersonal disorders. Indicators are the targets of trigger-decoded interpretations which are offered to illuminate the deep unconscious basis of these maladaptations and to enable patients to insightfully resolve them.

Intellectualizations – The generic term for all non-narrative communications. Intellectualizations include general descriptions, speculations, analyses, evaluations, formulations, interpretations, and the like. These communications tend to be single-meaning messages with manifest contents and implications, but little or no encoded meaning.

Interpretation, deep unconscious – See interpretation, strong adaptive.

Interpretation, strong adaptive – The means by which encoded narrative themes that convey patients' deep unconscious perceptions and processing activities are decoded in light of their evocative triggers. To be accepted as sound and truly loving, these interpretations must obtain encoded deep unconscious validation.

Interpretation, trigger-decoded – See interpretation, strong adaptive.

Intervention – An all-inclusive term that refers to everything of import that a therapist says and does not say, and does and does not do, in doing psychotherapy. There are many kinds of interventions, but only two classes obtain encoded, deep unconscious validation: Trigger-decoded interpretations and frame-sustaining and frame-securing managements of the ground rules of therapy.

Love, conscious – In psychotherapy, a patient's or therapist's directly experienced feelings of affection, caring, and the like for the other member of the therapeutic dyad. It is all but impossible to determine the actual nature of such love, true of false, through direct, manifest explorations, so expressions of conscious love must be validated deep unconsciously for them to be accepted as truly loving. For patients' conscious love, this determination is made in the therapy sessions, while therapists' conscious love must be assessed through private efforts at self-processing.

Love, deep unconscious – In psychotherapy, a patient's or therapist's feelings of affection, caring, and the like that is expressed solely through encoded narrative imagery. This type of love in patients towards their therapists tends to be genuine and true, and usually follows a helpful, deep unconsciously validated, truly loving intervention by a therapist.

Love, false – A form of love that is not validated by the deep unconscious system through its encoded themes. Conscious love is often false, while deep unconscious love is almost always true in nature.

Love, transference-based – The classical psychoanalytic belief that patients' love for their therapists, which feels real to them, is not real because the love actually is being directed towards a person in the early life of the patient. The love is, then, misdirected and a product of a patient's template for loving others as derived from his or her early life experiences. See also transference.

Love, true – A loving expression that is validated by the deep unconscious system of the emotion-processing mind. When forthcoming from patients, it usually follows a deep unconsciously validated intervention. True love for therapists by patient is only rarely consciously felt and conveyed, but when it does appear, it tends to be fleeting and is not accompanied by demands for satisfaction by the therapist.

Manifest contents – The surface meanings of communication. For dreams, they are the dream as dreamt.

Matrix, three-dimensional – The deep unconscious basis for loving expressions in psychotherapy. They include the evolved architecture of the emotion-processing mind, the ground rules and framework of psychotherapy, and the vicissitudes of death-related issues, past and present, for both patient and the therapist. These three aspects of emotional life form the underpinnings for, and are the driving forces behind, the course of love in psychotherapy.

Meaning, encoded – The meanings of manifest narrative messages that can be ascertained solely by trigger decoding the narrative themes.

Meaning, decoded – The results of applying the process of trigger decoding to narrative themes.

Meaning, implied – The meanings of manifest messages that can be abstracted or extracted from the manifest contents of intellectualizations and narratives.

Meaning, manifest – See manifest contents.

Messages, encoded – Narrative communications with both manifest or surface, consciously accessible meanings and latent or encoded, unconscious and inaccessible meanings. The encoded meanings can be accessed by decoding the manifest themes in light of the triggers that have activated the deep unconscious system to generate themes that reflect its perceptions and adaptive processing activities.

Mind-centered approaches, to psychotherapy – Theories of psychotherapy that propose that emotional maladaptations arise primarily from intrapsychic conflicts and anxiety-provoking unconscious fantasies and memories. These theories are weakly adaptive in nature.

Misalliance, therapeutic – An unconscious collusion between a patient and therapist designed to undermine therapeutic progress.

Module, mental – A collection of mental faculties – e.g., perception, thinking, reasoning, etc. – organized around a central adaptive task. The mental module that has evolved to adapt to emotionally-charged, traumatic triggering events and their meanings is called 'the emotion-processing mind.' See also emotion-processing mind, the.

Morality and ethics subsystem, of the deep unconscious mind – A postulated subsystem of the emotion-processing mind that operates outside of conscious awareness, doing so on the basis of a universal, archetypal set of ideal moral and ethical standards. The system enforces these standards by unconsciously orchestrating self-punishing actions and choices for non-compliance and self-directed rewards and sound decisions for compliance. Deep unconscious guilt is its hallmark. In psychotherapy, the moral positions of both patients and therapists are expressed through their adherence or non-adherence to the archetypal frame.

Narrative – The generic terms for all storied communications. As adaptive responses to triggering events, they are two-tiered messages, in that they convey a manifest set of directly stated meanings (along with their implications) and a more powerful, latent, indirectly stated or encoded set of meanings that are camouflaged in the same manifest themes.

Narrative, coincidental – A story or disguised dream that is not manifestly about an issue at hand, but is mentioned in passing in the course of a therapeutic exploration. These narrative are fraught with trigger-evoked deep unconscious meanings.

Narrative, origination – A dream, or a story that a patient composes during a psychotherapy session, that serves as a source of guided associations.

Natural selection – The natural process first described by Darwin and Wallace through which organisms who develop mutations and variations that enable them to survive best under adversely changing environmental conditions are favorably reproduced.

Non-narrative expressions – See intellectualizations.

Non-validation, of therapists' interventions – See validation, absence of deep unconsciously.

Origination narrative – See narrative, origination.

Patient-love – The loving feelings and behaviors of patients towards their psychotherapists. The love may be expressed directly and consciously, may be enacted or demand satisfaction by the therapist, or may come forth through encoded images and deep unconsciously.

Perception, conscious – An all-inclusive term used to convey the reception of incoming stimuli – visual, auditory, and otherwise – that register in awareness, along with their directly experienced meanings and their many implications.

Perception, subliminal – See perception, unconscious.

Perception, unconscious – An all-inclusive term, identical to subliminal perception, that alludes to the reception of various incoming stimuli – visual, auditory and otherwise – that register outside of awareness, along with their unconsciously experienced meanings and implications.

Predator death anxiety – See death anxiety, predator.

Predatory death anxiety – See death anxiety, predatory.

Psychoanalysis – Defined by Freud as the study of the unconscious, transferences, resistances, and infantile sexuality. It is redefined by the strong adaptive approach as the investigation of emotional cognition and of conscious and unconscious human adaptations to emotionally-charged triggering events.

Psychodynamic – A term used to describe approaches to the emotional life in which conscious and unconscious needs and conflicts, and external dangers, are seen as its driving force.

Psychotherapy – An effort by a therapist to help a patient to favorably resolve and insightfully modify emotional maladaptations.

Psychotherapy, deviant-frame – The form of therapy that unfolds under frame-modified conditions. Such therapies foster the turn to falsely loving expressions by both patients and therapists.

Psychotherapy, secured-frame – The form of therapy that unfolds within ideal conditions. Such therapies foster the turn to truly loving expressions by both patients and therapists.

Psychotherapy, self-processing – A new form of private, personal self-analysis for psychotherapists that makes use of the clinical precepts of the strong adaptive approach.

Reality-centered approaches, to psychotherapy – Theories of emotional dysfunctions that are centered around failures to cope with traumatic, death-related environmental events. These theories are strongly adaptive and they stress the role played by unconscious experiences of external events in emotional life and its treatment.

Rectification, models of – Frame-securing correctives that are encoded by patients in their narrative communications when their therapists modify or fail to invoke an ideal ground rule for a psychotherapy experience.

Resistance – A broad term used to allude to all obstacles to therapeutic progress that are expressed by patients. The strong adaptive approach views all resistances as interactional products of the bipersonal field, with contributions from both therapist and patient. There are two basic forms of resistance: Gross behavioral and communicative. See also counter-resistances.

Resistance, communicative – An obstacle to the progress of psychotherapy in which a patient, in the presence of an active emotionally-charged trigger, does not express viable encoded themes and/or fails to represent, manifestly or in encoded form, the trigger to which he or she is trying to adapt.

Resistance, interactional – Obstacles to the progress of psychotherapy that are products of the bipersonal field and thus have contributions from both patient and therapist.

Selection factor – An environmental challenge, broadly defined, that helps to shape the mutations that are most successful in enabling organisms to survive a fresh environmental threat.

Self-processing – See psychotherapy, self-processing.

Setting – A term that alludes to the physical conditions of psychotherapy, including the location of the therapist's office and the details of its many features.

Strong adaptive approach, the – The paradigm of psychoanalysis and psychotherapy whose basic thesis is that conscious and unconscious efforts to adapt to environmental conditions and traumatic triggering events are the fundamental task of the emotion-processing mind.

Structural theory, of psychoanalysis – The classical psychoanalytic theory of the mind, first published by Freud in 1923, that envisions three basic systems: Ego, id, and superego.

System, conscious – The adaptive system of the emotion-processing mind that operates with awareness and works over contents that are directly known or potentially knowable. This system is protected by the Message Analyzing Center which directs many overly-threatening, non-emergency events and meanings of events to the deep unconscious system for processing, barring these contents from direct awareness. This mental process is known clinically as 'conscious system denial' because an external reality has been prevented from registering consciously. See also denial, conscious system.

System, deep unconscious – The adaptive system of the emotion-processing mind that draws on unconscious perceptions and operates outside of awareness. It has many archetypal features including its distinctive adaptive preferences, exceedingly wise knowledge-base, moral values, sensitivities to death-related stimuli, and the like. It has three major subsystems: Adaptive wisdom, morality and ethics, and danger-sensitive. The conceptualization of this system is radically different from the weak adaptive conceptualizations of the unconscious aspects of the ego, id, and superego.

System overload – A general term used to refer to situations in which the processing capabilities of the conscious system of the emotion-processing mind are taxed well beyond its adaptive capabilities and resources. In the face of stimuli and events that threaten to overload the conscious system, the human mind tends to make extensive use of denial and the obliteration of incoming events and their meanings.

Themes, bridging – A term used to refer to themes found in patients' narratives – e.g., dreams, stories, and storied associations to origination narratives – that connect or link up to meanings of their evocative triggers. These themes trace a path from a manifest image to its deep unconscious context and meaning.

Themes, pool of – A collection of trigger-evoked encoded themes that facilitate trigger-decoded interpretations and frame-securing therapeutic efforts. See also dream-associational network.

Therapist-love – The loving feelings and behaviors of therapists towards their patients.

Topographic theory, of psychoanalysis – The classical psychoanalytic theory of the mind that envisions two basic systems, Ucs. and Pcs.-Cs. The strong adaptive approach makes use of an extensively modified version of this theory in that it postulates the existence of a conscious and deep unconscious system whose properties and operations are striking different from those proposed by Freud for the systems Ucs. and Pcs.-Cs.

Transference – The classical psychoanalytic belief that patients' loving and hostile feeling towards the psychoanalyst are based on unconscious misperceptions and projections caused by past relationships and interactions, and by the templates for loving that these interactions shaped for the patient. The term also is currently used to allude to all of a patient's inner mentally- and historically-derived feelings, perceptions, and behaviors towards a therapist, some of them triggered by innocuous interventions of the therapist. See also love, transference-based.

Trauma, traumatic event – An emotionally-charged event that causes psychological and/or physical harm to an extent that activates not only conscious adaptive responses, but also those that are deep unconscious as well. These incidents can be emotionally damaging and may leave lasting effects on the psyche. By and large, the emotion-processing mind has evolved primarily to adapt to death-related, traumatic incidents.

Trigger, anticipated – An intervention that a therapist plans or is expected to make.

Trigger decoding – See decoding trigger.

Trigger, triggering event – An emotionally-charged incident, verbal and/or physical, that activates the emotion-processing mind. These events are, with few exceptions, unconsciously death-related and traumatic in nature.

Unconscious, deep system – See system, deep unconscious.

Validation, absence of, deep unconsciously – Encoded storied responses to therapists' interventions in which negatively toned themes such as harmful, inappropriately seductive, blind, or ignorant people appear. Such themes indicate that the therapist has intervened erroneously and they call for reformulation of the patient's material.

Validation, conscious – Patients' manifest agreement or support for a therapist's intervention. This level of confirmation is highly suspect and often serves patients' defensive needs rather than the pursuit of deep insight. These responses can be accepted as reliable only if they are followed by deep unconscious validation of the intervention in question.

Validation, deep unconscious – The encoded confirmation of the essential correctness and insight-offering qualities of a therapist's intervention, which takes the form of encoded stories that feature helpful and wise people, rewarding events, and other positive themes. This kind of response indicates that an interpretation or ground rule securing effort has been properly carried out and is serving the healing process. It comes in two forms: Cognitive and interpersonal.

Validation, deep unconscious, cognitive – Deep unconscious affirmation of a therapist's intervention through responsive encoded images whose meanings and implications extend the therapist's previous intervention and broadens the patient's insight into a current emotional issue.

Validation, deep unconscious, interpersonal – Deep unconscious affirmations of a therapist's intervention through responsive encoded images of individuals who are wise, helpful, constructive, and capable.

Validation, of therapists' interventions – Patients' affirmations of their therapists' interventions. Expressed consciously, these responses are highly suspect and often in error, while expressed deep unconsciously, they are highly reliable and almost always on the mark. See also validation, conscious; validation, deep unconscious.

Weak adaptive approach – See approach, weak adaptive.

Wisdom, subsystem, of the deep unconscious mind – A hypothesized subsystem of the deep unconscious mind that operates on the basis of a remarkable, archetypal knowledge-base, superb adaptive resources, and extraordinary processing capabilities. In the emotional realm, the subsystem's operations are reflected in trigger-evoked narratives which encode the subsystem's perceptions and adaptive solutions in response to incoming traumatic triggering events. Deep unconscious adaptive wisdom far exceeds conscious adaptive wisdom in all spheres of functioning.

Index

196